Elements of Military Strategy

An Historical Approach

Archer Jones

PRAEGER

Westport, Connecticut
London

Library of Congress Cataloging-in-Publication Data

Jones, Archer, 1926–
    Elements of military strategy : an historical approach / Archer
Jones.
        p.   cm.
    Includes bibliographical references and index.
    ISBN 0–275–95526–5 (alk. paper).—ISBN 0–275–95527–3 (pbk. :
alk. paper)
    1. Strategy—Case studies.   2. World War, 1939–1945—Campaigns—
Pacific Ocean.   I. Title.
    U162.J66   1996
    355.4—dc20   95–52705

British Library Cataloguing in Publication Data is available.

Library of Congress Catalog Card Number: 95–52705
ISBN: 0–275–95526–5
       0–275–95527–3 (pbk.)

First published in 1996

Praeger Publishers, 88 Post Road West, Westport, CT 06881
An imprint of Greenwood Publishing Group, Inc.

Printed in the United States of America

The paper used in this book complies with the
Permanent Paper Standard issued by the National
Information Standards Organization (Z39.48–1984).

10 9 8 7 6 5 4 3 2 1

for
Joanne Leach Jones

Contents

Preface   ix
Introduction   xiii

I. Operations within a Base Area

1. The English Colonists' Warfare against the Native
   Americans, 1607–1676   3

2. The United States in the Second Seminole War   19

3. The United States in the Great Sioux War, 1876–1877   25

II. Operations from a Remote Base Area

4. The Commerce-Raiding War in the Atlantic, 1940–1945   35

5. Air Warfare in Northwestern Europe, 1940–1945   47

6. The Allied Western Europe Campaign, 1944–1945   57

7. The United States in the Pacific in World War II   87

8. The Strategy of the Korean War   141

9. The Persian Gulf Conflict of 1990–1991   147

III. Operations with a Mixture of Base Area Access

10. The United States in Vietnam   161

IV. Some Unifying Elements

11. Political Aspects   199

12. The Principles of War and Some Related Ideas   205

13. Some Factors Affecting Strategic Choices and Outcomes   221

Appendix A: Weapons and Strategy in the Twentieth Century   237
Appendix B: Maps and Diagrams   241
Suggested Readings   251
Index   253

Preface

In order to emphasize the limitations of this book, the title purposely does not begin with *The*. This book deals with only some of the elements of military strategy. The experience of recently reading an article about the strategy of some campaigns with which I was familiar, and understanding not a sentence, gives me ample assurance that this book treats the subject on an elementary level. Yet, because its components have constituted some of the basic ideas in strategy for over two millennia, it is unlikely to mislead readers or give them a faulty foundation for more-sophisticated works.

This book uses history in two ways: as the source of ideas about strategy and as examples to illustrate the elements by showing their application to specific campaigns and their utility in understanding the role of strategy in military operations. To accomplish this, it uses different land, sea, and air campaigns. Over one-fifth of the book discusses the U.S. war against Japan in the Pacific because that campaign so well illustrated and compared the independent and interdependent operations of land, sea, and air power.

The book aims to appeal to readers of military history by giving them some ideas helpful in making use of strategy in their reading of military and related history. Thus the examples are intended to not only illustrate strategic ideas induced from history but also to show the utility of this way of organizing military strategy. For students of the military aspects of current events, this book seeks to give added insight and to shed light on hypotheses about the outcomes of different courses of action.

This work has its antecedents in nineteenth-century books that used examples from military history to teach operational strategy. The most prominent of these in English, which appeared in the middle of the century, are by two English generals: P. L. MacDougall's *The Theory of War* and Edward Bruce Hamley's *The Operations of War Explained and Illustrated.* These expound Napoleonic strategy, follow Jomini's approach, and give examples of the application of the ideas with accounts of campaigns, mostly drawn from European military history. Toward the end of the century, an American officer, John Bigelow, Jr., authored *The Principles of Strategy Illustrated Mainly from American Campaigns.* He added some distinctive, but largely ignored, strategic ideas and employed the same approach as the earlier volumes.

In using mostly American examples and going beyond an exposition of Napoleonic operational strategy, this present work follows in Bigelow's footsteps. The ideas come from the significant contributions to strategic thought and to our comprehension of the Napoleonic military past made by Antoine Henri Jomini, Karl von Clausewitz, and Jean Lambert Alphonse Colin. For understanding twentieth-century war, I learned from B. H. Liddell Hart, J. F. C. Fuller, and Mao Tse-tung. Like the earlier authorities, these also had gained many of their insights from military history and experience and used military history to elucidate them.

Sea and air warfare and strategy have lacked land war's longer tradition of military thought, two notable authorities being A. T. Mahan and Giulio Douhet. Their ideas, like those of the interpreters of warfare on land, have contributed to comprehending the strategy of wars occurring after they wrote. Neither the strategy of nuclear war and its deterrence nor the cost-benefit, economic approach to strategy seemed to fit well in this book.

The study that went into preparing my 1987 *The Art of War in the Western World* made possible a synthesis and extension of the ideas of others. With modifications, these offered a workable set of interpretations that facilitated the understanding of a large body of events drawn from the military history of the Western world. The utility of these interpretations for such a broad spectrum of military events suggested a book that followed the example of Bigelow. Further, stressing the twentieth century seemed wise in order to give air power its properly prominent place. Nevertheless, warfare on land receives more attention because it is more complex than war on the sea and in the air if only because the earth is a less yielding medium than the sea or air. Readers of *The Art of War in the Western World* will find the content of chapters 4, 5, and 6 familiar and will recognize the ideas used to explain strategy in the other chapters.

Readers may skip some chapters, but those who read chapter 10 would benefit from having first read chapters 1 through 3. Readers who have learned all they want to know about strategy by the time they finish chapter 11 could omit the thorough recapitulation in chapters 12 and 13.

I express my gratitude to the University of Richmond for allowing me to use the library and to the nearly omniscient staff in the reference room. I owe even greater thanks to the Tuckahoe Branch of the Henrico County

Library, where the system always works the way its designers imagined that it might. I am particularly grateful to the staff, who always display a cordial alacrity in responding to every question and request. I little used the library's proficiency in securing interlibrary loans because I could avail myself of the thoroughness with which it had responded to its patrons' interest in twentieth-century military history.

Among many individuals who have given me aid, I am particularly indebted to Alberto Bin, Robert A. Doughty, Paddy Griffith, Janice McKenney, Allan R. Millett, Eugene Rasor, Edwin H. Simmons, Pierre Vanderputten, George M. Van Sant, and T. R. Young II. I am especially grateful to the following who read the original draft manuscript—transformed, thanks to their critiques: James R. Arnold; Warren W. Hassler, Jr.; Lee Kennett; Malcolm Muir, Jr.; and Alexander Wellford. Richard Hill read not only the first but parts of subsequent drafts and gave me invaluable help on the Persian Gulf conflict and the capabilities of the newest weapons. I have acknowledged my wife, my most important editor and writing coach, by dedicating the volume to her.

I am immensely grateful to Ned Henson for doing such a fine job with the maps and diagrams in so short a time. Any defects in these are my responsibility, as are all errors of fact and interpretation in the whole work.

Introduction

The purpose of this introduction is to present the definition used for military strategy and then succinctly outline the book's approach to the subject. Because of strategy's dependence on logistics and tactics, these are summarized also. Thus the introduction seeks to prepare the reader for the presentation of some elements of military strategy.

The objective for military strategy used herein is the depletion of the military force of an adversary. The definition of political-military strategy, a companion term, is the use of military force to attain political or related objectives directly, rather than by depleting an adversary's military force. Of course, military strategy usually endeavored to implement political or comparable objectives but sought to attain them indirectly, by depleting the hostile military force sufficiently to gain an ascendancy adequate to attain the war's political goals.

Depletion means reduction by consuming or destroying. Any military operation, including the mere existence of armed forces in a period of profound peace, results in depletion. Soldiers, sailors, and airmen die of accidents as well as natural causes; equipment, from typewriters to bilge pumps, wears out; and a vigorous program of training, most desirable at all times, uses up much combat and logistical equipment. The same wear and tear takes place during war and so depletes armed forces independently of any hostile action.

Depletion of this kind, as well as the relatively small number of casualties and other losses incident to patrolling and skirmishing, or even the greater number resulting from a major conflict, usually receives the label attrition, the steady gradual wearing away of military force. Because this word sometimes refers to a particular kind of strategy, it is reserved for that use and

not as synonymous with depletion. A favored means of depletion is one
that inflicts large losses in a short time, such as a particularly successful
battle or a maneuver that captures a major hostile force.

So depletion is a product of all military operations and has political
significance in that it is a cost of war to each antagonist. The comparative
rate of depletion in relation to the available force on each side and the
attractiveness of the war's aims often tend to define the political significance
of depletion. Some of this book's examples illustrate this relation between
military strategy and political objectives as well as offer instances of political-military strategy.

This treatment of military strategy will omit any consideration of the
very elaborate strategy developed for nuclear war. It does not belong here,
partly because, having so much to do with deterrence, it is as much political
as military. The other difficulty with including it is that we have no history
of nuclear wars from which to induce or to which to apply strategic ideas.
To contain the length and maintain the focus, the book omitted many other
germain topics, such as command, control, communications, and, particularly, intelligence.

Armed forces had two strategic means available for depleting their adversary's military forces: combat and depriving the opponent's armed forces
of supplies, weapons, recruits, or other resources needed to function. The
former method is easily labeled combat strategy, the latter suitably termed
logistic strategy. The two strategies frequently appeared in the historical
examples in contexts that illustrated their meaning and use. There were
also two means of carrying out these two strategies. One used the raid, a
transitory presence in hostile territory to make a destructive incursion. The
other, called persisting strategy, had the objective of conquering a significant portion of the territory under the adversary's control. This book refers
to these two pairs, combat and logistic and raiding and persisting, as comprehensive strategy. These are used in lieu of other terms, such as conventional and unconventional warfare. They conveniently fall into a strategy
matrix that applies to warfare on land and sea and in the air (see Figure
I.1).

Thus there are four possible combinations of the strategic means of depletion: combat + persisting, combat + raiding, logistic + persisting, and
logistic + raiding. The strategy of any military operation is almost certain
to fall into one of the four possible combinations; the use of one combination does not preclude the simultaneous use of others. This family of
strategies also implemented political-military strategy.

Guerrilla warfare and other sorts of unconventional war usually took
advantage of the dominance of raiding. Often guerrillas gained a benefit
from the location of their base area. Rather than defining guerrilla warfare
as a distinct sort of strategy, it seemed more useful to employ the categories
of comprehensive strategy and, by using other factors, such as the ratio of

Figure I.1
Strategy Matrix

	PERSISTING	**RAIDING**
COMBAT		
LOGISTIC		

military force to the area of operations, make it easier to understand how guerrilla forces operated and the conditions under which they had success.

The execution of comprehensive strategies had considerable dependence on operational strategy, now frequently called operational art. I chose the term operational strategy to connect it with its roots, for it originally constituted the whole body of strategy when the term strategy first came into use. When it emerged from the experiences of the eighteenth century and Napoleonic warfare, it relied on the traditional ideas of concentration in space and time and on attaining surprise in order to concentrate against weakness on the offensive and strength on the defensive. Its distinctive element was the turning movement in which one force reached its adversary's rear and so compelled it to fight at a disadvantage or to surrender.

These concepts underlay the operational stategy of the deployment and use of armed forces on land and sea and in the air. They had as their basic assumption that concentrating against weakness on the offensive and against strength on the defensive were essential to success and were the means of winning with the least effort. The aim of winning with the least effort also guided the choice among the four comprehensive strategies. For example, the Roman political and military leader, Julius Caesar, distinguished between combat and logistic strategies and labeled them as winning by steel and winning by hunger. In stating his preference for winning by hunger rather than by steel, he drew a conclusion from his experience in finding his enemies more vulnerable to a logistic than to a combat strategy. Like Caesar, many other great commanders used least effort as their principal guide in making strategic military decisions.

Both comprehensive and operational strategies depended on tactics and logistics, the two foundations upon which military strategy necessarily stood. Thus strategic possibilities and decisions were, to a considerable degree, dependent variables of the pertinent tactical and logistical conditions. This dependence resulted because tactics—the organization, weapons, and the mode of combat of forces fighting on land and sea and in the air—had much to do with what was possible for strategy. This was also true for logistics, the means of providing shelter for the armed forces but, more importantly, for supplying them with food, fuel, ammunition, and other necessaries, and with the movement of the forces themselves.

Logistics had importance equal to tactics because so much of strategy is contingent upon the movement possibilities of the contending forces and on the supply of a force after a movement. In spite of its being so much a part of every day civil life, it requires a brief introduction. Logistics had two keys to its understanding. The most important was the need for a base, best conceived of as a productive area from which a military force, on land or sea or in the air, may draw the supplies that it needs. As late as the middle of the nineteenth century, European armies could supply themselves in the traditional manner by drawing most of their supplies from the countryside in which they operated.

Since, typically, battles were rare, as often were small combats, armies needed little beyond food for the men and horses. Clothing usually lasted the soldiers for a year of campaigning, and local artisans could often repair or replace wagons and gun carriages. Thus armies frequently operated within their base areas and, by being able to move about within them, could go to the sources rather than have to transport supplies even moderate distances. Only in sieges, which required the concentration of large numbers of men and much artillery and ammunition, did armies have to transport most of their supplies from a distant base area.

In the twentieth century, transportation became an increasingly important aspect of logistics. The larger armies, characteristic of Europe in that century, could not live on the country in which they campaigned. Further, their size brought them into greater contact with each other, and this involved frequent skirmishing, sieges, and battles. So, in addition to moving immense quantities of food and fuel for these huge armies, the supply organizations had to transport much ammunition and many replacement weapons, equipment, and people.

Thus transportation became the second key to logistics, often essential for keeping the forces in touch with their base areas. Facilities for movement kept pace with the growth of the forces, not only for supplying them from a distant base but for giving them superior strategic mobility. Before the middle of the nineteenth century, armies had made their strategic movements by their men walking and the navies by their ships sailing. With the coming of the steam engine, fleets and ships carrying armies could move against the wind at sea, or current on rivers, and railroads offered a fine supplement and even a substitute for rivers and canals. In the First World War the motor truck became important for moving troops as well as sup-

Table I.1

Mode	Cents per ton/mile
water	.3
pipeline	.4
rail	1.3
truck	6.0
air	19.8

plies, and in the Second World War the airplane assumed a significant logistic role.

Without a base area, an armed force would perish, and no source of necessaries could function as a base area unless the force had transportation for access to it. So the logistics of supply had to do with keeping the armed forces on land and sea and in the air in touch with their base areas. This may still mean that an army operates within a base area and draws the bulk of what it needs from it, or a force may have long lines of land, sea, and even air communication to link it with its base area.

The strategic movement of the armies themselves also depended on the same kinds of transportation that conveyed their supplies. Navies and air forces have the same need for a base, but it is usually at a distance, as ships can no longer beach themselves on shore to search for water and food, and aircraft never could. For strategic movement, ships and aircraft could always move themselves rapidly, but they still depended on finding anchorages, landing fields, and supply arrangements at their destination.

Because of the role of transportation in supply and strategic movement, its efficiency was a paramount concern. In a market economy, cost is a good index of efficiency, so the comparative cost of different modes of transport in the United States in the 1960s will provide a useful guide to understanding this aspect of logistics. Table I.1 charts the various modes of transportation and their costs in cents per ton/mile from *Moody's Transportation Manual* for 1969.

Of course, there were other modes of transportation still in use. Animal traction of wagons was one—the horse, for example, being faster, more dependable, and more productive than the ox but costing more to feed. Less efficient than wheeled vehicles, but essential in the absence of suitable roads, was carriage on the backs of different animals, including mules and human beings. Humans could also function with handcarts and bicycles, being able to move them on roads that would not accommodate a horse or ox and wagon. All of these are far less efficient for moving supplies than the transport used in the United States in the 1960s. Navies often had access to water communication and air forces to air transport, and armies could still make strategic movements on foot.

Hence many forms of transportation, having very diverse costs, could contribute to meeting the logistic needs of armies, navies, and air forces. But on the relative ease of supply and of movement hinged strategic opportunities, offensive and defensive, just as the relative tactical balance also conditioned strategic decisions. Because of the significance of the physical relation of military operations to their base areas, the book has divided examples of strategy into three groups, depending on this relationship: supply largely through campaigning within a base area, supply principally from a remote base area, and operations depending on a mixture of the two systems.

Tactics is far different from most civil life, consisting of the methods and conduct of fighting and the requisite organization, equipment, deployment, and maneuver. Combat at the tactical level is not usually an end in itself but rather a means of achieving strategic goals. Thus tactical conditions and possibilities profoundly influence strategy. The differences between land, sea, and air combat require a separate presentation for the tactics of each. The subject lends itself to treatment in terms of three of its aspects: group and individual combat, the fortified defense, and mounted combat. Throughout, the problems of attack and defense will animate the exposition of these modes of combat. Although there are many similarities and useful analogies between land combat and that on the sea and in the air, the differences are so great that a description of these introduces the sea and air combat.

Traditionally soldiers fought either as individuals or as part of a group. To make it effective, its members had to learn to work together in order to cooperate in a common endeavor according to an agreed-on tactical system. Only in this way could they make the most of the strength of the team. Though drill, exercises, and maneuvers helped prepare the infantry for combat, the battle remained unrehearsed and improvised according to some rules and concepts, now called doctrine, and the experience and momentary inspiration of the leaders. In ancient times, groups of soldiers usually fought in a line, but most often one with several ranks. If fighting hand-to-hand, they arrayed themselves shoulder to shoulder. They stood close so as to provide mutual support and protect each other's side but still allow room to wield sword or spear.

The men had also practiced marching together, could move on command in different directions, and could run forward a short distance while maintaining their formation. Their movements did require much practice to execute while still being formed so as to offer each other mutual support in fighting. So they sought to make a movable wall from which they could strike with their spears or swords and either stand fast or charge at a run, all men having practiced this working together in formation. Thus the Romans defeated barbarians who, lacking organization, drill, and discipline, often pitted an aggregate of individuals against men trained to work together according to a common tactical method.

Because of this early and long dependence on an array in line, the tactics of the group earned the label line. Fighting among the Greeks displayed individuals fighting against groups while also exhibiting the nature of conflict between different weapon systems. Whereas most Greeks wore heavy armor and fought in line with spears and swords, some wore little or no armor and shot arrows or threw javelins.

Yet, instead of grouping themselves into a line, the bow and javelin men dispersed to fight as individuals. Faced by a line of armored infantry, they kept their distance as they shot their arrows or threw their javelins. If the line charged them, they would immediately run away. They easily eluded the charging line because, lacking heavy armor, they could run faster. Further, as individuals, rather than having to conform to the movements of a group, they could choose any direction for their flight and run as fast as they could. Still, as soon as the pursuing line halted, they turned about again to come close enough to shoot an arrow or throw a javelin.

These individuals employed tactics called skirmishing when they avoided close combat and used their better mobility to keep their distance and inflict casualties on the troops in line. On the other hand, without the coordination of the group, they lacked the ability to concentrate their force or otherwise maneuver and so had difficulty gaining and holding ground.

The success of these individuals also depended on being part of a weapon system intrinsically superior to the armored man equipped to fight at close quarters. His armor, well adapted to protect against a sword or spear, did not cover him completely and so left him vulnerable to the skirmishers who could pelt him with missiles with impunity. But, when elite Persian archers used lines to array themselves against the Greeks, the armored men charged and came to close quarters with the Persian bowmen, unable to flee quickly enough because of their dense formation. In these contests the armored Greeks won complete victories against the unarmored Persians. This experience demonstrates that the bow/javelin weapon system, though having an essential advantage over the armored footman, depended for this dominance on the use of skirmishing tactics.

Line and skirmishing tactics continued to have importance, and the availability of inherently ascendant weapon systems has also exercised a greater or lesser influence over tactics to the present. A comparison with the child's game of paper, rock, and scissors illustrates the importance of the superior weapon system. Using the fist to represent rock, their palm paper, and two fingers scissors, two or three children simultaneously showed one of the three. The child with his open palm won over the child with a fist because paper will cover rock, but the possessor of the rock defeated the holder of scissors because a rock will break scissors, and scissors triumphed over paper because they will cut it. The tacticians' usual response to the vulnerability created by the superior weapon system was to combine weapon systems into teams so that one in a team would have dominance over any antagonist.

Fortifications had importance almost from the beginning of warfare. Villages and towns usually had some, and often forts or castles guarded communications routes and provided places of refuge for inhabitants of villages too small to warrant their own walled defense.

Long ago soldiers and military engineers developed principles for fortification. These simple concepts have endured to this day because they have proven the best way to enable fortifications to magnify the power of the defenders. Traditionally they have offered a physical barrier to an attacker as well as given protection from the assailants' missiles. Walls, frequently supplemented by ditches, long fulfilled both of these functions and also lent themselves to implementing another principle, successive lines of defense. The important medieval city of Constantinople had, for example, three concentric walls, the outer the lowest and the inner the highest. Thus, should attackers get through the first wall, they would find their position on the captured wall much lower than, and vulnerable to arrows shot from, the next wall.

Although most cities could not afford the successive lines of Constantinople's triple walls, all city defenses and most castles utilized the crucially important principle, mutual support. Walls achieved this by having towers inserted at intervals or, instead, employed bastions, an outward projection of the wall. From these vantage points, the garrisons of the town or fort could shoot parallel to the walls and so at any assailants of the walls or adjacent towers. Since they could then shoot at the attackers' more vulnerable sides, the defenders gained an immensely important tactical advantage. Thus, in the most effective method of defense, soldiers defended each other rather than themselves, relying on the superior effectiveness of crossfire.

Even though the development of the cannon made obsolete the high, vulnerable walls of castles and cities, permanent fortifications retained their importance. By sinking the walls until they were no higher than the edge of the ditch, military engineers made them proof against the besiegers' artillery unless it had a position on the opposite lip of the ditch. So to position artillery usually required weeks or months of digging to move forward the guns, gunners, and supporting soldiers through a system of ditches dug to protect their progress from the defenders' usually very powerful artillery.

It took some time for humans to learn to ride on horseback, and it remained very difficult because it was a long time before they invented stirrups. This helps explain why the horsemen long fought only as skirmishers, keeping their distance and using javelins and bows. Yet Alexander the Great trained some of his men to wear armor and fight at close quarters with swords and lances. Still they could not grip the horse tightly enough to attack armored footmen in front; with their feet on firm ground the infantry could best the stirrupless mounted man. Thus the new weapon system had no intrinsic superiority over the armored foot soldier.

But Alexander used his new cavalry to ride around the line of the opposing infantry and assail its flank or rear where the soldiers were unprepared to defend themselves. This flank attack had long been the goal of commanders of infantry. Despite this, they had always found that, because of its cumbersome line formation, the foot soldiers could rarely reach the flank of the opposing infantry before it had maneuvered to face them. If the flanking troops used their rapid-moving march formation in column, they could outflank their adversary but would be in the wrong formation to attack. Alexander's horsemen solved this problem by having the speed to reach the enemy's flank before it could maneuver to face them and still be prepared to fight without changing formation. So Alexander's new cavalry became an offensive weapon system, one with mobility superior to the adversary's to enable it to outflank the adversary and the ability to use the same formation in which it moved to assail the weak flank or rear. So he formed for battle by placing the cavalry on the flanks and the armored infantry in the center with the skirmishers ahead of them. Europeans used this plan and array for battle for over 2,000 years.

Long before people mounted horses, they had mounted themselves on logs, rafts, and boats on the water. By the time of Alexander the Great they had capacious sailing ships for cargo and sleek, oar-driven galleys for war. Only just over 200 years ago warriors went aloft in balloons and now also in airplanes and rockets. The tactics of these two kinds of mounted warfare have significant parallels with, as well as major differences from, combat on land. In strategy, however, they are essentially alike.

The role of strategy shows itself well when one uses Aristotle's ancient tool of analysis—the four causes—to examine the nature of military operations on land, sea, and air. Aristotle's four causes are the material, formal, efficient, and final causes. He believed that, to understand anything, we have to know that out of which something comes, is made of, what he called the *material* cause (matter). We must also known the form, structure, the pattern, the design, or, in Aristotle's words, the *formal* cause (form). But some agency, person, or force is necessary to impose the formal cause (form) on the material cause (matter). That agency Aristotle called the *efficient* cause. Finally, Aristotle felt that everything has to have a purpose, goal, function, or end. He called this "why" the *final* cause.

The construction of a piece of furniture can illustrate his analytical approach. A man goes to his shop to make a coffee table. The material cause of the table is the wood, the screws, the paint or varnish, all the materials used in making the table. The formal cause is the pattern or design he follows in his work. The efficient cause is primarily the craftsman himself, along with the tools he uses to impose the design on the whole project. The final cause is the ultimate purpose of the project, in this case a piece of furniture that will fulfill the function of a coffee table. Or perhaps he wants to surprise his wife on her birthday.

In a military operation the material cause is the armed forces. In addition to the people, weapon systems, equipment, and supplies, the physical features, including climate and weather, are part of the material cause. The military organization is the efficient cause, and this comprises the commanders, staffs, and all of the executives who make the organization effective in carrying out its missions. The tactical doctrine, base area and other logistic arrangements, and, particularly, strategy constitute the formal cause. The final cause is the objective of the battle, campaign, or war.

A familiar campaign from the American Civil War can illustrate these four causes as applied to strategy. In late April and in May 1863 General Ulysses S. Grant marched his Union army south on the west side of the Mississippi River, thus beginning his final campaign against Vicksburg. The navy ferried him across to the east bank of the river, about 30 miles south of Vicksburg, and he drove back the Confederate forces at the Battle of Port Gibson. Then, having received supplies, he resumed his march, going northeast, fought again when he drove the Confederates from the city of Jackson, turned west, and defeated the Confederates once more at the battle of Champion's Hill. He commenced the siege of Vicksburg when the Confederate commander, General Pemberton, withdrew his army into that fortified city.

The three battles, Port Gibson, Jackson, and Champion's Hill, have the same material cause: Grant's veteran army, including the navy and its boats that ferried the army and moved its supplies. Another part of the material cause was central Mississippi in May, with an abundance of hay for horses and chickens and other food for the men. The formal cause included the method of dispersion of force that enabled the Union army in the battles to drive back the rebels by threatening to outflank them. The efficient cause consisted of Grant, his three corps commanders—the able Sherman and McPherson, the inept McClernand—and the other executives that supplied as well as maneuvered and fought the army.

The three battles had the same final cause: to facilitate Grant's turning movement, a 270-degree circuit around Vicksburg. This made it possible for him to carry out his operational strategy of turning Vicksburg from the west, reaching its rear, and then forcing its evacuation or, thanks to the bungling of General Pemberton, besieging it and capturing the city and the entire defending army. This drastic depletion of the enemy, not an expected result of the campaign, was also a great victory for combat strategy. Grant rightly shared the credit for the victory with Pemberton by always referring to him as his "best friend."

The successful Vicksburg campaign was part of the combat needed to implement its final cause, the comprehensive logistic strategy of conquering Southern territory and thus depleting the rebel armies by depriving them of their sources of recruits, supplies, and weapons for maintaining the strength of their military forces. This logistic military strategy for winning the war had as its final cause the United States' Civil War objective of saving the Union.

Clearly Aristotle's four causes would apply as well to understanding the tactics that enabled the soldiers to move so easily from march to combat formation and the logistics of changing from supply of the bulk of the food for Union troops from water communications with a remote base area to living on the Mississippi countryside. But these appropriate tactics and logistics would each have a final cause outside of itself, usually the strategy of the campaign that ultimately led to the final cause of the war. So there was a hierarchy of final causes, one for each level of war, from the tactics used in combat to the objective of saving the Union.

Part I

Operations within a Base Area

Armies either drew their supplies from the area in which they operated or relied on a remote base area. For most of the history of warfare, armies have obtained the bulk of their supplies from the area in which they campaigned, as in the campaigns in chapters 1, 2, and 3. They could operate within their base areas because, combat being infrequent, food constituted their main need.

Chapter 1

The English Colonists' Warfare against the Native Americans, 1607–1676

In April 1607, English settlers landed on the coast of a land they would call Virginia. When they sent a small, armed party ashore, a group of five native Americans ambushed the newcomers and wounded two of them. The attackers only withdrew when one of the Englishmen finally managed to fire his handgun. This experience forecast the major role warfare would play in the survival of the colony then established at Jamestown.

LOGISTICS

Although the English colonists at Jamestown initially drew their supplies from England, they soon cleared some of the densely forested land and began to grow their own food. Yet they remained dependent on commerce with Europe for the export of their cash crop, tobacco, and the import of manufactures and many luxuries. Like the English, the natives relied on heavily forested eastern Virginia for their supplies. In addition to gaining much meat from hunting turkeys, deer, and other game, they used systematic fishing, blocking streams with weirs. They also depended heavily on the western hemisphere's distinctive crop, the very nutritious maize or corn. They cultivated it in clearings in the forest. Thus both antagonists campaigned in the same base area, a situation not then unusual in warfare elsewhere in the world.

TACTICS

The colonists came equipped for the infantry combat they knew in Europe, some with armor and long pikes to withstand the charge of sabre-armed cavalry and others with handguns to shoot at infantry or cavalry. Few settlers had any military knowledge or experience, but they possessed books explaining how to handle pikes and muskets and how to form and march to execute line tactics. None of their books explained much about skirmishing, and they would have considerable adapting to do to cope with the tactical conditions in their new world.

Except for a small amount of copper used as ornaments, the technology of the native Americans on the eastern seaboard was that of the Stone Age. The absence of metal affected their weapons primarily by depriving them of swords. But stone could supply an adequate head for an ax or club and made suitable points for a spear or arrow. The natives used spears and hatchets instead of swords and employed shields but wore little body armor. So, backward as the Stone Age sounds, it did not affect combat at close quarters in a critical way.

Yet the native Americans depended primarily on missiles, relying principally on the bow. Because their economy depended much on hunting, the men had acquired the strength to pull their comparatively weak bow and the skill to aim it without any military training or special practice at all. In addition to accuracy acquired in hunting, the bowmen could perform in rapid succession the sequence of notching the arrow, drawing the bow, aiming, and releasing the arrow. Since the horse had long since disappeared from North America, the natives all fought as infantry.

With skilled use of their bows, the natives had a far-superior weapon system to that of the Europeans. Even if the colonists had extensive practice with their guns, they would have had difficulty shooting more than one shot a minute, a time in which the archer could shoot five or six arrows. Moreover, the English, inexperienced as marksmen, lacked practice and used an inherently inaccurate and undependable weapon, the matchlock.

The matchlock fired with a match, a long cord impregnated with gunpowder that would burn slowly. After the gunner had inserted powder and ball into his smoothbore weapon, he would ram in wadding to keep the ball and powder from falling out of the gun's barrel. Then he would put some powder into a tiny pan beside a hole in the rear of the barrel that would let the flame from the burning powder into the powder charge in the gun's barrel. Then he would grasp his burning match, which he had kept at a distance lest a spark ignite the gunpowder he poured into the barrel or the pan. Having attached his match to a bracket near the pan and blown on it to make it smolder briskly, he took aim and pulled a trigger that moved the bracket and put the match in contact with the pan. If the powder had not fallen out, it would flash in the pan and then probably ignite the powder in the gun barrel. With the possibilities of the match going out, spilled or wetted powder, or a flash in the pan that did not reach the charge, there was a 50 percent chance that the gun would not shoot.

Inferior in accuracy, dependability, and rate of fire, the matchlock in the hands of the inexpert colonist had another disadvantage. It would not shoot unless the match was burning. To light it was difficult in the era before the invention of the wooden or cardboard match with a head coated with a substance that friction could ignite. Before such friction matches, starting a fire involved striking a flint against a piece of steel to generate sparks that lit an inflammable material called tinder; this, in turn, provided ignition for a sulphur-tipped splint of wood called a spunk or match. Because of this slow, uncertain process, users of a matchlock had such a great concern to keep their match burning that they often kept both ends lit so as to still have a source of ignition should one end go out. Clearly, keeping matches alight would only occur were combat imminent. This meant that the matchlock was rarely ready to shoot in an unexpected emergency.

Still, the colonists' weapon system did have one advantage over the natives' bow. The matchlock's high velocity and the large-bore, heavy, soft bullet meant that almost any hit would make a serious wound and usually knock down the wounded man.

The colonists quickly found technological solutions to much of their inferiority. As pikes had no use against bowmen, all colonists used guns. They immediately began importing wheel locks, a gun that worked on the principle of a cigarette lighter and did not require a match. Cocking the wheel lock required using a wrench to operate a ratchet to wind up a spring-loaded metal wheel. When released by a trigger, the rough wheel rubbed against pyrites, a mineral that readily produced the sparks, which ignited the powder in the pan. Soon they could replace the matchlock with the simpler snaphance. A primitive flintlock, it relied on a flint, held by a trigger-actuated hammer, striking steel. This gave the settlers a more dependable weapon that was ready to shoot at any time and one that could fire two or, with much practice, even three shots per minute. Still, the settler had a weapon system inferior to the natives'.

But the colonists acquired from the outset a major and unexpected tactical advantage, one that did not at all belong to the tactical methods brought from Europe. The initial complement of weapons had included not just the pikes but the armor of the pikemen. The colonists immediately saw that the pikeman's armor could stop an arrow. So the English soon carried a gun and, in spite of the hot, humid climate of coastal Virginia, wore armor. This proved a major advantage for inexperienced men pitting the inaccurate, slow-firing, unreliable gun against the rapid-shooting bow in highly skilled hands.

The colonists suffered no shortage of armor because the English government gladly sent much armor left over from earlier military eras. Though obsolete, this armor was proof against Indian arrows.

A census of weapons taken in the Jamestown colony in the winter of 1623–1624 revealed how well armed was a population of 1,232; with about 700 men able to bear arms, the colony had 1,039 guns and 661 outfits of armor, including plate, chain, and quilted fabric. The colonists learned how to use these weapons, all able-bodied men being in the militia and attending drill as often as once a month. Here they practiced the techniques of loading and firing and learned the line tactics of forming and maneuvering together as a group. But neither this drill nor even their arrow-proof armor enabled them to cope with the Indian skirmishing tactics of individual combat for which their native culture and economy perfectly equipped them.

The English made thorough use of the fortified defense, beginning with their settlement at Jamestown. They surrounded it with a triangular stockade as a barrier and concentrated their firepower in bastions at each of the three corners. Besides having men with handguns, they mounted cannon there that could shoot either cannon balls or a charge of small shot at the flanks of any attackers trying to scale, batter down, or burn the stockade. Thus assailants on any of the three sides would receive crossfire from the bastions on each on their flanks, and the same crossfire defended the bastions themselves.

The natives lived under very weak governments in a society that valued individual liberty. Except that both societies relied on the citizen soldier, their military system was the antithesis of the colonists' compulsory membership in the militia. Indians participating in a military expedition were exclusively volunteers at liberty to depart whenever they no longer had an interest in the operation. Thus their culture adapted them well to the individual action needed for skirmishing, and their experience as hunters equipped them to perform admirably.

The practice of stealth in stalking game gave the native warrior precisely the technique and skill needed to surprise and harm an opponent and then elude pursuit. The Indians valued surprise in their warfare just as much as they did in shooting game in the woods. They knew that a surprised adversary would be unready and weak. Their skill as skirmishers enabled them to defeat any English offensive against them in the wooded terrain characteristic of the region. Lacking the skills of these master skirmishers, the colonists could only oppose them with clumsy and ineffective group action. In spite of having the superior weapon system of the armored handgunner, they could not cope with skirmishers who shot their arrows unexpectedly and then vanished into the woods only to shoot again from a new vantage point. The settlers only had the upper hand when they fought on the defensive in the rare open spaces or defended themselves with the fortified defense of wooden stockades. Without fortifications, they relied on the maneuvers characteristic of line troops.

When the colonists defended, they would choose a position on a well-reconnoitered piece of cleared land, usually forming their armored infantry in a defensive line. They fired individually, the then-approved manner, with soldiers moving to the front to fire and then going back to reload. This method, rather than volleys of simultaneous shots, would permit a steady, aimed fire that usually discouraged any native skirmishers who thought of venturing into the cleared ground to seek the cover of a tree stump to shoot arrows at their armored antagonists. Thus the defenders with a good field of fire had an advantage over attackers.

The natives could have completely altered the tactical situation by resorting to hand-to-hand combat with hatchets and spears, easily done by running through the limited danger presented by the slow-firing guns. Although most colonists wore armor, few had swords, meaning that they would have had to defend themselves by using their guns as clubs. But such an assault would have required more powerful leaders and a higher degree of group action than the natives usually possessed. Moreover, for this kind of attack, as well as skirmishing on open ground, the Indians would likely have thought it foolish to face a strong and unsurprised enemy. Thus they, like most wise warriors, preferred to win with the least effort by assailing weakness rather than strength and knew that only a surprised opponent would be unready and weak.

This situation also illustrated what was often another strength of the defense, the ability to refuse to fight. Had the English taken the offensive against the natives, the natives would surely have retreated and, except for a force disorganized by defeat, retreat was usually superior to pursuit. Also, once the pursuing Jamestown settlers had entered the woods, the Indians would doubtless have counterattacked, using their highly effective skirmishing tactics in the wooded terrain.

While the English gained a tactical advantage by the innovation of reintroducing armor, they had at their disposal, in cavalry, a weapon system intrinsically superior to the native skirmishers. The armored European cavalry could have easily ridden down the Indian bowmen and used their sabres to defeat them with the same ease as they could European musketeers who lacked the protection of pikemen. The natives' lack of any tradition of group action would have made it difficult for them to create the formations essential to the effectiveness of the pike, much less devise and execute the formation that combined them with the bowmen. But the densely forested nature of the country precluded the employment of cavalry and so deprived the Europeans of the use of a weapon system that could have given them tactical dominance and with it strategic victory through a combat strategy.

STRATEGY

The raiding strategy used by the natives against the English invaders closely resembled that which they employed in their own warfare. Lacking the European's concept of ownership of and sovereignty over land, they naturally thought in terms of raids. These usually had such objectives as booty, vengeance, or the repute gained by a successful raid. On the other hand, the colonists aim of establishing settlements enjoined a persisting strategy.

Some of the English leaders had military experience in the English participation in the war of the Dutch and Spaniards for control of territory in the Netherlands. Here they saw both sides pursuing a persisting strategy as they besieged and defended cities and struggled to protect the country not just against conquest but against raids. The Dutch were particularly thorough in building fortified lines, connecting cities and forts with a line of earth and wood fortifications 150 miles long.

WARFARE IN VIRGINIA

The Indian strategy centered on the raid, the brief incursion to take booty, intimidate an enemy, and withdraw quickly. They used it against the colonists and, in doing so, implicitly followed an essentially political-military strategy of trying to make the colonists so uncomfortable that they would halt their expansion or even return to England. On the other hand, the colonists followed a persisting strategy of gradually taking more land and organizing it in the European manner into privately owned farms.

The natives' destructive raids and their intimidating practice of torturing some of their prisoners could accomplish the objectives of a persisting strategy. If pursued unremittingly and ruthlessly, these political raids often had caused the submission of their native adversaries or, sometimes, their emigration, leaving behind to the conquerors fields, woods full of game, and streams and rivers with weirs for taking fish. They applied the same strategy against the English invaders.

Their raiding strategy lent itself well to concentration against weakness, the major tenet of their strategy. They made the most of the raid's advantage of a broad choice of objectives to attack and the many opportunities for bringing greater numbers against lesser. In war, few prospective assailants deliberately warn their foe, but many take inadequate precautions to keep their intentions secret; the Indians, however, accustomed to the futility of hunting if the stalker warned the quarry, were assiduous in avoiding giving any hint of an imminent attack. Most of their surprises were, however, tactical. It proved difficult to achieve the strategic surprise of planning and executing major raids without the intended recipient learning that such operations impended.

The natives' surprise attacks produced very brief conflicts. If they did not kill the defenders or provoke and allow their flight, a battle would result as soon as the attacked had recovered from the surprise and began to make a representative resistance. Since this would raise the probability of the Indians sustaining serious casualties, it marked a propitious moment for the raiders to withdraw.

A French explorer succinctly summarized the harmony of the Indians' raiding strategy with their abhorrence of warfare with heavy casualties: "They make war by strategem, surprise, or ambush, despising us as fools for exposing ourselves to be shot at like marks. A man's valor with them consists in their cunning, and he is deemed the greatest who employs the most art in surprising his enemy; they never strike a blow unless they think themselves sure of retreat, and the loss of many men is an infamous crime laid to the charge of the party." Another European used an elegant simile to characterize their raiding strategy: They "approach like foxes, fight like lions, and disappear like birds."

The English, who settled at Jamestown in 1607, needed the Indians' lack of political unity, because though numerous initially, disease and hardships constantly reduced the colonists' numbers. Further they faced an apparently powerful monarch, Powhatan, who held sway over all of the tribes in tidewater Virginia. Fortunately for the English, he could not mobilize the military resources of his loose confederation of thirty tribes.

In contrast to the political, logistical, and strategic reasons that prevented the Indians from confronting the invaders with a sustained campaign, the colony had ample political unity and organization as well as a militia system that required all men to arm themselves and participate in a military unit that trained as often as once a month. This militia acted only on the defensive in emergencies, all men turning out on the alarm of an actual or expected hostile raid.

For an offensive campaign requiring sustained operations, the colony created an ad hoc force by drawing men from various militia companies. Such an approach had the disadvantage of throwing together men from different communities who lacked experience serving together, but it had the merit that often in such units the volunteers outnumbered the drafted men. Such forces conducted the offensive campaigns that lasted days or weeks. Because all men had received similar rudimentary drill and the captain and other leaders often had superior experience and ability, the force had—for an essentially civilian group—considerable military capability and, often numbering a hundred men or less, doubtless quickly developed a sense of community.

Following the well-established European tradition of reliance on the fortified defense, the English built small stockaded forts as they began to move away from their exclusive concentration at Jamestown. This reliance on the fortified defense enhanced its strength and placed the militia in a position where, in shooting from behind walls, the tactical situation placed the minimum demand upon the courage and skill of the amateur soldiers.

The stockades gave a place of refuge against the natives' raids and thus helped the colonists cling to their settlements and land. The commitment and investment represented by these improvements meant that the English invaders could not very easily consider the alternative of moving when subjected to repeated raids. So only a persisting strategy could remove them once they had settled on the land and found steady employment. The natives' raiding strategy, essentially aimed at political intimidation, would fail unless it could inflict greater destruction and more severe loss of life and offer no prospect of cessation.

THE ENGLISH LOGISTIC STRATEGIES

Still the English needed to do more than merely endure raids that destroyed property and wounded or killed isolated individuals or groups. So to their persisting strategy of steady, fortified encroachment they added what proved a formidable raiding strategy of their own. They decided on these easily because they early realized the ascendancy of the raider in the elusiveness of the natives who had "so many lurking places to escape the execution of the sword by flight" and, even if discovered, being "as swift as Roebuck," were not to be caught and brought to battle against their will. Recognizing the raiders' offensive advantage and the primacy of retreat over pursuit, the English turned to raids, but these implemented a military as well as a political strategy. So they clearly discerned that logistic strategy offered the path of least effort and were fortunate to find that easily executed raids fully met their needs.

The native dependence on corn for food and for balance in their diet made them vulnerable to a logistic strategy directed at the crops in the fields and, less easily found, the crops stored to supply food until the next harvest. By raiding these, the English could accomplish the military objective of depleting the vigor and aggressiveness of the native militia. Because of the number of navigable rivers, much of the country and the natives' fields as well as their weirs for catching fish were accessible by boat. This made them vulnerable to raids by the English, whose larger, cannon-armed boats gave them untrammeled use of the waterways and thus a degree of initiative. So the settlers began to retaliate by conducting their own raids. On one essentially political raid they not only burnt several enemy villages but captured and killed a tribe's queen and her children.

This ruthlessness prevailed on both sides. The torturing of prisoners was part of the Indian military culture; killing women and children or, later, selling prisoners as slaves came readily to the English, engaged as they were in a struggle for survival. So the war continued, the Indians successfully ambushing parties as large as fourteen and the settlers using the secure mobility given by the rivers to strike at cornfields and villages of the Indians' base area. On finding a field of corn, the colonial expeditionary force would deploy, some in line to protect the others who cut and burned the corn. The natives would assemble but would not attempt to cross the open ground to assail the armored militia with their loaded flintlocks ready to fire. Instead, they watched in dismay as their winter food supplies disappeared.

Further, the English expanded their defensive arrangements, closing with palisades the peninsulas of farmland formed by loops in the rivers. Then the English captured Powhatan's daughter Pocahontas, worked at Christianizing her, and had prominent colonist John Rolfe interested in marrying her. Because political marriages, as well as making a prisoner of enemy royalty, had long constituted a staple of European politics, the Jamestown governor in 1614, Sir Thomas Dale, understood the political potential of the situation.

He then conducted a major raid against Powhatan's capital on the Pamunkey River. Sailing with 150 men down the James River and up the York, Sir Thomas passed Indians on the banks shooting at the flotilla and halted long enough to land, engage the enemy, and burn 40 huts. Having resumed its voyage, the little army reached Powhatan's city, finding 400 natives ready to fight. But Governor Dale began negotiations, which led to the marriage of Pocahontas and Rolfe and a peace between Powhatan and the English colonists.

This peace facilitated the agricultural expansion of the colony and its prosperity through the cultivation and export of tobacco. By 1619 the population had reached 400, a representative assembly had met, and new colonists flocked in. The peace also promoted a decline in military readiness, though most settlements had palisades and the colonists guns and armor.

But in March 1622, Powhatan's brother and the new ruler of the confederacy, the portly and ferocious Opechancanough, had skillfully organized the concentration in time of a simultaneous series of surprise raids against most of the exposed settlements. Communities that made a determined resistance against these raiders found that the natives did not long prosecute a siege of a house or stockade. Yet over 200 colonists, a quarter of the population, died in the fierce forays. In April, the raids subsided, in part as a result of the Indians' inability to maintain so high a level of mobilization. The English then availed themselves of the opportunity to organize their military forces while, for the most part, still remaining in the strong points in which they had taken refuge.

In the summer, they were able to carry on some of their agriculture, as did the natives, for whom the corn crop took precedence over warfare. Because, unlike wheat, corn did not require harvesting at the time of ripening, in September the English used 300 volunteers to conduct a series of logistic raids against the Indians. The campaign began with a raid that had the objective of crippling the native base area by burning huts, taking or ruining stored corn, and destroying crops standing in the fields. This was the first of ten such raids conducted in the fall.

The raids of the natives in the spring of 1622 had had the implicit political objective of making Virginia too painful a place for the English to remain and had so far attained their objective that the governor did consider abandoning the settlements on the west side of Chesapeake Bay and retiring to its eastern shore. The English raids pursued no such political end; rather, they aimed to employ a logistic military strategy to cripple the native armed forces. Since the Indians' sporadically mobilized militia embraced, like the colonists', a large part of the eligible male population, the logistic strategy had to aim at the food supply of the entire population.

Thus, as the English reported, their logistic raids "burnte their Townes, destroyed theire wears & corne" because, as they emphasized, they could not pursue a combat strategy against "an enemy nott suddenlie to be destroyed with the sworde by reason of theire swiftness of foote and advantages of the woodes, to which, upon all our assaultes, they retyre." So finding their antagonist so adept at exploiting the ascendancy of retreat over pursuit, the settlers had no temptation to pursue a combat strategy and had ample opportunity to apply a logistic strategy to "worke the ruine and destruction" of their elusive enemy by "cutting downe theire Corne in the fitt season."

The colonists' raiding strategy owed much of its success to the natives' unwillingness to meet the settlers in battle in the open. Here the discipline of a group of men in line with guns and body armor had a tactical and a psychological advantage over an adversary who knew nothing but the individual action of the skirmisher and felt great reluctance to abandon the cover of the forest to risk high casualties against armored men.

The logistic effect of the raids showed itself in the spring of 1623 when, after a year of mutual raiding of varying intensity, Opechancanough proposed peace, and the settlers arranged a parley to which they invited many Indians, including Opechancanough himself. The English opened the proceedings by serving wine, reserving particular barrels of poisoned wine for the natives. When the wine had disabled many of their adversaries, they opened fire. As many as 200 died, but Opechancanough survived both poison and gunfire. Such dealings seemed only fair in a war against heathens who threatened the colonists' very existence; and the natives had hardly acted more scrupulously, having begun their raids in March by coming to have a friendly breakfast with their colonist neighbors as a prelude to a sudden attack at the breakfast table. Moreover, few Christians would have thought that promises made to heathens were binding.

Even after this lethally deceitful peace conference, the natives, surprisingly, still made a truce. But the English broke it with six big harvesttime raids and more in the fall to find stored provisions. One battle illustrates the advantages the colonists enjoyed in this and the next year's raiding campaigns. Sixty well-armored settlers landed at the site of an Indian village with extensive corn fields. Not surprising the enemy by their obvious approach on the river, the small colonial expedition found 800 bowmen at hand to defend the vital harvest. Yet the raiders then devoted two days to cutting down corn, 24 men doing this while the remaining 36 held the Indians at bay with much of the fighting "in open fielde." When the English departed, with 16 wounded, they believed that they had cut enough corn to feed 4,000 men for 12 months.

And so the war continued. The Virginia legislature required the palisading of houses and institutionalized the logistic strategy by directing that "at the beginning of July next the inhabitants of every corporation shall fall upon their adjoining savages as we did last year." Thus the legislature prescribed a strategy of logistic raids, and the natives continued theirs. The raids of both antagonists also had a positive logistic goal, the capture of needed food from the enemy. The Indians coped with the logistic strategy by increasing their fishing, some withdrawal westward, and cultivating fields the colonists did not know of.

The implicit political strategy of the natives did inspire dread among the settlers, but not enough to cause an emigration back across the Atlantic or even across Chesapeake Bay. As their main response, in addition to their logistic raids, the colonists intensified the defensive aspects of their basic persisting strategy. In addition to requiring the palisading of houses, the legislature supported building between the York and the James rivers a stockade six miles long, studded with blockhouses within gunshot of each other. The government guarded this barrier, which protected a peninsula of 150,000 acres, by giving settlers 50 acres and occupancy of one of the little forts if they maintained and defended the wall.

In 1632 the adversaries made a durable truce, one in part reflecting the political impact of the colonists' raids. This one lasted until April 1644 when Opechancanough repeated his surprise attack of 1622, this time killing 500 settlers; but these numbered only about 6 percent of a far more numerous population than in 1622. The long palisade across the York-James peninsula proved its worth, no raiders crossing it. The far more powerful colony responded in June 1644 by sending out an army of 300 men to follow the usual strategy of burning Indian villages and hurting the corn crops. The 300-man army campaigned for more than a month while two smaller forces carried out similar raids. All together 500 men participated. Among these were native allies whose skill as guides, scouts, and skirmishers gave a valuable tactical balance to the English expeditionary forces.

In the summer of 1645 Opechancanough proposed peace. When the colonists used the opportunity to make an unexpected attack on the Indian peace delegation, Opechancanough again escaped. Another year of this campaigning ended with Opechancanough, infirm and carried on a litter, fleeing a colonial cavalry detachment. When the horsemen captured their wily adversary, one of the militiamen took impromptu revenge for the Indian raids by fatally shooting him in the back.

The death of such an inveterate foe helped pave the way for the peace concluded in the fall of 1646. The political agreement created separate settler and native areas, some still occupied three centuries later; but the colony's promise to protect the Indians from their enemies showed that the English dominated.

Thus the colonists, few in number and constantly depleted by disease, managed first to survive and then to overcome the hostility of numerous warlike natives skilled at skirmishing and using a sophisticated raiding strategy.

The possession of sailing ships, whether a 200-ton, cannon-armed merchant ship or a pinnace of less than 30 feet, gave the English superior facilities for two of logistics' principal functions, transporting supplies and moving troops. This ability to use the rivers for conducting their raids played a crucial part in making possible the colonists' successful logistic raiding strategy. If the raiders had needed to carry out all of their movements overland to their objective, they would almost always have had to march through forests where they would constantly have had to face the adept skirmishing of the Indians and suffer severe losses in morale and men.

The colonists' combination of persisting and raiding strategies coped admirably with the three major constraints faced by soldiers of that time. Their persisting strategy dealt with the large amount of space of Powhatan and Opechancanough's domain, which, though tiny compared to the continent, was vast in relation to the small number of colonists during the first decades of colonization. Instead of seeking to conquer the Indian confederacy or otherwise exercise an extensive political sway over the natives, the settlers confined themselves to appropriating the land they could use for agriculture and effectively occupy. By fortifying thoroughly, they gave themselves a high ratio of their force to the space they occupied.

Nothing better typified the persisting strategy of conquest than the systematic, fortified advance of the English colonists against the resistance of their formidable opponents nor showed better how this incremental approach overcame the obstacle a large amount of space could present for a persisting strategy.

Having thus combined a persisting and a raiding strategy to overcome the low ratio of force to space, the ascendancy of the raider, and the primacy of retreat over pursuit, the English turned the dominance of the tactical defense to their own advantage when they fortified their conquests.

THE NEW ENGLAND SETTLEMENT

The colonists of New England had quite a different experience from those in Virginia. The Pilgrims, who landed on an arm of Cape Cod Bay in 1620, learned from Virginia's experience and came with armor as well as guns. After an initial clash, the English made peace with the few natives who had survived a terrible epidemic in 1616–1617. Ten years later thousands of well-organized and thoroughly prepared Puritan immigrants began landing in present-day Massachusetts and soon spread to Connecticut and Rhode Island. Like the Pilgrims, they came armed with guns and armor and found the natives depopulated by disease. But this situation did not lead the colonists to neglect their defenses, and they formed a militia that, well armed, met for ten training sessions a year.

When a new tribe, the aggressive Pequots, invaded the area, the English and the powerful Narragansett tribe combined against them. Learning that many Pequots had gathered in two villages, an Anglo-Narragansett force of 450 moved against them. By surprising the careless Pequots and surrounding a village early in the morning, they turned the palisaded village into a trap when the colonists fired through the chinks between the stockade's logs, thus having a crossfire within the village whose dwellings often would not stop a bullet. Then, setting the buildings alight, the Anglo-Indian force killed the few that escaped the flaming huts, the fire accounting for most; a contemporary noted that the gruesome event presented the "fearful sight to see them thus frying in the Fire, and the streams of Blood quenching the same; and horrible was the stink and scent thereof." The Pequots lost 400 dead, half warriors and half women and children.

Pequot reinforcements arrived from the other village but, on facing a fusillade, adopted skirmishing tactics of shooting from behind rocks and trees. Satisfied with the brilliant results of their combat strategy, the English then withdrew, their Indian allies covering their retreat.

So, instead of the Virginians' logistic raids, they added to their persisting strategy successful combat raids to deplete the native forces, the attack on the Pequot village exemplifying this strategy. But almost 40 years later, New Englanders found that they would have to fight under substantially different strategic and tactical conditions from those of their quick victory over the Pequots.

THE TWO ENGLISH STRATEGIES OF KING PHILIP'S WAR

In 1675–1676 over 50,000 New England colonists and their Indian allies fought King Philip's War. A comparatively few natives began hostilities in an attempt to stem the tide of English immigration that was rapidly displacing them. The principal military change since the Pequot War was that, to counter the English armor, the Indians had given up their bows and adopted guns, also more effective for hunting. Because of the presence of roads and much cleared land, the settlers had created some mounted militia units.

War began in June 1675 on the eastern side of Narragansett Bay when Philip, chief of the small Wampanoag tribe, inaugurated a campaign of raids against neighboring villages where New England farmers as well as artisans and merchants dwelt. These raids, like those employed by Indians in Virginia, had the implicit political objective of intimidating the settlers. The militia mobilized, searched for the native raiders, but found the wily chief too elusive and soon learned that he had marched north, where he joined the friendly Nipmuk tribe. Together they raided settlements in eastern Massachusetts and the Connecticut River valley. Pursuit of him and his band failed once more, as had other efforts, and only again demonstrated the primacy of retreat over pursuit and the strategic superiority of raiding. A contemporary had already used a cogent metaphor to point out this basis of the failure of the settlers combat strategy: "We were too ready to think that we could easyly supresse that flea; but now we find that all the craft is in catching of them, and that in the meane while they give us many a soare nip." This was a lesson that the New Englanders, inexperienced in war, were just learning.

Having a wider scope for action, the larger native forces did not limit their operations to raids against towns. In one instance, a large group ambushed a party of 25 cavalry, killing or wounding eight and then wounding two more as they charged through the natives to make good their escape to a small village. Here the pursuing Indians surrounded them in a fortified house on a hill. For two days the dismounted cavalrymen faced steady gunfire as they successfully thwarted efforts to burn the house. Then another force of cavalry arrived, rode through the besiegers, and strengthened the defense. The natives, having burned all the other buildings in town, withdrew.

The summer war of raids prompted the colonies to agree in September to raise an army of 1,000 men. Most exposed towns erected garrison houses, strong buildings with loopholes for shooting and, usually, an overhanging second floor. This overhang substituted for an adjacent wall or house that traditionally protected each other with crossfire. The overhang permitted observation of the garrison houses' walls and gave an opportunity to shoot downward. When raiders attacked Springfield, the largest town in the region, the 500 inhabitants were safe in several of these fortified houses when the arrival of a relief force caused the natives to withdraw; yet the natives had burned more than a third of the town's buildings.

When the raids subsided with the cooler weather of the fall, the colonial leaders could see only devastation of towns with little apparent loss on the raiders' part to compensate. Philip's campaign had exemplified the dominance of raiders. The thinly settled country enabled the raiders to move easily in spite of the hostility of the armed settlers.

In early winter King Philip's warriors inaugurated a series of raids, initially attacking the Massachusetts towns in the vicinity of Boston. Having been driven from the traditional base area, the Indians began the new raids with the capture of food as a major motive. But they also followed the pattern of killing and destruction designed to intimidate. Two separate forces seemed engaged in a coordinated campaign.

On 10 February 1676 a native force of perhaps as many as 400 attacked Lancaster, a town west of Boston on the fringe of settlement. Although five of the six garrison houses held out, the settlers lost 50, either killed or taken prisoner. The raiders acquired much valuable booty before burning most of the buildings and withdrawing upon the approach of a party of 40 active duty men from a nearby town. Six weeks later, the surviving colonists evacuated the ruins of the town of Lancaster.

Eleven days after the attack on Lancaster, 300 natives struck the town of Medfield, southwest of and nearer Boston than Lancaster. Unlike Lancaster's defense force of only militia, Medfield had a garrison of 100 active troops in addition to their 100 militia. Still, the natives used surprise to assail this strong garrison where it was weakest. They did this by infiltrating men into the town at night, taking up vantage points, and beginning hostilities by shooting the inhabitants as they came out of their houses in the morning. This attack put Medfield's garrison on the defensive and enabled the raiders to burn over 40 buildings and take much booty. Then, expecting that the firing of the cannon in the town's fort would soon bring reinforcements, they quickly withdrew. Burning the bridge as they crossed the river, the raiders had no pursuers.

Accompanying these major operations were smaller raids into the thickly settled part of the colonies, one of which burned a few buildings in Weymouth, near the coast southeast of Boston. Another, at an unexpected place far from the frontier, occurred on 21 March when raiders killed 11 people only three miles from Plymouth, on the coast and the oldest town in New England. The next day Indians struck Groton, far to the northwest, taking much plunder, burning dwellings and barns, but leaving the garrison houses holding out. At Northampton, on the Connecticut River and over 60 miles west of Groton, the natives made an unsuccessful raid the day following. Finding a garrison of active troops, the raiders promptly fled, taking only a few horses and sheep.

This late winter surge of big and little raids caused the evacuation of several large Massachusetts towns and the government's recommendation that the inhabitants of the smaller communities take refuge in the larger. Having sent a mounted force of 300 west to search for Indians, the Massachusetts government suffered disappointment when the horsemen pursued some natives only until they escaped by crossing a river on a raft. The raids even led to a proposal to erect an 8-foot palisade to join several lakes to make a defensive line 12 miles long.

In spite of this demonstration of the superiority of raiders over the persisting defense and the ineffectiveness of most of the New Englanders' combat strategy pursuits, the native leaders were beginning to see that they could never prevail against the numerous, determined, and heavily armed English. And, having integrated native allies into their forces, the colonists themselves were developing a skill in operations that would give more promise of success for their combat strategy.

In May discouragement about the prospects of victory combined with pressing logistical needs to cause Philip to suspend his raids. Just as the raids ended, the colonists pushed their combat strategy with as much vigor as their own agricultural needs would permit. The first major colonial success fully combined combat and logistical objectives.

When natives gathered in the upper Connecticut River valley to fish at a falls, plant crops, and take cattle from a nearby settler village, they gave the English an opportunity that those nearby siezed by surprising the natives as they slept soundly after a roast beef dinner. The fleeing natives left behind camp, food, gunpowder, guns, and forges for repairing guns.

Then comprehending their adversaries' real logistical distress, the English leaders modified their strategy to include raids into native territory aimed at disrupting the growing of crops, interrupting fishing, and finding any remaining caches of food. Of course, the same raiders also sought battle with the foe and, by keeping them in motion to evade combat with the Puritan detachments, further diminished their supplies and morale.

The English practice of killing prisoners or selling them to the West Indies as slaves tended to inspire in the natives a fanatical courage in combat. But, when the settlers did not apply this to groups that voluntarily offered surrender, this encouraged such submissions. Desperate for food and without any secure base area, the Indians who had menaced their adversaries with apparently irresistible raids disintegrated during the summer.

Inexperienced at the beginning of this war and lacking the Virginians' advantage of armor protection, the New Englanders had little conception of any but a combat strategy. But they learned quickly and, in part adventitiously, merged their combat with a logistic strategy and had the happy experience of not finding the strategies in conflict in the last months of the war. Then they, like the Virginia colonists before them, added to their defensive, fortified, persisting strategy one of logistic raids.

One factor indispensable both in Virginia and in New England was the proximity of the base area from which the hostile natives drew their supplies. Had the Indian raiders come from a great distance and lived on the loot of their forays while in colonial territory, the strategic situation would have been quite different. Then the raiders could have withdrawn to their distant base area for rest, recuperation, and preparation for the next raid.

Chapter 2

The United States
in the Second Seminole War

Perhaps as many as 5,000 Seminole Indians inhabited the Florida peninsula in 1835. At this time the original Spanish and the more numerous U.S. immigrants had settled in the north and along the northeast coast, near the old town of St. Augustine. Living by farming and hunting, the Seminoles dwelt in villages, each with its own chief and with no formal central government. When the United States tried to induce them to move to a reservation west of the Mississippi River, some had agreed but most had resisted. Finally, in the fall of 1835 war broke out between the United States and those Seminoles who did not wish to move.

LOGISTICS

For supply in the United States' wars against the natives, both continued to rely heavily on the area of operations, but the U.S. forces depended much on accumulating supplies in advance of a campaign. Because men could carry enough food for five or more days, the belligerents could conduct brief campaigns without having to forage for anything but water.

TACTICS

In spite of changes in weapons, tactics had altered little since the seventeenth century. The pike had disappeared, superseded for defense against cavalry by the addition of a removable bayonet to the barrel of the handgun, the musket.

Armies had experimented with the use of rifles, but many still preferred the smoothbore because its ease of reloading gave it a much higher rate of fire. The loading method for rifles preferred by hunters and mostly employed in North America used a ball that would go easily down the barrel. To provide the needed tight fit, the riflemen placed it in the middle of a small piece of greased leather or cloth, called a patch. They then carefully centered the ball and patch over the muzzle of the barrel and easily rammed the slippery patch and its ball down on the powder charge. But this process took time because of the care needed to be sure that the patch and ball were exactly centered before ramming; the riflemen needed this care to be sure that they would not become misaligned or separated during the ramming and thus have a faulty shot or require starting the loading over. Upon firing, the patch provided the necessary seal and enabled the rifling to impart its spin, the heat of the explosion not having time to burn it. In the Seminole War, the natives fought with their hunting rifles and the U.S. forces employed both rifles and smoothbores.

STRATEGY

The United States had had success in their campaigns against the natives in the South by attacking and destroying their villages. Because typically the Indians had fought to defend their villages, U.S. forces had depleted them in combat as well as implemented a logistic strategy by destroying their habitations, food, and cattle. But the Second Seminole War would give few opportunities to strike the major combat and logistic blows that had quickly decided earlier wars. This left the United States without a strategy for the war.

The Seminoles almost always employed a raiding strategy and continued to rely on surprise to assail weakness and win with the least effort. But the many conflicts with the natives had long ago prepared their adversaries for this. In 1791, for example, President Washington thus warned General Arthur St. Clair as he began his campaign against the Indians: "Beware of surprise; trust not the Indian; leave not your arms for the moment; and when you halt for the night be sure to fortify your camp—again and again, General, beware of surprise."

Seminole strategy consisted of raids against the U.S. settlers. These were implicitly logistic in that the Seminoles took food and useful property and political in that they killed some settlers. In addition the Seminole leaders began the war with two meticulously planned operations: one to kill Wiley Thompson, the hated U.S. Indian agent, and the other to defeat a U.S. military force.

THE INITIAL MAJOR OPERATIONS

The Seminoles killed Thompson by patiently lying in wait outside the fort where he lived. When, on 28 December 1835, Thompson and his guest took a stroll after lunch, 14 bullets of a fusillade from the concealed natives struck him down, his guest dying also.

At the same time, the natives ambushed Major Francis L. Dade's column of 108 regular troops as it moved from one fort to another. When the column came into a fairly open pine wood, 180 concealed Seminoles rose and brought down half the column with their first volley. The troops promptly retreated and built a triangular breastwork. But this gave them limited protection from the fire of the natives who also took cover near them and maintained a steady fire. Finally, with most of the remaining soldiers wounded in the head or neck, Dade's Battle ended. Only three soldiers survived. The natives celebrated the achievement of their war aims, but they had helped provoke a big war.

The U.S. forces then took their first offensive action with a blow against a major Seminole settlement along the Withlacoochee River. Colonel Duncan Clinch, the first of many U.S. commanders in the war, employed a force of 250 regulars and over 500 volunteers. The troops moved slowly, giving the natives time to prepare an ambush at the ford over the river. But Colonel Clinch inadvertently thwarted them by not using the ford.

Instead, the army crossed a deep part of the river, six or seven at a time, using a leaky canoe found at the spot. When the regulars had crossed, they formed, marched ahead into a clearing, and rested until Seminole warriors, concealed in the thick woods, opened fire. The troops then formed into line and conducted a bayonet charge against the natives. True to their traditional skirmishing tactics, the Indians promptly withdrew, disappearing into the woods. The regulars suffered 63 casualties, the natives eight. After this Battle of the Withlacoochee, Colonel Clinch withdrew, never reaching the settlement. This proved an operation representative of many in the war.

The unmapped and unexplored terrain presented many problems for the U.S. forces. Mostly flat, it alternated between areas thinly wooded with pines and hammocks and densely forested higher ground. Their knowledge of the country gave the Seminoles a distinct advantage for both finding and evading their adversary in carrying on their raiding strategy.

GENERAL SCOTT'S CAMPAIGN

Early in 1836 General Winfield Scott took command, having an augmented force of regulars and more volunteers raised for short periods of service. He would have about 4,000 men to engage the Seminoles. Very capable and learned in modern large-scale warfare, Scott planned an envelopment by three columns converging from north, east, and south. They were to advance simultaneously in late March 1836 and coordinate their movements by firing a cannon morning and night.

The northern column under Colonel Clinch easily crossed the Withlacoochee with wheeled flatboats brought for the purpose. The natives fired

on the crossing but inflicted few casualties before withdrawing when the
line troops charged. But Clinch found no other enemy, having driven the
Seminoles, he presumed, into the hands of the other columns. The southern
column had moved slowly, Indian skirmishers harassing it all the way; but
it too found no other adversary. The force coming from the east, which
also suffered from skirmishers as they crossed rivers, arrived five days late
and also found no one to fight. The envelopment, an essay in combat strategy, had most emphatically failed.

Scott's effort had failed to engage the enemy because he campaigned with
only 4,000 men in a theater of operations three-fourths the size of Massachusetts. So the U.S. commanders would have to discard combat strategy
and, like their forefathers in Virginia and New England, find an effective
means of combatting an adversary so adept at skirmishing tactics and raiding strategy.

THE UNITED STATES EVOLVES A LOGISTIC STRATEGY

Scott's successor, General Richard K. Call, endeavored to establish four
bases, supplied by steamboat, from which U.S. units could penetrate the
Indians' principal base area along the Withlacoochee and nearby. He had
wished to advance in the summer when he could find crops in the fields
vulnerable to destruction, but he could not complete his logistic preparations in time.

General Call's first offensive reached the Withlacoochee, but the Indians
prevented a crossing. The second offensive reached the heart of the native
base area, discovered and burned three vacant villages, and found, attacked, and counted 20 bodies of a hostile force. It also captured baggage
and horses. His further movements resulted in skirmishes with the natives
but little more logistic damage.

Call's successor, General Thomas S. Jesup, continued the strategy of logistic raids into the Seminole base area. Although they rarely found or
destroyed any Indian depots, they did have a significant effect because, to
avoid conflict with these powerful mobile contingents, the natives had to
remove their supplies and equipment to safe locations. This made Jesup's
operation work as a logistic strategy, slowly depleting the Indians by the
wear and tear of movement.

The United States increased its strength, and not just with more regulars.
The navy augmented its contribution when sailors garrisoned forts, and the
commandant of the marine corps assumed personal command of the substantial marine contingent. This enabled General Jesup to build and hold
more forts, which further threatened the Seminoles.

He augmented the effect of more forts by having seven strong forces
engaged in systematic patrolling. Since these contingents were small enough
to invite attack, they acted according to Washington's advice. When five

or six hundred natives pounced on a camped patrol in a predawn attack, the fortified defense of a log breastwork saved them.

A joint navy and army patrol even used canoes to penetrate the swampy area of south Florida. By the close of the war, the navy was employing seven ships and 140 dugout canoes. In addition to the navy and marines and the volunteer forces, Jesup had nearly two-thirds of the regular army at his disposal. Such a large force with so much of it in motion increased the opportunity for finding a native camp.

But the Seminoles' willingness to fight a battle led to a notable victory for Colonel Zachary Taylor and his troops. The natives took a position on a hammock, having prepared by clearing a field of fire through tall grass and cutting notches in the trees to steady their aim. With over 1,000 men, mostly regulars, Taylor had a two-to-one numerical superiority. As he arrayed his men for the frontal attack, he rejected a suggestion to assail the Seminole flank. But, after his attackers suffered heavily and fell back, he changed his mind and sent his reserve to turn the enemy flank. This precipitated the Indian withdrawal and ended the Battle of Okeechobee. Although the U.S. forces suffered 138 casualties and the natives 25, this tactical defeat became a U.S. victory because the enemy retreated. Yet, the next day, when the troops collected 300 cattle and 100 ponies, Taylor did gain a substantial logistic victory.

But Jesup won the biggest victory of the war when he invited the Seminoles for a peace conference, and, as they waited for a decision from Washington, he broke the flag of truce and sent all 500 west of the Mississippi. Jesup's effective, if nefarious, method clashed with the view of most regular army officers that the natives were in the right, only acting as patriots, and that the United States waged an unjust war.

When General Taylor succeeded Jesup, he accentuated the existing logistic strategy, dividing much of the country into squares, 20 miles by 20 miles, building a small fort in each, and prescribing daily patrolling within it. He also facilitated control by building more roads. In eight months he had built 53 new fortified points and 848 miles of wagon road. This increase in force seriously inhibited Seminole raids and other movements.

The army extended its strategy to a thorough exploration of the country and continued it until no spot remained uninvestigated. This paid large dividends when the troops discovered three major bases, one deep in a big swamp. The soldiers also found crops growing in the swamps and, altogether, uncovered 500 acres of crops. This tightening of the control of the countryside better implemented the logistic persisting strategy while making movement to the west more attractive. The harassment of the natives, which resulted from this persisting logistic strategy, caused many natives to decide to go to the western reservation.

When, in 1842, the government finally accepted the army's reiterated recommendation to leave the remaining Seminoles alone if they stayed in the far South, the Second Seminole war ended.

So the U.S. forces, far larger and more amply supplied than those available to the Virginia and New England colonists 200 years before, had required more than six years to attain victory. Since the Seminole and the colonists' war demonstrated the superiority of raiding strategy, the far greater space available to the Seminoles accounts for the longer war. It did so by making a persisting logistic strategy so difficult to implement. Of course, the lack of settlers using the fortified defense made it impossible to use the method of the seventeenth-century colonists. But, by studding the country with forts and linking them by persistent, aggressive patrolling, the army raised the ratio of force to space, gained many of the advantages of a persisting strategy, and contributed to the political settlement.

Chapter 3

The United States in the Great Sioux War, 1876–1877

The war between the United States and the Sioux Indians and their allies began in early 1876 when the United States wished to transplant many of the Indians from eastern Montana to a reservation in the southern part of the Dakota territory. Further, to give better access to the gold discovered in the Black Hills, the United States wanted to remove that area from the Indian's reservation. The natives particularly resented the loss of this picturesque and revered wooded area. Thus the Indians, and the Sioux in particular, had a very serious grievance when the United States ordered them to move from Montana to southern Dakota by the end of January 1876. When they failed to comply, army troops, under capable and experienced General George Crook, began an advance north in Wyoming to compel them to move.

LOGISTICS

This war took place in the Northern Great Plains, a rolling grassy area populated by large numbers of bison, called buffalo, which filled the natives' need for food, clothing, material for tents, and much else. In a further contrast with the forested East, the natives used horses, acquired and bred from those brought by the Spaniards to North America. Because the grass sustained the horses and the bison, the natives could live and supply themselves in a vast territory of thousands of square miles.

The region offered the same resources to the regular troops whom the army employed in this campaign. But the army was less prepared to feed itself as exclusively from bison and the area's other products. That steamboats could navigate the Missouri and some of its tributaries that ran through the area gave the army some access to its remote base area.

TACTICS

Since the time of the Seminole War, the rifle had undergone a major transformation. The introduction of the breechloader more than doubled the rate of reloading and of fire and made it possible to do so, not standing as with the muzzleloader, but with the very substantial protection of the prone position. In addition to sabre and pistol, cavalry also carried the new rifle for fighting on foot. The Indian also relied on the rifle, which he could use while mounted or on foot.

STRATEGY

The skill of the well-mounted native riders meant that they could easily avoid combat, moving effortlessly away over the plains' vast spaces. The army had already learned that by exercising their option to avoid combat, the Indians could baffle any U.S. combat strategy. Many natives spent the warm weather moving from place to place, finding fresh grass for their horses, hunting the bison, and accumulating meat to carry them through the winter. This lack of herds, crops, and villages to destroy seemed to preclude the use of a logistic strategy.

But the climate in the northern plains made it possible to implement a logistic strategy through a winter campaign. The region had a very severe winter, the average January low temperature being nearly 0 degrees Fahrenheit. The average obscured the great fluctuations in temperature, typical of the continental climate. When the chinook winds from the west brought balmy days, temperatures could be as warm as the 50s. But just as often there could be blizzards and cold as severe as 30 degrees below zero and records approaching 50 degrees below. The predominant north wind, normally quite strong, produced a chill that often made the effective temperature lower by 20 and even 40 or 50 degrees.

Instead of moving as they did in the warm weather, the natives coped with these winters by building villages where they stored their winter food supply and spent the season avoiding exposure to the fierce weather. Thus immobilized, Indians' villages and their supplies became vulnerable to a logistic strategy if the army could keep moving in such weather. This is exactly what the army attempted when General Crook advanced northward in Wyoming to compel the natives to move.

Although the army was used to winter campaigning, this operation did not go well. The unseasonable cold in March froze thermometers and caused an officer with Crook to complain to the general in chief that two months' campaigning in that weather had aged him five years.

It may also have contributed to his bungling performance in leading the advance. Having surprised a native settlement and captured its horses and food, he was unready when the Sioux counterattacked, allowing them to recapture the horses. He completed the fiasco by destroying the food he had taken. Since that food was to have supplied the U.S. troops, General Crook had to fall back to his base, thus ending the campaign. So the army had to have a summer campaign to enforce the government's requirements and to use a combat, rather than a logistic, strategy. Although the army command knew the virtual futility of trying a combat strategy, it had little choice and so devised a plan that resembled General Scott's in the Seminole War. Because of the natives' strong opposition to the government's desires, the army would experience more combat than it expected.

THE LITTLE BIG HORN CAMPAIGN

For this operation the army had doubtless the most accomplished and capable chain of command in its history. The commander in chief, President U. S. Grant, had as the army's general chief his Civil War collaborator, General W. T. Sherman. The leadership for the summer campaign came from five distinguished Civil War veterans: Lieutenant General P. H. Sheridan, commander of the theater of operations; Brigadier General Alfred Terry; Brigadier General George Crook; Colonel John Gibbon; and Lieutenant Colonel George Custer.

For the summer, Sheridan planned three converging movements that took place in a far larger theater of operations than had Scott's in Florida. Colonel Gibbon, for example, had to march his detachment of 400 men 600 miles from western Montana to meet the others in the East. General Crook would again move north from Wyoming into Montana, and General Terry would march the 300 miles west from Bismarck to the junction point in eastern Montana. His cavalry, under Custer, and his infantry together numbered 1,100 men.

Ready for war, the Indians had concentrated their forces, supplied them by moving periodically to new sources of grass and buffalo, and remained south of the Yellowstone River. Colonel Gibbon, the first to reach the eastern Montana rendezvous, remained north of the Yellowstone, alert for the Sioux army, believed to be at least 1,500 strong. Both Gibbon and the Sioux awaited the arrival of Crook and Terry.

Having crossed into Montana by 10 June, Crook met the Sioux on Rosebud Creek. He had 1,300 men, all cavalry or infantry on mules. The Indians, with about the same number, began the action with an attack, and after a battle with each alternating assaults, both combatants retreated. The United States lost 10 dead, killed 36 Indians, and expended 25,000 rounds of ammunition. After this Battle of Rosebud Creek, the usually aggressive General Crook fell back 40 miles and waited a month for reinforcements.

His men made the most of the Montana summer, catching 15,000 trout, while their general, by abandoning concentration in time, thus gave the Sioux ample opportunity to concentrate in space against Terry.

The Battle of Rosebud Creek was unusual in that it occurred at all. The Indians usually avoided battles and, when they fought, stayed on the defensive. But the strength of their grievance against the United States changed their strategy. Situated between the converging forces with perhaps 3,000 men, they could concentrate in space on interior lines of operation, striking first Crook and then Terry. So a strategy of converging on exterior lines to keep the natives from escaping made Sheridan's forces vulnerable to concentration on interior lines of operation.

By the time of the battle on the Rosebud, of which they were unaware, Terry and Gibbon had united and now searched for the natives and for word of Crook. Ordinarily this would have availed them little, but the Indians, with the veterans of the fight on the Rosebud rejoined, wanted a battle. Even though Crook had retreated and the Indian force now concentrating against him was probably 3,000 strong, Terry's men were not in peril. He had in his and Gibbon's force 1,500 disciplined regular toops with which to oppose militia, one that was quite indifferently equipped with a very heterogeneous armament. So he disposed his forces on the assumptions that the Sioux army was about the size of his own, that Crook was active in the field, and that the major problem was to forestall an Indian escape. In his determination not to have the natives elude him, he attempted an envelopment with his and Gibbon's infantry going to the right and Custer and the cavalry to the left.

Custer was equally determined that the enemy should not escape and thus divided his forces in order to envelop his adversary. So, while he led the main body ahead, Custer detailed two subordinates, Reno and Benteen, to lead two separate detachments to envelop from the left while he moved forward on the right.

Since Custer's cavalry approached the Sioux before Terry, the Sioux concentrated against him, making their initial contact with Major Reno. Perceiving himself assailed by a large number of natives, the major assumed the defensive and waited for Custer. This attack held Reno while the bulk of the Sioux army concentrated against Custer.

So, instead of Custer and Terry enveloping the natives, the Sioux had interior lines to concentrate against Custer and may even have had interior lines between Custer's two wings, his own and Reno's. The Sioux surrounded Custer's cavalry, who dismounted to fight in a very exposed position. Then, true to their skirmishing tradition in tactics, the natives took cover and kept up a steady fire until the Battle of the Little Big Horn ended with the extinction of Custer and his men. Custer's force perished just as had Major Dade's at the beginning of the war with the Seminoles. By the time Terry reached the place where Custer had fought, the victorious Sioux army had withdrawn.

In seeking envelopment and striving for concentration in time, Sheridan and all of the generals were quite aware that they were operating on ex-terior lines and exposing themselves to concentration in space. But they did not believe that this had any significance because the Indians never at-tacked. Of course, if they could have had perfectly synchronized concen-tration in time, they could have won.

The army responded to the defeat by sending large reinforcements to Terry and Crook, who marched around an area five times the size of Mas-sachusetts. They encountered no natives, but General Sheridan had not expected that they would, only feeling it necessary to do something. For decisive action, he waited for a winter campaign.

THE WINTER CAMPAIGN OF 1876–1877

The winter campaign implemented a logistic strategy by endeavoring to deprive the natives of their winter supplies. In this respect it closely resem-bled the logistic strategy used in seventeenth-century Virginia. The army took advantage of its superior resources, particularly in pack mules, ample food, and, especially, warm clothing. An early and significant victory by General Crook made an auspicious beginning for the campaign.

On 4 November 1876 he moved north in Wyoming with 2,200 men. On 24 November a scout reported the location of an Indian winter camp. Crook sent forward 1,100 cavalry who arrived in time to carry out an early morning surprise attack the next day. Awakened from a sound sleep, most natives had to leave the camp hurriedly, some warriors with little more than their rifles and ammunition. After a day-long struggle, the U.S. troops captured the village of 200 huts. While 400 warriors held the bluff above the village, the soldiers completed the burning of the huts and the destruc-tion of their contents, particularly clothing and the winter's supply of meat. They then withdrew, taking with them 700 captured horses.

The defeated and dispossessed natives then retreated north to Montana. That night they experienced 30-degree-below-zero cold, which killed 11 babies, injured many adults, caused more deaths later, and further demor-alized the victims of a major victory for the army's logistic strategy. Crook achieved nothing else of note—but did not need to.

In eastern Montana the army had planned another winter logistic cam-paign. This consisted of building a fort and stationing a regiment of infan-try along the Yellowstone River. When Colonel Nelson A. Miles brought his regiment of 500 men to the Yellowstone in the summer, preparation began. Miles, one of the ablest soldiers in the army, then built a fortified base on the Yellowstone from which he would conduct his operations. He stocked it with tons of hay and firewood for the winter as well as food and medical supplies. These came by steamer until the runoff of the summer rains ended, the river level dropped, and supplies came by wagon trains.

On 18 October Miles set out with infantry, artillery, and supply wagons. The supplies were to support the infantry in a winter campaign to destroy the Sioux villages and supplies or, at least, to force them to spend the winter moving from camp to camp with the resulting loss of supplies and equipment. Harried by Miles, a large group of Sioux tried to drive him away, but this interrupted their final hunting of the season and the noise of the gunfire frightened the buffalo away.

After returning to his base for rest and resupply, Miles set out on 5 November for what would prove to be a 50-day campaign in which he scoured the area between the Yellowstone and Missouri rivers. Although he eventually spread his coverage by dividing his force into three detachments, he had no tangible success until almost the end of the campaign.

Still, this activity compelled the natives to move, thus doing them unmeasured harm by steadily depleting their logistic base by the wear and tear of constant movement, including the complete uprooting of winter villages, which involved dismantling teepees and moving them and their contents, usually through snow and often in intense cold. The vicissitudes of the natives are well understood by noting the hardships of the lavishly equipped and supplied army. The army's method of continuing to march in a blizzard shows the difficulty of this winter campaigning. Though unable to see through the snow, the troops kept going, following a compass course. They moved in single file, keeping in touch with one another. As the lead soldier became exhausted by opening the path through the deep snow, he dropped to the rear and another took the arduous front position.

Two of Miles's detachments returned without finding any Sioux, one having marched 558 miles without making significant contact. The natives eluded the remaining detachment under Lieutenant Baldwin by crossing the Missouri River on the ice and then, by making the river bank a defensive position, stymied Baldwin. Then marching through a blizzard and temperatures of 35 degrees below zero, the lieutenant reached Fort Peck, replenished his supplies, and set out on a renewed march, carrying 40 of his sick or exhausted men in wagons.

Early in the afternoon of 18 December he saw smoke, and his reconnaissance found an Indian camp ahead, near Ash Creek. Baldwin moved forward rapidly, the feeble men joining in the attack, and attained complete surprise. With most of the warriors away hunting, the people in the camp fled. The army destroyed 90 huts, captured 60 horses, and burned the food and buffalo furs they could not carry away.

The native warriors followed Baldwin's force, but, its camp fortified by the wagons and cargo, the detachment repulsed the attack. Reinforced by troops who marched out from the base, Baldwin's debilitated men returned to the base on 23 December, having marched 716 miles in 50 days. The

mileage was a measure of his harassment and depletion of the enemy accomplished before the very substantial success of the Ash Creek surprise.

Colonel Miles planned yet another campaign, one into the area south of
the Yellowstone River. His men might be tired, but they would be even
better equipped. They had improved buffalo overcoats, which reached their
ankles and had collars that could turn well above their ears. A doctor with
the regiment believed that the troops had on too many clothes and that
their long overcoats impeded their marching. But on this campaign he said
that he was cold on two days, even though he wore the following:

two pair of woolen socks

buffalo mocassins and leggings

buffalo overshoes

two pair of drawers, one of them buckskin

two pair of pants, one made out of a blanket

five shirts, one of buckskin and one made of a blanket

a coat and a buffalo overcoat

a blanket cap that could cover the face

a muffler

buckskin gloves inside blanket-lined buckskin mittens

The doctor's clothing amply illustrates a relationship between logistics and
strategy.

The contrast of this elaborate equipment with the comparatively meager
provision of the natives shows how powerful a logistic strategy was Miles's
marches, which merely made the logistically ill-prepared adversary conform
to his movements.

On 29 December Miles moved out of his base with most of his men and
his two cannon disguised as supply wagons. With scouts and an advanced
guard ahead, his careful march had flank and rear guards also. Like a
Roman army, he started and halted early, in a defensible position with time
for the troops to improve it.

It was well that he took these precautions because Crazy Horse, who
commanded the natives, planned an ambush; but Miles detected the presence of the Sioux. After a day of feeling each other out and a failed Sioux
night attack, a battle began with the natives making a determined strike
until a blizzard halted the battle.

That the Indians fought a battle at all is a testimonial to the effectiveness
of Miles's logistic strategy, as well as to the depth of their feeling about
the issue at stake in the war. The battle had no military importance but
did have significant political impact by adding substantially to the discouragement already felt by the Sioux and their allies.

Fortuitously, at this propitious moment, the United States changed its peace terms to allow the natives to stay in their traditional location and keep their rifles and horses. By the spring, Chief Crazy Horse and 3,000 others had agreed to these terms. So, before the logistic strategy could deplete the Indians' military power, its political effect and a change in U.S. peace terms ended the Great Sioux War.

The failure of the U.S. summer campaign has received most of the attention devoted to this war. The failure came because of the ability of the Sioux to refuse battle when operating in a base area in which they, like the Seminoles, could move in any direction. The army could do likewise, but, with pursuit having no advantage over retreat, it could not effectively implement a combat strategy. Nor, as the experience in the Seminole War had shown, was it easy to carry out a logistic strategy under these circumstances.

But the army had long known this and had learned how to use the climate of the northern plains to make possible a logistic strategy.

Part II

Operations from a Remote Base Area

When armies had to remain long in one place, as for sieges, or were too large for the region to support, they had to operate from a remote base area. Part II deals with armies dependent on distant bases and with sea and air forces, which have always depended on a remote base.

Chapter 4

The Commerce-Raiding War in the Atlantic, 1940–1945

In World War II the far-superior British fleet had control of the Atlantic, preventing the Germans from using it for trade and permitting the flow of commerce between the British Isles and the rest of the world. This dominance of the Atlantic sea lanes was essential to the British economy and to any land or air campaign Britain and the United States wished to conduct against their common enemies, Germany and Italy. Yet the German navy challenged this command of the sea by application of a raiding strategy.

LOGISTICS

When warships depended on sail, they could carry enough food and water for months at sea. With the introduction of the steamer, they could no longer linger at sea. But, by World War II, most warships, using oil instead of coal, could refuel at sea fairly easily. Their vulnerable tankers, however, depended on a remote base area.

TACTICS AND STRATEGY

For several hundred years, command of the sea hinged on outnumbering the adversary in big ships with great firepower and thick wooden sides or, later, steel armor. Even so, the exercise of this command depended on cruisers, which were smaller, faster ships that protected the commerce and military movements of the stronger, often convoying groups of ships. They also interdicted similar movements of the weaker sea power. This application of command corresponded to persisting strategy on land and had its closest parallel in the blockade of enemy ports.

The tasks of the cruisers had great importance because the weaker sea power naturally responded to the persisting logistic strategy of blockade with a logistic raiding strategy against the dominant power's commerce. In the eighteenth-century wars between Britain and France, for example, the British blockaded the main French ports while, from the smaller ones, the French sent out commerce raiders that would capture or sink hundreds of British merchant ships during each year of the long wars.

By the 1880s, the steam-powered, steel, armored battleship had an established design: about four big guns firing a shell as heavy as 1,000 pounds, armor as thick as 16 inches, and speed as high as 14 knots. In combat they were much superior to cruisers, but only on the defense. Since the cruisers' higher speed enabled them to outrun battleships, the bigger ships could dominate where they were but could not destroy the weaker. Inasmuch as battleships cost too much to have enough to protect commerce or guard convoys, cruisers would usually fight cruisers in the attack and defense of commercial and military movements.

So the demands imposed by the raiding strategy conditioned tactics and the design of cruisers. By the 1880s cruisers varied in size, but many carried 4-inch or larger guns, firing shells weighing 30 to 50 pounds. Called protected cruisers, they had no side armor but a thin, concave, steel deck that joined the ships' sides below the waterline, thus protecting the engines and the magazines for powder and shells. Still, this type of defense left the waterline and the ships' buoyancy vulnerable to the gunfire of other cruisers.

By varying the combination of firepower, speed, and the thickness of the deck and gun shields, sailors and naval architects strove to increase the power and utility of cruisers. This included introducing the armored cruiser, which became commonplace in the British and French navies after 1900. Its armored waterline gave more security to the engine and magazines as well as conserving buoyancy. Typically armored cruisers had higher speed and a very powerful armament, usually 6-inch guns and some as large as 9.2 inches, firing a 380-pound shell. These attributes made the armored cruiser a weapon system inherently dominant over the protected cruiser and so better for attacking and defending commerce and convoys. Inevitably it gained a role in scouting, fending off enemy cruisers engaged in this work and backing up its own. In 1906, on the eve of World War I, the British brought forth another new type, the battle cruiser, an armored cruiser with the 12-inch guns then typical of battleships. Further, it had a speed of 25 knots, two knots faster than the armored and other cruisers of the time. Thus the British had created a class of ship having an inherent advantage over the armored cruiser.

Although the speeds of cruisers had increased by the outbreak of World War I in 1914, the effort to create fundamentally dominant naval weapon systems worked as expected when, off the Falkland Islands in December

1914, a German squadron of two armored and three protected cruisers met a British squadron containing two battle cruisers, three armored cruisers, and two protected cruisers.

The battle cruisers, with 12-inch guns and 25-knot speed, pursued the German armored cruisers with 210-mm (8.27-in.) guns and 22.5-knot speed, easily overtaking and defeating them at a range of 12,000 yards, a distance at which the German shells could not pierce the British armor. While the battle cruisers sank the armored cruisers, the British armored cruisers pursued the fleeing German protected cruisers, a difficult task because they had little or no speed advantage over the newer German cruisers. The fastest of the three German cruisers soon escaped its pursuers.

But one of the British armored cruisers, the *Cornwall,* slowly gained on its quarry, the unarmored German *Leipzig.* The British ship's fourteen 6-inch guns fired a shell three times as heavy as the *Leipzig*'s ten 105-mm (4.13-in.) guns. After a long chase, the *Cornwall* closed the range sufficiently to score enough hits to slow the *Leipzig* to 15 knots and put her at the *Cornwall*'s mercy. She continued fighting until she sank with only 18 survivors. The four-inch armor of the Cornwall meant that the 18 hits she received harmed not a man on the ship.

In the contest between the remaining ships, the British armored cruiser *Kent,* identical to the *Cornwall,* pursued the German protected cruiser *Nurnberg,* similar to the *Leipzig* in armament. But over eight miles separated the racing ships, and sunset approached. The British captain exceeded his ship's designed speed by adding to the coal in his boiler fires his ship's furniture and other painted and varnished wood. But his visibility never improved because, as the *Kent,* gained on the *Nurnberg,* the darker it became. Then, in twilight, some of the German ship's boiler tubes failed, reducing its speed, and allowing the *Kent* to come within 3,000 yards. At this range the gunners could see the target and quickly sank the German ship with only seven survivors. The *Kent,* armored like the *Cornwall,* received 36 hits but suffered only 16 casualties.

Before World War I, Germany had built many battleships in an attempt to rival the British for command of the sea, but before World War II they built very powerful commerce raiders instead. These included four battleships with battle-cruiser speed, two of 32,000 tons and two of 42,000 tons. Their speed would enable them to outrun battleships, and their armor and firepower would allow them to overwhelm convoy escorts and quickly destroy the ships. In addition, the Germans built for commerce raiding three armored cruisers with the exceptionally powerful armament of six 283-mm (11.14-in.) guns, but a speed of only 26 knots, easily overtaken by the intrinsically superior battle-cruiser weapon system. But, when designed and built, the British had only three battle cruisers, and by World War II the Allies had only five, France having built two.

It happened that, early in the war, three British cruisers overtook one of the raiding German armored cruisers, the *Graf Spee,* named after the admiral defeated at the Battle of the Falkland Islands. It fought them near the mouth of the River Plate, defeating but not sinking the more lightly armed and armored British ships, and took refuge in the Uraguayan port of Montevideo. When Uraguayan authorities forced the ship to leave the harbor, the German captain expected the early arrival of an Allied battle cruiser, either the French *Strasbourg* (30 knots, eight 330-mm [13-in.] guns) or the British *Renown* (30 knots, six 15-in. guns). The captain scuttled his ship outside the harbor rather than suffer the fate of Admiral Spee by facing the superior speed, armor, and firepower of an inherently dominant weapon system.

A year and a half later, when one of the big battleships, the *Bismarck,* made a commerce raid, the British pursued and sank it before it could sink a convoy. These surface raiders did some damage, caused the Allies much anxiety, but proved ineffective as raiders compared with the submarine, a weapon system with both tactical and strategic antecedents.

THE TORPEDO AND THE SUBMARINE

The Whitehead automobile torpedo developed into a weapon system whose potential seized the imagination of naval tacticians. Invented in 1866, this slender, pointed projectile moved underwater, propelled by a compressed-air engine and kept on its course by a gyroscope. Its first use in combat, by a British cruiser against a Peruvian warship, proved a humiliating failure for the Whitehead torpedo. The lookouts on the Peruvian ship saw the torpedo coming, its course clearly visible from the bubbles of its compressed-air exhaust. The somewhat antiquated Peruvian ship, originally designed for the navy of the Confederate States of America, turned away and outran the ten-knots-per-hour torpedo. Improvements followed, and by the twentieth century torpedoes could make 30 knots.

Yet this new weapon gave rise to a family of small, fast boats to attack battleships and cruisers with torpedoes. These torpedo boats employed a naval version of skirmishing tactics when they attacked at high speed on erratic courses, launched their torpedoes at close range, and then dashed away. Some naval thinkers saw in the torpedo boat a weapon system essentially dominant over the battleship. But, because torpedo boats were too small to be sea going, they could only dominate battleships in such situations as coast defense.

Navies responded to this threat by adding to their ships' armament small, rapid-firing cannon to fight off torpedo boats. Further they created yet another weapon system with a fundamental advantage, the torpedo-boat destroyer. Larger than a torpedo boat and faster, this ship, soon called simply a destroyer, could use its guns to sink torpedo boats and its speed to avoid their torpedoes and to catch the boats. But soon destroyers carried torpedoes as well, filling some of the role of torpedo boats and, as they grew in size, eventually assuming some of the functions of cruisers.

Devalued by the destroyer and the anti-torpedo-boat armament of larger ships, the torpedo boat continued in a new guise, the diving torpedo boat, or submarine. Not perfected until the eve of World War I, this small boat cruised on the surface with a diesel engine that also charged the batteries that powered the submarine's electric motors for submerged operation. If it spotted an adversary, the submarine would dive, either to escape or attack. Submerged, it could move as fast as eight knots, for a brief period, using its battery-powered electric motors, which required no oxygen. Seeing the surface vessel through a periscope, the captain fired the torpedoes by aiming the submarine. At the outbreak of World War I in 1914, all navies had submarines, the British and French the most, but no one knew how effective they might be. One authority thought they would drive surface ships from the sea and, on the eve of World War I, a British naval officer was convinced that "the submarine is only a toy; it can easily be driven off by a machine gun or a well-directed rifle bullet."

When the First World War began, the German navy, with its surface ships confined to port by the blockade of the superior British navy, early sent to sea its little flotilla of submarines, called U-boats. Inexperienced in war and apprehensive that the black smoke from their primitive diesel engines would reveal their location, German submarine commanders also felt concern about their boats' disconcerting tendency to bob to the surface when they fired a torpedo. Yet they soon proved the value of the submarine.

The most spectacular success came in the second month of the war when a submarine observed three huge British armored cruisers patrolling off the coast of Holland. Unobserved, the German submarine U-9 took advantage of the ships' steady speed and straight course to torpedo one of the 12,000-ton cruisers. When it immediately began to sink and the other two ships halted and stood by to pick up survivors, the submarine torpedoed first one and then the other, the sinking ships aggregating more than 50 times its own weight. Never again would any ship steer such a predictable course or be as naive as to stand by to pick up survivors.

Early in the war, surface ships could look for a submarine's periscope and then try to ram it. Often ships waited in an area where a submarine had dived for it to come to the surface when its batteries had discharged. As submarines improved and their captains became more skillful, these methods had little chance of success.

But by 1917 the surface ships had the hydrophone, a listening device that could hear a submerged submarine if it were in motion. Ships thus equipped, especially the destroyer, which proved the ideal antisubmarine ship, could attack the submerged submarine with the depth charge, a cylinder containing explosives that could be set to explode at various depths. If it exploded near enough to a submarine, the increase in water pressure could cause serious leaks in the submarine's hull, and a direct hit would surely sink it. These two devices gave the destroyer an intrinsic ascendancy over the submarine. And, in spite of their elusiveness, submarines presented relatively little threat to warships. By steaming fast, preferably at 20 knots or more and zigzagging, warships made an almost impossible target for a torpedo.

But early in the war a German submarine captured a merchant ship, setting an important example for German naval thought. With a surface speed of 13 to 16 knots, adequate to overtake a freighter, and a gun of three to four inches, a submarine could easily force a merchant ship to surrender. It used its ability to dive only to escape warships. But, to make good its capture, it had to sink its prize, leaving the crew in lifeboats. Britain and her allies immediately began to equip their commercial vessels with guns. Still, with mostly obsolete guns available for this purpose and usually a crew of inept civilian seamen as gunners, merchant ships, thus armed, did not always forestall surface attack. But some freighters, called Q ships, would hide modern guns manned by a naval crew until a surfaced submarine drew close and was vulnerable to a surprise volley of well-aimed shells. The armed merchantman and the Q ship increasingly led the German navy to use scarce torpedoes to sink merchant ships without warning, thus directly causing civilian casualties at sea.

Thus having begun as a rival of the battleship, the World War I torpedo diving boat had such success in commerce raiding that the Germans thought it could win the war by sinking so many British ships that it could cripple Britain's economy and compel it to make peace. Hence the potential of a logistic raiding strategy had conditioned tactics and naval technology, and the Allies used the time-tested strategy of convoying to defeat the submarine raiders by concentrating the antisubmarine ships where the submarines would have to strike.

Many British admirals did not expect that the Germans would revive this failed logistic strategy in another war, and the small number of German submarines available at the beginning of the war tended to confirm their hypothesis. Further, to deal with the submarine in World War II, the British had Sonar or Asdic. It emitted high-frequency vibrations, which, when reflected back, gave the range and direction of submarines. This augmented the destroyer's dominance and helped make the British overconfident about their ability to deal with the submarine.

Nevertheless, they did begin a program of construction of antisubmarine vessels, smaller and slower than destroyers but nearly as effective. Yet, even with the world's largest merchant marine and shipbuilding facilities to match, the British shipyards would be hard pressed to build and repair warships and replace merchant ship losses. The defense of commerce would require all of this productive capacity as well as much tactical skill and strategic acumen, because Germany had an outstanding submarine admiral who had a strategy to counter the convoy.

CONCENTRATION IN CONVOYS AND WOLF PACKS

The submarine campaign started slowly because Germany began the war with only 27 submarines with a range adequate to operate easily in the Atlantic from German ports. The situation began to change in 1940 after the German conquest of Norway, defeat of France, and occupation of France's Atlantic coast. Then, with the addition of the well-situated Norwegian and French bases and an increasing number of submarines, the German fleet began a sustained and increasingly effective campaign of submarine raids against Atlantic commerce. This struggle clearly illustrates the role of concentration of force in operational strategy.

Soldiers, sailors, and airmen typically desired larger forces because numerical superiority provided one way to have greater strength than an antagonist. But a substitute for, and valuable supplement to, going to war with more force is its concentration. This is the principle underlying the old strategy of convoys for protecting merchant ships, applied by the British in the latter part of the First World War and resumed by them at the beginning of World War II.

Rather than using destroyers and other antisubmarine vessels for patrolling in search of the elusive diving boat, convoys concentrated them where they were most likely to meet their enemy, the submarine. Instead of an isolated and unprotected merchant ship, the World War II U-boat had to face several escorting patrol craft armed with depth charges and able to hunt with the new sonar detection system. Further, by substituting the targets of a few convoys for many individual ships spread over the sea, convoying made it more difficult for the German raiders to find their quarry. In World War II the German navy responded to concentration in convoys by using concentration itself.

The commander of the German submarines in World War II, the shrewd veteran of World War I submarine service, Admiral Karl Doenitz, used long-range radio communication to control his submarines from shore and direct their concentration against a convoy. Since convoys moved at the speed of the slowest ship, the U-boats had a surface speed about double that of convoys, more than enough to maneuver to concentrate ahead of a convoy. To find the convoys, the admiral spread his submarines across a likely part of the ocean, each watching for a convoy and reporting to him its own position. The submarines covered a sizable area because a convoy of 40 ships, for example, steaming in columns abreast occupied a considerable patch of ocean, especially with the visibility added by smoke from some steamers' smokestacks.

When a U-boat spotted and reported the position and course of a convoy,

Doenitz, knowing the location of his boats, ordered them to concentrate at a point to intercept and engage the convoy.

The assembled submarines, having concentrated in space, then concentrated in time by attacking simultaneously, thus outnumbering the defending escorts. The U-boats preferred to attack at night, remaining on the surface in order to have much better observation than a periscope could give; and, in doing so, they also exploited their small size and low profile to make themselves nearly invisible in the dark. A U-boat captain, who positioned himself in a lane between the convoy's ships, could torpedo as many as three ships, a fine night's work. Thus their tactics helped to elude the defenders, and their concentration in time outnumbered the escorts and confronted them with too-challenging a task. The concentration in space into "wolf packs" did resemble the cooperation of wolves in seeking their prey.

Admiral Doenitz's strategy of concentration against a convoy accentuated the importance of intelligence of enemy movements and caused each side to increase its information-collection efforts. The Germans, for example, supplemented their submarine reconnaissance by monitoring Anglo-American radio messages to determine ship locations and to decipher the coded messages. Such efforts could find out the course, or altered course, of a convoy. The British, American, and Canadian navies did the same thing. When they could find the point of concentration by tracking submarine movements or decoding Admiral Doenitz's instructions, they could change a convoy's course to avoid the wolf pack. Code breaking contributed much to both sides' maneuvers.

The same striving for better intelligence led to more use of aircraft for reconnaissance, with the Allies taking advantage of it the most. The British installed radar on their reconnaissance aircraft to aid in finding submarines. They also armed the planes, large bombers or flying boats, with depth charges and, like ground-attack aircraft, with machine guns and light cannon. Vulnerable to attack by such aircraft, the U-boats responded by equipping themselves with radar detectors; but the British then changed the frequency of their radars. When the Germans ran submerged in the day and only surfaced at night, the British prepared for this by equipping their airplanes with searchlights for night attacks on submarines found by radar.

Ultimately the Germans baffled the aircraft by equipping the submarines with snorkels, a small device above the water that let air through a pipe into the submerged submarine to enable it to operate its diesel engine below the surface. Because the snorkel was too small for radar detection and the U-boats could then cruise below the surface, they had ceased to be merely diving boats and had become, for a time, very nearly submarines. But remaining submerged inhibited their ability to find their quarry, and the Allies soon had more sensitive radar that could spot a snorkel.

The Allies strengthened their air reconnaisance and submarine-attack capabilities by adding small aircraft carriers to a convoy's vessels. With more escorts, they created support groups of antisubmarine ships that could come to the aid of an attacked convoy, thus making a defensive concentration against Doenitz's for the offensive. Because of their superior organization and good ability to keep in contact for tactical maneuver, the escorts and support groups had many of the advantages of fighting as a team. Yet the wolf packs, ad hoc assemblies, more resembled an aggregate of individuals.

GERMAN CONCENTRATION IN SPACE

But, all along, Admiral Doenitz had successfully used concentration in another way, by directing his forces on to the most vulnerable sea routes. For example, when he gained his French bases, the admiral moved some of his submarines to the coast of West Africa and the major part of his remaining boats westward in the Atlantic. In both areas his U-boats found convoys that had yet to meet their inbound escorts and were relying entirely on the difficulty of a single submarine finding a convoy. In markedly increasing their sinkings, his submarines showed that they had made the most of this concentration against weakness. In 1941 Doenitz again shifted his North Atlantic attack, moving it even farther west to avoid the augmented British air patrols.

When Germany went to war with the United States in December 1941, Doenitz immediately concentrated against the unconvoyed shipping on the U.S. Atlantic coast. To devise a way to operate any U-boats there required some imagination, because Germany lacked submarines with the range to cruise so far away. Because some German submarines relied for their water supply partly on tanks of fresh water and partly on distilling sea water, the submarine could use the water tanks for enough additional fuel to give adequate cruising time off the American coast. The result was acute crew discomfort from the partial dehydration of the inadequate distilled water ration but a "happy time" of sinking so many ships with so little hazard to themselves. When the U.S. Navy began convoying, the admiral made concentrations against weak escort arrangements in the Caribbean Sea and off the north coast of South America.

The campaigns in the Atlantic resulted in the defeat of the U-boats. In its most successful period the average life of a submarine reached 13 months; at the end of the war it was only three months. In the first year and a half of operations, the submarines sank more ships than British and American yards built. Thereafter, construction soared, kept pace with rising sinkings in 1942, and reached twenty times the shrunken sinking tonnages of the last year of the war.

In view of the poor German preparations for the war and slow acceleration of submarine construction, the navy brought inadequate resources to the war, especially when compared with the overwhelming productive capacity provided by U.S. shipyards for replacing losses and U.S. production for replacing lost cargoes. So operational strategy played no decisive role, but both sides demonstrated how effective concentration could be in conducting this potentially crucial naval campaign.

Yet the submarine campaigns again demonstrated the strategic ascendancy of raiders. They usually had the advantage of a choice of objective, thus creating a confusing ambiguity for the defenders. Not only would defenders be uncertain as to the raiders' target but doubtful of both the route of approach and of withdrawal.

The raiders also derived their strategic ascendancy from the possession of the initiative. A term more often used than defined, in its traditional military meaning *initiative* implies the freedom to act. For our purposes, we define it as the ability to strike something of value to an adversary while not having a similar vulnerability. Thus German submarines could raid Atlantic commerce while offering little or no commerce that the Allied submarines could assail. This meant that the British and Americans made their principal offensive blow against the submarines in World War II by bombing their bases. But the fortified defense, in the form of U-boat anchorages protected by thick, bombproof roofs of reinforced concrete, defeated the attacks.

The Allies' increased emphasis on intelligence of German movements and points of concentration made it a powerful antidote to the raiders' initiative. Thus, if Allied navies knew where the wolf pack would strike, they could evade the attack by rerouting the convoy or provide adequate defense by reinforcing the escort with a support group.

Whereas surprise made a military force weak and vulnerable, the warning given by excellent intelligence would assure strength through readiness. Because gaining surprise conferred the initiative, better and more-comprehensive intelligence would not only take away the initiative an antagonist might otherwise have possessed but would give it to the side who had secured the intelligence.

THE LAST BIG SURFACE RAID

Surface raiders usually had the raiders' advantage, but, toward the end of the war, the last German raider had little chance to surprise its adversary.

The campaign of German surface raiders, which had no potential for effecting the outcome of the war, ended as it had begun, with a battle, when the last active German fast battleship, the *Scharnhorst*, attempted to attack a convoy. Stationed on the Norwegian coast, north of the Arctic circle, it menaced convoys bound to the U.S.S.R. More dangerous to merchant ships than its main armament of nine 283-mm (11.14-in.) guns were its secondary and antiaircraft weapons of rapid-firing guns, twelve 150-mm

(5.9-in.) and fourteen 105-mm (4.13-in.). Steaming through a convoy and firing these 26 guns in all directions, the 32,000-ton *Scharnhorst* could quickly destroy many of the convoy's closely packed ships.

When it began such a cruise in December 1943, it missed the convoy but found itself shadowed by the three cruisers of the convoy's escort. Directed by the cruisers, the 38,000-ton British battleship *Duke of York* intercepted the German ship. Having thicker armor than the *Scharnhorst,* the British ship had little to fear from its 11-inch guns, but the armor of the German ship could not protect it against the *Duke of York*'s ten 14-inch guns, firing a shell over twice as heavy as the German's 11-inch. Though immediately damaged by the rapid and accurate salvos of the 14-inch guns, the 31-knot *Scharnhorst* made its escape by using its battle cruiser speed to outrun the 27-knot *Duke of York.*

Then the four British destroyers accompanying the British battleship pursued and drew abreast of the German ship after a three-hour chase. These versatile little 36-knot ships, barely 5 percent the size of the *Scharnhorst,* assumed their role as torpedo boats, and, acting like skirmishers on land, made confusing individual attacks on the German ship with torpedoes, reducing its speed to only 20 knots. Soon overtaking the *Scharnhorst,* the pursuing *Duke of York* used its big guns to reduce its adversary to a wreck. Then, with a searchlight illuminating the derelict in the darkness, cruisers and destroyers drew alongside the helpless ship and sunk it with salvos of torpedoes, ending the menace of this raider just as the defense had clearly overmastered the U-boat raids.

This victory, like that accumulated by many small successes against the submarine, made the sea lanes secure enough to support the land and air campaigns against Germany and Italy. And the strategy of the struggle for the north Atlantic, which had showed the elusiveness of raiders and the strength of the raid, would repeat itself in the air war, with the advantage belonging to the British and Americans. So the war in the air over Europe would resemble that at sea in this respect as well as in the part again played by offensive and defensive concentration.

Chapter 5

Air Warfare in Northwestern Europe, 1940–1945

The prolonged air war pitted Allied air forces against German, and each against the air defenses of the other's cities.

LOGISTICS

All aircraft depended on a remote base area and used the fortified defense in the same way as navies protected their ports, to secure their bases from hostile attack. This took the form of antiaircraft defenses against high- and low-altitude raids and provision of protected spaces for aircraft. For this, earth banks or concrete walls surrounded an airplane parking space on three sides, shielding it from bomb hits on three sides and also offering some protection from the machine-gun fire of low-flying airplanes.

TACTICS

Early antiaircraft guns for defense against low-level attack were no more than the infantry's machine guns mounted to fire upward. For defense against high-altitude attacks, the defenders often had telephone warnings from ground observers and, when the airplanes came closer, sound detection apparatus that would hear airplane motors at a distance. The detectors had receivers placed so that they could determine both the horizontal direction, or azimuth, and the elevation of the approaching planes. The sound equipment then gave this information to the range finder, enabling it immediately to take the approaching aircraft under observation. The range finder calculated speed and related data with a computer similar to that used on warships and by coast defense guns. The guns, initially field guns with different mountings, fired shells like those containing shrapnel, aimed to intersect the airplane's course and timed to explode when it reached the target. Against night raids, searchlights used the information from the sound detectors to find and illuminate the targets for the range finders. If it were too overcast to see the aircraft, it was too overcast for the aircraft to bomb the target. At night, cities would "black out" most of their lights to thwart night raiders.

Defense also depended on aircraft, and early in World War I air tactics had received their form from the development of the pursuit, or fighter, aircraft. Designed as a weapon system intrinsically superior to the reconnaissance and bombing airplanes, it fulfilled this function especially well when the pusher gave way to the more maneuverable tractor in which the pilot aimed his forward-firing machine guns by aiming the airplane.

At the outbreak of the war, most heavy bombers had two engines only, and only Britain and the United States envisioned using large numbers of four-engine bombers. Representative of the 1940 heavy bomber was the British Wellington bomber, which had two engines, a speed of 235 miles per hour, and a bomb load of 4,500 pounds. Its adversary, the German fighter plane, the Me 109, had a speed of 354 miles per hour and an armament of three 20-mm (.79-in.) cannon and two machine guns. By 1944 the Wellington had given way to the four-engine Lancaster, a little faster and with a bomb load of 18,000 pounds. It faced faster and better armed and armored German fighters and, though it carried eight machine guns, the Lancaster depended on night bombing as its main defense. In daylight the fighter naturally had an advantage over the bomber. Its tactics usually, like skirmishers, prescribed individual action by pilots to approach the bomber at high speed from its most vulnerable angle. Designs of improved bombers sought to give the larger planes the ability to fire a machine gun in any direction. But the bomber flew a straight and level course, and the fighter, a smaller target, approached at a much higher speed, possibly flying an erratic course, and with a rapidly changing range.

Airmen and designers endeavored to give the daylight bomber the ability to defend itself. The name of the U.S. B-17 bomber, Flying Fortress, indicates the defensive concept. Initially the 295-mile-per-hour aircraft carried five .303-inch machine guns, mounted in different positions so as to give an all-around defense. When trials by the British indicated the inadequacy of this defense, the new armament consisted of eight .5-inch machine guns in four turrets plus five in single mountings. The new armament strengthened the line tactics planned to cope with the skirmishing tactics of individual fighters. Formations of bombers would concentrate the fire of each plane's machine guns against the single attacking fighter. But lack of central command and fire coordination made the plan complex to carry out because of the difficulty of the proper gunner on each bomber seeing the same assailant soon enough to act together. Further, when large battles took place between bombers and fighters, the fighters would concentrate in time. So the fighter was the dominant weapon system, and its skirmishing tactics triumphed over the line.

STRATEGY

Many in Europe and America saw airplanes as having a mission independent of their effect on land and sea warfare. Airmen developed their ideas before anyone could see the immense impact aircraft would have in radically extending the range of sea combat and in becoming part of the dramatic and significant restoration of mounted combat on land. One of those who envisioned a separate role for air power was a British airman, Hugh Trenchard, who, late in World War I, pointed out that independent air action could have both a "moral and material effect."

Soon after World War I an Italian soldier, General Giulio Douhet, gave the fullest presentation of these effects, advancing the thesis that a powerful air force could circumvent the World War I ground deadlock of the fortified defense by flying over the siege lines. He argued that deep strikes into the hostile country could make two contributions to victory, each potentially decisive by itself. He saw one effect as essentially political, terrorizing the hostile population by bombing cities. Although such a strategy of political intimidation by raids went back to ancient times, it would have vastly augmented political significance because of popular literacy and public participation in government. Thus a demoralized population could have a decisive influence on public policy by insisting on peace to secure the cessation of air raids.

Further, Douhet believed that the airplane would be especially effective as a raider—its great speed and freedom from ground obstacles would accentuate its elusiveness and enhance the traditional dominance of raiders over defenders.

The second aspect of his thesis also fit the novel conditions of the First World War. The war's prolonged sieges, instead of the traditional mixture of intermittent battles and sieges, had made military operations much more dependent on industrial production. General Douhet recognized that by ignoring the armies and bombing the factories that supplied them, air power could use a logistic strategy to provide a shortcut to victory. Thus he argued for a powerful air force, not for a combat strategy of assailing the hostile armed forces but the logistic objective of the cities that provided their weapons and munitions and the political objective of demoralizing the civilian population.

Arguing from the airplane's ability to increase the traditional dominance of raiders over defenders, the general believed that the bombers would always get through. Thus he argued against dissipation of resources on the less effective defense against air attack and the concentration of all military effort on the dominant offensive and the bombers to execute it.

Although World War I hardly gave his theses a fair trial, it certainly offered no encouragement. The Germans had maintained consistent bombing raids on the United Kingdom from early 1915 until the spring of 1918; yet this did not hinder industrial production nor induce a popular demand to end the war in order to halt the bombing. And the German bombing of British cities in 1940–1941 seemed to have little more effect. With the yet-larger airplanes and even-greater numbers wielded by air forces built in accordance with Douhet's theses, British and American airmen believed that they could attain victory through air power.

THE BATTLE OF BRITAIN

In the summer of 1940 the Germans made an effort to gain a thorough dominance over the British air force. This meant destroying so many of its fighter planes that German bombers could easily attack any target and, particularly, make possible an invasion of England by the German army. It could do this because the air force could then drive Britain's navy from the channel between England and France, enabling Germany's superior army to invade.

To compel Britain's Royal Air Force to fight, they attacked British cities and then airfields, precipitating the Battle of Britain. Then the British committed their fighter aircraft to defending the airfields in aerial combat against German bombers and their escorting fighters.

Because the Royal Air Force had a considerable number of excellent fighter planes and well-trained and mostly seasoned pilots, they inflicted heavy losses on the attackers. They endeavored to use their best fighter, the Spitfire, to engage the German fighters and the 30-miles-per-hour slower Hurricane against the bombers. Since both had eight machine guns, the German fighters would meet their match and the bombers a deadly adversary. The Royal Air Force also had the advantage of fighting on the strategic defensive. This increased their effective fighter strength because the German fighters, flying farther to the arena of combat, had less fighting time in the air than the British planes, fighting near their air bases.

Because Britain had a higher rate of aircraft production than Germany, the Royal Air Force was winning a contest in which it had downed twice as many planes as the Germans. Moreover, the Germans lost a higher proportion of pilots because the British pilots of crashed airplanes that reached the ground safely usually did so in friendly territory, whereas most downed German pilots became British prisoners or landed in the English Channel where many drowned. Greatly overestimating British losses, the Germans continued their campaign for a month and a half before fully realizing that they were losing. From the fall into the spring of 1941 they carried out night bombing raids against British cities, particularly London. Though far more punishing, these raids were akin to those of the First World War in their objective of making the war unpleasant for British civilians. They also demonstrated the effectiveness of large numbers of small incendiary bombs for setting fire to the cities. During the day British fighters dominated Britain's skies and gained complete superiority when the bulk of the German air force moved to support the army in the 1941 war with the U.S.S.R.

Still, the Battle of Britain offers an instance of one air force having the initiative against another. The German air force, designed primarily as an adjunct to the army, had a bomber force admirably suited for attacking British air fields. The Royal Air Force, smaller overall and which, on the other hand, had stressed attack and defense of cities and industrial targets, had few aircraft suitable for such missions as assailing airfields. Since the Germans could attack air bases with far more effect than the British, this gave them the initiative and forced the British onto the defensive in a fight for the life of their air force.

Further, the Germans' initiative received reinforcement from the greater ease with which they could reach British cities. They derived this advantage from their army's victory, which gave them occupation of airfields in the Netherlands, Belgium, and France. These placed their bombers much closer to British cities than the Royal Air Force was to German population centers. So the German air force possessed a clear initiative to compel the Royal Air Force to fight but lacked the numbers to defeat the British fighters, especially when they had the advantage of the strategic defensive in fighting near their own bases. In this instance geography combined with the preexisting composition of the two air forces to confer on one the initiative.

Air raiders had a strategic advantage similar to that of the submarines, but in the beginning they had the additional benefit of not facing a defensive concentration comparable to a convoy. Instead, British cities lacked good defenses. Still, the Germans had bombers mostly ill-adapted to that mission, lacking in bomb capacity, and without adequate doctrine or experience for night bombing.

THE BRITISH BOMBING OFFENSIVE

Whereas the Germans bombed Britain at night with bombers intended for working with their ground forces, the British, who had bombers designed for air power's independent role, began using them against German cities. In spite of good defensive armament, such as the Wellington bomber's five machine guns in three turrets, Britain's Royal Air Force found that poorly coordinated group action failed emphatically when contending with the skillfuly piloted German Me 109 fighter. Thus Britain's Bomber

Command early abandoned daylight raids in favor of the comparative security of night attacks.

This decision, made for tactical reasons, had significant strategic implications. At night the bombers had difficulty not only in finding their targets but even the targets' city. A study in the summer of 1941 showed that, of aircraft that succeeded in finding the target, only one-fifth of the bombs fell within five miles of the target. Thus British night bombing, unable to aim at anything as specific as a factory, had to give up seeking material effect and aim primarily at the political objective of attacking enemy morale and seeking to make the war so costly in human terms that the public would compel the government to abandon the war. In practice this meant bombing cities to destroy houses and kill people.

But early results were very disappointing. In 1941 the Royal Air Force's Bomber Command lost 700 planes without doing very much damage to any cities. In addition to inaccuracy, the relatively small bomb loads of the two-engine bombers prevented the raids from doing serious damage. But by 1942 two developments would give the bombing program a real opportunity: the delivery of four-engine airplanes able to carry double the load, and the development of electronic navigational aids to find the target cities and pathfinder groups to mark them.

Bombing strategy had already concentrated in space routinely by attacking only one or two cities in a night. To this Air Marshal Sir Arthur Harris, Bomber Command's dedicated new chief, added concentration in time. Instead of the usual practice of the attacking bombers arriving in successive groups, Harris planned to bunch the attacking planes. The Germans, as in all World War I bombing operations, had used the incremental system in their 1940–1941 raids on British cities. Using such a succession of attacks had the advantage of making the operation simpler for pilots and reducing the possibility of midair collisions.

Instead of giving the antiaircraft defenses time to concentrate on successive groups of aircraft, concentration in time could more than saturate the defense, enabling many planes to pass the guns unengaged. Further, Harris saw that such concentration could overcome another key element in the defense, the target town's fire department. This would give maximum effect to the large number of incendiary bombs that the bombers routinely carried.

Lastly, the air marshal sought the maximum effect for his concentrations by directing them at a weak objective, the town of Lübeck. An old commercial city with a population of 150,000, it had the narrow streets and many wooden buildings characteristic of a city that had flourished in the Middle Ages. In the attack at the end of March 1942, 234 bombers dropped 300 tons of bombs, almost half incendiary. The strategy worked. The fires, overwhelming the fire department and destroying much of the town, made the first such emphatic blow against any German city.

Bomber Command followed this up with a similar attack against a smaller city, Rostock, and, at the end of May, against Cologne, a city with a population of 678,000. For this formidable objective Harris brought 1,000 planes, all he could muster, including those in training. Although they delivered only a little over 3,000 pounds per plane, well over half the weight was in incendiary bombs. The aircraft passed over the city in two and a half hours instead of the seven hours that the old method would have required. In spite of so many planes he achieved no result comparable to Lübeck. Yet, in a sense, the Royal Air Force was marking time, waiting for more and bigger bombers. They would be ready in 1943, as would the heavy bombers of the U.S. Eighth Air Force, based in Britain.

THE UNITED STATES JOINS THE BOMBING CAMPAIGN

The Americans had always planned to use large four-engine aircraft for an independent mission and brought many to England. Further, with their augmented defensive armament, the U.S. airmen believed that group defensive tactics would work against individual German fighters. In 1942 the Eighth Air Force began conducting small daylight raids against industrial targets, gaining combat experience as their force gradually expanded. Thus the Allies had a division of labor: the British attacked German morale at night, and the United States assailed industrial targets with daylight's more accurate aiming.

As the Allies prepared to attack day and night with larger forces of enhanced quality, the Germans had been perfecting their defenses. Their antiaircraft guns had radar for finding the target and soon for directing the guns. But the fighters, by night as well as by day, provided the most effective defense. Defenders received an alert from a radar warning line near the coast, which identified the bombers and directed the fighters. So they engaged them before the raiders reached the target. This intelligence and control system considerably nullified the raiders' initiative. Further, this could give the defenders the ability to surprise the raiders, particularly by attacking the bombers on their return flight. And, increasingly, this intelligence and control system could concentrate more fighters against the attackers. Soon night fighters had their own radars to enable the pilot to find and engage the bombers in the dark. Further, as one would expect, the bomber campaign contributed to the German decision to make dramatic increases in aircraft production: from 15,000 in 1942, to 25,000 in 1943, to 40,000 in 1944. The output increasingly emphasized fighters, which reached peak monthly production of 4,000 in September 1944.

The Royal Air Force began sustained major operations first in 1943, using its augmented strength to strike the city of Hamburg. To destroy a city with a population of 1,682,000, Air Marshal Harris planned a sequence of several raids in quick succession. The first, in July 1943, employed 718 four-engine planes and 73 with two engines. Although the destruction was limited and only about 1,500 people died, the high-explosive bombs broke many water mains, a result that had much significance for the next night raid. On the next two days 225 U.S. bombers attacked Hamburg's submarine yards and engine plant. Though few bombs actually hit the target, only a few missed the city.

The next night Bomber Command repeated its first raid, the bomb load including over 600,000 4-pound incendiary bombs. The bombs hit a built-up section of the city with multistory buildings and soon created a fire that overmatched the fire department, still fighting old fires from earlier raids and handicapped by so many broken water mains. Again fire engulfed much of the affected part of the city, its temperature reaching 1,500 degrees Fahrenheit. The oxygen required to fuel it caused winds with velocities as high as 70 miles per hour blowing toward the fire. These uprooted trees, and carried them, human beings, and much else into the fire. It destroyed over 8,000 acres and killed over 40,000 people. Two subsequent raids added comparatively little to the destruction.

Now Air Marshal Harris felt able to hunt the biggest game of all, believing that if he destroyed Berlin, he would win the war. With 4,332,000 people, it was the largest city on the continent of Europe and the fourth largest in the world. Further, it was a new city, largely built in the nineteenth and twentieth centuries with many stout buildings and wide streets. Moreover, it had well-developed air defenses, work having begun after a token raid in 1940. Thus Harris concentrated not only against strength rather than weakness but also against a distant city, one that would expose his airplanes to attack long before they reached their objective and long after.

The campaign against Berlin lasted from November 1943 to March 1944 and involved sixteen huge night raids. The Germans naturally responded to this concentration against Berlin with their own defensive concentration of night fighters drawn from distant areas and fire-fighting reinforcements from other cities. The force making the last attack lost 9 percent of its aircraft. Other raids had lost this heavily, a rate above the 7 percent Bomber Command believed too high to sustain. Berlin and the German air force had won. So, when both concentrated, the defense won. In selecting Berlin and holding to that objective, Bomber Command forfeited the raider's inherent advantage of the initiative and the opportunity offered by surprise and attack against weakness.

While the British engaged Berlin, the Germans were improving their tactics for assailing daylight bombers. This included steadily enhancing their defenses and adding firepower to their fighters. They had a twin-engine fighter, the Me 110, which had proved vulnerable to British single-engine fighters but found its niche in attacking bomber formations with its 37-mm (1.46-in.) and two 30-mm (1.18-in.) cannon. Moreover, the bombers' formations proved good targets for 210-mm (8.27-in.) rockets fired from beyond the range of the bombers' guns. The Me 110 carried four of these and, with its cannon, outranged the bombers' machine guns, thus becoming a completely dominant weapons system.

Meanwhile, the U.S. Eighth Air Force, with a strength of 500 four-engine bombers, was conducting a campaign in daylight against critical German economic targets: the aircraft industry as most important, followed by ball-bearing factories and then petroleum, particularly the synthetic oil production facilities. In August, the first large raid, 376 big bombers, flew to strike two targets deep in Germany and about 100 miles apart: the ball-bearing works at Schweinfurt and the aircraft factory at Regensburg. The raids lost 60 planes, mostly to fighters and more than double the British loss ceiling of 7 percent.

Losses amounted to 10 to 20 percent and, of a raid of 229 planes, the Germans shot down 60, and the Americans had to scrap 30 of those that succeeded in returning to base. Nor were the Germans suffering as much as the Americans believed, losing, for example, only 40 fighters combating a raid in which the Americans lost 128 four-engine bombers. The U.S. command would have been even more discouraged had it known how successful the Germans were in increasing their production of aircraft and other war material.

After giving attention to closer targets where a fighter escort helped protect the bombers, the Eighth Air Force launched five successive raids deep into Germany. The last, 291 planes to Schweinfurt again, lost 60 aircraft, over 20 percent of those engaged. Clearly groups of unescorted bombers were no match for the cannon-armed fighters and the rockets of the twin-engine Me 110. Thereafter, the day bombers struck only targets close enough to England for fighters to accompany the raiders. There is an obvious parallel between the escorted bombers and the escorted convoys, one quite apt in view of the bombers' mission to carry explosives to Germany and the corresponding task of merchant ships.

The circumscribed range of escorted raids changed in the spring when U.S. fighters acquired auxiliary fuel tanks that they could jettison when they had to engage in air combat. These gave the bombers escorts to almost all objectives. But, just at this time, British and American big bombers transferred their primary effort to raiding the communications of the area in France where the armies expected to land for the Allied invasion of the continent. This change in priority lasted through most of the summer.

Then the Eighth Air Force could resume devoting its primary attention to German industry, employing a force of 2,000 bombers and ample escorts. The German aircraft industry having proven difficult to cripple, the bombers concentrated on two objectives: oil production and railway transportation. The enormous force of bombers, backed by two crews for each aircraft and having the aid of 1,200 bombers based in Italy, produced impressive results by the end of 1944. Oil output fell from 316,000 tons in March to 17,000 tons in the fall. The number of railway cars available weekly dropped from 900,000 to 214,000 by December 1944.

Belittled by Air Marshal Harris as "panacea" objectives, the raids against two of Germany's material resources crippled its economy by throttling the railroads while its armed forces slowly ran down as they exhausted their inventories of fuel and their engines stopped. So, just as the Allied armies completed their defeat of the German ground forces, the bombing had at last implemented an effective logistic strategy.

The campaign against morale enjoyed no such success, the public stoically maintaining its resistance in spite of 600,000 fatalities and 800,000 serious injuries.

Chapter 6

The Allied Western Europe Campaign, 1944–1945

The successful campaign by British, American, Canadian, and other Allied navies and air forces to make the sea lanes secure permitted the invasions of North Africa in 1942, Italy in 1943, and finally the much more elaborate and hazardous landing in France in 1944. Sea transport of food, fuel, raw materials, and a multitude of civilian and military products sustained Britain's fully mobilized war economy at maximum output and made possible bringing its armed forces to a peak in quantity and quality. Ocean freight also moved and supplied U.S. and Canadian armies in the United Kingdom. Dominant British and American air forces and the diversion of the majority of German air strength to the Russian and Italian fronts assured the security of Allied fleets and armies from serious injury from the German air force.

The comparative safety of the sea lanes also made possible the overall Allied strategy for concentration. First, it precluded any significant communication between the Germans and Japanese. Further, because the U.S.S.R. had frontiers with German and Japanese possessions, it could mount major offensives against either. As the sea lanes enabled Britain and the United States also to concentrate against either adversary, the Allies had interior lines of operation. Thus they were situated between their two antagonists and could make a concentration in space of their main effort against first one and then the other. Since the U.S.S.R. had by far the most powerful Allied army and had most of it committed first to halting and then to driving back the German invasion, Germany was clearly the necessary objective of the first concentration if the U.S.S.R. was to participate; and without the participation of the Soviet Union's army and air force, there could be no concentration in space.

LOGISTICS

Following the establishment of reasonably secure communication with the remote base areas, the remaining logistic task was the invasion of north-western Europe. Moving and landing the forces in France would constitute a prodigious logistic feat, but the continuing challenge of maintaining an adequate link of the armies with their base areas conditioned strategy right up to the end of the war.

TACTICS

As usual in land war, tactical possibilities exerted a profound influence on the combat. The tactics employed represented the maturing of a new tactical era, one that witnessed the reemergence of mounted combat after its almost total eclipse in the decades before and in most of the First World War.

In the 1860s the rapidly shooting breech-loading rifle called seriously into question the tactical viability of cavalry. When, in the 1890s the magazine rifle again doubled the rate of rifle fire to as many as 15 aimed shots per minute, the big target of the horseman had no place on a battlefield with infantry armed in the new way. Though cavalry had thus lost its tactical function, it retained its strategic roles in reconnaissance and raiding of communications.

In World War I the immense armies of the European nations so filled the theaters of operation that, with armies always in contact and the soldiers thoroughly entrenching themselves, no flanks remained. This not only baffled strategy, but cavalry, never able to cope with fortifications, had no flanks around which to ride to carry out its strategic functions of reconnaissance and raiding. This occurred at a time when the dependence of armies on links with remote base areas by railroad had made the raiding of communications far more effective and significant, the American Civil War having clearly demonstrated the damage cavalry raids could do to railroads.

Early in the war the machine gun began to assume an importance equal to that of the magazine rifle. At the beginning of World War I most machine guns were heavy, water-cooled weapons mounted on a tripod or similar support and firing at least 400 shots per minute. By preventing overheating as it does for an automobile engine, water cooling permitted great sustained fire, ten guns once firing a million shots in half a day.

The British Army began the war with four machine guns for each battalion and, like other armies, finished it with about 60. Much of this increase had taken the form of the light machine gun or automatic rifle. The heavy machine gun excelled on the defense, and the mobility of the light machine gun enabled it to accompany infantry on the offensive.

The World War I emphasis on the fortified defense enhanced the importance of artillery. Both sides had the support of large quantities of powerful guns directed by observers in the front lines as well as in balloons and airplanes. The observers in balloons and at the front had telephones to communicate with the artillery, those in airplanes eventually having wireless. The guns could fire shrapnel, a shell filled with small pellets that, exploding in the air above advancing troops, sprayed them from above with a cone of pellets. Or they could employ high-explosive shells that would churn the ground and also disperse at high velocity the fragments into which the explosion had blown the shell. Shrapnel supplied the motive for the belligerents to return to steel helmets.

The British and French, who attacked the Germans in France in 1915–1918, naturally relied on traditional siege methods. To destroy the entrenchments, they had to fire for days, even weeks, thus showing the Germans exactly where they planned to attack. In 1917 the British used 2,300 cannon for seven days to fire 3,000,000 shells at the Germans on the six-mile front they besieged. With the aid of some huge mines exploded under the enemy lines, the British advanced two miles in one day. But, true to the principle of successive lines of defense, this did not drive through all of the German fortifications. And the Germans industriously built additional defense lines in their rear.

These sieges, called battles, which advanced a few miles, often lasted for months and sometimes caused hundreds of thousands of casualties. Yet they had one thing in common with most of the battles in the past: They rarely affected the strategic situation. Warfare on the western front had reached this state not only on account of the tactical condition of enhanced firepower but because the belligerents, having millions of men, had such a high ratio of force to the space of the theater of war.

It was in this siege warfare of armies without flanks that the Americans had their first experience of large-scale military operations in the twentieth century and their first since their own Civil War. The U.S. Army quickly adopted the well-developed techniques of attack and defense evolved by the belligerents since 1914.

The offensive based on the siege model with its long bombardment sacrificed surprise and any chance of breaking through the fortified zone. This led the French, British, and German armies to develop an offensive plan based on a short, intense, and accurate bombardment, followed by an attack by troops in small groups with light machine guns and small mortars as well as rifles and hand grenades. Infiltrating between the defenders' strong points, they pushed ahead deeper into the defense while the men following them overcame the surrounded strong points and opened routes for more troops and light artillery to reinforce the attackers.

THE RESTORATION OF CAVALRY IN A TACTICAL ROLE

Seeking a technological solution to the trench deadlock, the British developed a huge armored land ship to cross trenches and the French an armored self-propelled field gun, which crossed trenches badly. Then, in 1917, the French designed a true tank and ordered 4,000 of the small, simple machines from the Renault automobile company. The Germans remained skeptical of tanks, in part because a senior German staff officer was present for the first, and quite inept, attack by French self-propelled guns. Each of the ungainly vehicles went into battle carrying its reserve gasoline supply in a can on the roof! But few became incinerators, because most mired in the mud. The German officer reported that tanks had no military value.

Although the Allies had produced a weapon system with a fundamental advantage over infantry and machine guns, the tanks could not make a breakthrough because, about two miles behind every front trench line, the tanks would encounter the line of field guns providing artillery support for the first-line troops. These guns could bring a rapid and devastating direct fire of high-explosive shells against the tanks.

THE DEVELOPMENT OF TANKS AND ANTITANK WEAPONS

During the period between the World Wars, armies developed antitank guns, the German 37-mm (1.46-in.), adopted by the U.S. Army, being representative. As the war progressed, antitank guns, like tanks, increased in size, the Germans ending the war using an 88-mm (3.46-in.) antitank gun weighing 11,000 pounds. The contrast with the 952-pound weight of the 37-mm indicates the loss in mobility. The best Allied gun, the 3-inch British 17 pounder, weighed only 4,600 pounds, was less cumbersome, yet could penetrate thicker armor than the 88-mm gun.

On the defensive, the antitank gun had an intrinsic dominance over the tank. Usually emplaced in groups with good fields of fire, the gun offered a small target, one usually having some natural cover. Its high-velocity, flat-trajectory fire could hit the prominent target of a tank and pierce its armor. In a similar defensive stance, the tank could be just as effective but cost considerably more than the gun and the truck or tractor for its movement.

The steady loss of mobility of antitank guns found a partial remedy in the rocket launcher, which a soldier could fire while holding it on his shoulder. Normally a rocket's low velocity would deprive it of much penetrating power, but this one used a shaped charge to pierce the armor with the heat and force of the bursting of the rocket's explosive charge. The rocket exploded outside of the tank, but, by shaping the charge around a hollow cone at the tip of the rocket, the design directed the explosion forward against and through the armor. Thus the gases of the explosion entered the tank, spewing the inside with the molten metal of the tank's pierced armor. Able to penetrate the thinner armor of a tank's side or rear, the light antitank rocket became a valuable weapon for the infantry. The United States nicknamed its version the bazooka because of its resemblance to an elaborate kazoo played by the comedian Bob Burns.

In the two decades between the first and second world wars, the tank improved tremendously in its speed and mechanical reliability. The five miles per hour of the early tanks gave way to speeds over thirty miles per hour. This, and much-enhanced reliability, gave the tanks of the 1930s excellent strategical as well as tactical mobility.

As the war progressed, tanks in production received modifications, the German model IV, for example, increasing its armor thickness 150 percent, more than doubling the power of its gun, and increasing its weight from 17 to 25 tons. New tanks had more firepower and protection, the Germans building the largest, called the Tiger and nicknamed the furniture van by the soldiers. Tanks proved superb antitank weapons when they deployed like antitank guns especially when it could make only its turret visible.

The United States devoted most of its tank production to the 30-ton Sherman with good speed and reliability, armor as thick as 100 mm (2.95 in.), and, at first, armed with a low-velocity 75-mm (2.95-in.) gun; by 1944 it had a 3-inch gun of good muzzle velocity. It overmatched the German model IV but was at a serious disadvantage against the newer tanks. The British improved their version by mounting their superb 17 pounder antitank gun.

World War II witnessed the full-fledged development of self-propelled artillery. The Germans and Russians had many of these, well armored and with high-velocity guns, that fulfilled many of the functions of tanks. But other forces, particularly the U.S. Army, had stressed howitzers on self-propelled tracked carriages. This enabled the artillery more easily to keep up with the tank forces and go into action promptly. Since most of these howitzer carriages also had some armor and carried a machine gun, they had protection against infantry.

A similar trend affected infantry. Foot soldiers had long mounted themselves on horses for strategic mobility but dismounted to fight. In the Second as well as the First World War, trucks filled the horses' function in giving infantry mounted strategic mobility. But, particularly in the maneuvers and combat of armored divisions, the foot soldiers needed tracked carriers for cross-country mobility. Pioneered by the Germans, these versatile vehicles gained increased mobility by having wheels in front but tracks in the rear. The U.S. Army improved on this model by giving it the same armor and machine gun as the self-propelled howitzer. Now infantry could enter combat with reduced vulnerability.

Even without antitank guns, infantry could present a serious threat to tanks. This is exemplified in the experience of a French officer during an offensive in World War I. When leading his platoon over the brow of a hill, he saw a French tank below, surrounded by German soldiers. The Germans had halted the tank by jamming its tracks with a log. Now some men tried to pry open the door with their bayonets, while others sought to put a hand grenade into the ventilator. The tank was powerless because the infantry was too close to shoot. With the German soldiers so absorbed with the tank that they failed to notice the French platoon, the officer had his men shoot them down with several unexpected volleys.

This rescue indicates why French tank doctrine prescribed platoons of three tanks, one with a 37-mm gun in the lead and two armed with machine guns on either side and a little to the rear. Thus the lead tank used its cannon to demolish German machine gun positions, while the other two used the crossfire of their machine guns to protect each other and the cannon tank against infantry. World War I gave the Germans the need and the opportunity to become expert in using infantry to defeat tanks, a tradition which carried over into World War II.

German soldiers received help from an antitank grenade and, more importantly, from the portable rocket launcher similar to the bazooka. With this handy weapon, a bold individual could creep up on a solitary tank and fire his rocket at its thinly armored side or rear; on the defense he could wait hidden until it passed and then shoot it in a vulnerable spot. So, when all armies prescribed that tanks and infantry would work together, the protection of the tanks was one of the benefits expected from the familiar tactical device of combination of arms.

The tactical array also included aircraft guns and antiaircraft weapons. In its battle interventions, the aircraft had a fundamental dominance over the infantry and the tank. The vulnerability of ground objects to air attack thus gave the antiaircraft artillery a major role. Although it could not provide a perfect defense against air attack, it had the attribute of an intrinsically dominant weapon system because it could inflict such losses as to make it too costly for aircraft to assail well-defended targets.

Though truly the cavalry of the air, the airplane had difficulty in making its tactical contribution to a battle because it had so much difficulty telling friend from foe. But it excelled at cavalry's strategic functions of reconnaissance, raids against logistic installations and supply movements, and attacks against troops on the march, traditionally a vulnerable and important objective. In defending these targets, antiaircraft guns had their greatest importance.

So tacticians attempted to exploit essentially dominant weapons systems, while trying to foil them by combination of arms. In World War II this had more tactical importance than any time since warfare in the Renaissance.

Yet the distinctive capabilities of line and skirmishing tactics continued to assert themselves. The typical infantryman on a World War II battlefield needed antitank gun protection, but he could, by adopting the elusiveness of the skirmisher, contribute to his own defense. Further, he could provide essential assistance to tanks in their attack and, with infiltration tactics, penetrate a defense and defeat the antitank guns. Thus infantry had to assume a line role in the defense to protect the antitank defense from hostile infantry supporting any attack relying on tanks. And, as before, infantry had many occasions to fight each other without the participation of the twentieth-century weapon systems.

STRATEGY

In World War I the Allies' plans for the campaigns in France stressed a combat strategy: to deplete the German forces, to implement the implicit logistic strategy of taking territory from the Germans, and to achieve the important objective of liberating occupied French and Belgian areas. But the fortified defense had defeated major French offensives in 1915 and 1917 and the main Anglo-French effort in 1916.

This had led the British to look upon these sieges as an opportunity to deplete the German army by the gradual process of attrition. Because, by 1917, they had so many cannon and such immense supplies of ammunition, they believed that their attacks could inflict more manpower losses than they themselves would suffer. For the summer and fall campaign of 1917, for example, they estimated that German casualties would amount to as many as 200,000 men per month. This calculation enabled them to see victory through attrition by comparing these estimated casualties with the 450,000 young Germans who became eligible for military service in 1917. But the Germans did not have nearly such large losses. In fact, they incurred far fewer casualties than the 346,000 the British suffered in the summer and fall, a figure about equal to the number of young men in the British Isles who reached military age in 1917. So attrition worked against the British.

But the British and French, who had more experience with the offensive than the Germans, had perfected the artillery techniques for a very accurate surprise bombardment and tactical methods much like the German infiltration tactics. They had these ready for offensives in 1918; but they faced a German effort to win the war by separating the British and French armies. The offensive, directed primarily against the British, began in March 1918. It broke through the fortified front but soon met Allied reserves, which contained the advance. It frightened the Allies enough for them to appoint, for the first time, a commander for all of the forces fighting on the western front. The choice of the French General Ferdinand Foch proved wise, and his success led to his promotion to the rank of marshal.

The Germans followed their first offensive with a succession of three more, all intended to lead up to the final drive to separate the British and French armies. But this never came, because the fifth preparatory offensive ended suddenly when struck in the flank by 21 divisions with 820 tanks, the first of Foch's offensives.

Foch had the objective of driving the Germans back and bringing the Allied armies into Germany at a minimum cost. Just two days after the conclusion of his offensive that had halted and pushed back the last German drive, he launched the second of a series of consecutive, rather than simultaneous, offensives. Even the very successful four-week Anglo-French drive that began on 8 August embodied successive short phases. The British Fourth Army began the offensive, succeeded two days later by the French Third Army attack to the south, followed a week later by the French Tenth Army still farther south, next, in four days and to the north, by the British Third Army, and in five more days the British First Army still farther north. This pattern had much success in avoiding engagement with German reserves by discontinuing the attack as they arrived but resuming it in another place. A week later the United States made its first offensive, brief and successful, in the St. Mihiel sector. Thus these attacks were primarily concentrations in space rather than time.

Shortly after the conclusion of the St. Mihiel operation, the Allies had made a transition to concentration in time, beginning four offensives between 26 and 29 September, including the Americans and the French in the Meuse-Argonne region. The opening of the these offensives reinforced the effect on German official opinion of the loss of an ally when Bulgaria signed an armistice on 3 October. Three days later Germany requested an armistice, and negotiations began. Thus the simultaneous offensives had a political effect. Offensives continued until the end of the war while the German armies fell back and armistice negotiations continued; and on 11 November Germany accepted the Allies' stringent armistice terms. Through its part in this series of victorious offensives the U.S. Army learned to cope with the modern fortified defense and had ample experience for study and instruction in its branch and staff schools in the succeeding two decades.

So, upon this experience and a comparable background on the part of the other allies, the staffs would plan the 1944 invasion of France and the commanders would conduct it. But, by the time of the landing in France, World War II had provided other models for warfare in western Europe.

THE FRANCO-GERMAN CAMPAIGN OF MAY 1940

The campaign of May 1940 between the French and the Germans had an immediate outcome, one not anticipated by foreign observers or the participants, including the Germans. As in 1914, the Germans avoided the heavily fortified French frontier and drove into Belgium where the French met them in greater strength than in 1914. But the Germans also attacked through the Ardennes Forest part of Belgium, a rugged country through which an army could move only with difficulty. Here they used seven of their ten armored divisions and supported them with three motorized divisions and many foot-marching troops with horse-drawn artillery and transport.

The ten elite divisions, with good combat experience against Poland the previous September, gained strategic surprise by their unexpected route of attack. Thus they met French divisions composed largely of reservists, many a number of years away from their period of active duty training. To the astonishment of the German command, but not to the younger officers leading the armored units, they quickly broke through the French defenses and, to the alarm of some of their superiors, pushed forward until they had reached the rear of the French and British armies in Belgium.

The Germans had made a strategic turning movement that drove the Belgians from the war and inflicted such a disastrous defeat on the French and British armies that they lacked sufficient forces to defend France against the renewed German offensive in June. This inadvertent masterpiece of combat strategy—the turning movement—had won the war. The Germans made a propaganda victory of it as well, claiming that they had planned it that way and that it was a new kind of war, blitzkrieg, or lightning war.

The secret lay not in armored and motorized divisions, of which the French had as many as the Germans, but in their use as strategically offensive forces. Just as the tactically offensive weapons systems, the cavalry of old and its successor the tank, could use their better mobility to go around the enemy flank, so the Germans used a concentration of armored and motorized divisions against a surprised opponent to pierce the front and thus create a flank. With this the Germans used the better strategic mobility of their armored and motorized divisions to turn the adversary's flank; thus they blocked the Allied retreat, having the advantage of the tactical defensive. The strong effort of other German troops to fight their way directly through Belgium probably provided an important distraction.

The immediate U.S. reaction to this campaign combined tactical innovation with strategic mobility. Seeing that a huge, unexpected concentration of tanks on a narrow front could overwhelm almost any antitank defense, the army created weapons and established an organization to cope with this threat. It originated tank destroyer units and placed them under a separate command, one distinct from the other units in their assigned area. These included towed antitank guns and "tank destroyers"—fast, thinly armored, tracked vehicles with powerful antitank guns. This separate organization and direct chain of command to a higher headquarters would facilitate an extremely rapid concentration of tank destroyer units at the point where an enemy was making his overwhelming tank assault. Thus an exceptionally rapid defensive concentration would counteract the surprise tank assault.

But, when the army fought Germany, the German army had no capability to make such an overwhelming tank attack and, in fact, German doctrine viewed tanks not as an independent force but as part of a team of infantry, artillery, and aircraft. Still, the tank destroyer organization not only showed the army's emphasis on mobility but represented an imaginative and operationally well-conceived response to a strategic menace that the opening campaigns of World War II initially seemed to forecast.

The U.S. Army readied itself for the strategic consequences of the 1940 campaign in other ways: It created many armored divisions and so completely motorized its infantry divisions that the addition of a few trucks would make any division a motorized division. Hence, even though staying with many of the concepts learned in 1918, the army equipped itself for a different war, one of high mobility forecast in the strategy of the French-German campaign of May 1940. In particular, the army gave great emphasis to the cavalry of the air.

By 1940, aircraft designed to function as cavalry had changed markedly since 1918, when the British Bristol F2B had two machine guns and carried 240 pounds of bombs. In 1940 the twin-engine U.S. A-20 carried 2,600 pounds of bombs and would soon exchange its machine guns for four 20-mm (.79-in.) cannon. Instead of an attack bomber, the Germans made good use of a dive bomber, the Stuka. But the attack bomber became the Allied mainstay, easily created by modifying fighters into fighter bombers. Their machine gun and cannon armament made them very effective against such targets as railroad trains and highway traffic. Because of the difficulty of assailing tactical targets in World War II, the attack and fighter bombers would devote their most telling efforts to the cavalry's traditional strategic roles of reconnaissance and raiding the enemy's rear.

But these ground-attack aircraft, and larger bombers too, could make a distinctive tactical contribution by offering a critical supplement to, or substitution for, artillery when the task did not require artillery's traditional precision in aim. A significant instance occurred early in World War II when, in May 1940, these airplanes played a crucial role in the battle to cross the Meuse River at Sedan in the German campaign against France. The Germans needed to cross the river quickly, before more French troops arrived, but had very little artillery. An attack by 120 dive bombers supplied the deficiency, and the crossing succeeded.

PLANNING THE INVASION OF FRANCE

Logistics and combat merged in a distinctive way when soldiers and sailors coped with the problem of invading the continent. The need for fighter aircraft to protect the land as well as the sea forces from German bombers and torpedo planes meant that the planners limited their choice of landing places to those within the short range of fighter aircraft based in Britain. Remaining this close to British airfields also gave the soldiers the advantage of the full support of bombers, particularly the tactical air forces, which provided the armies' cavalry of the air.

The requirement for ports to supply the armies after they had landed and begun their campaign placed another constraint on the choice of the landing area. Neither Calais nor its neighboring ports had the capacity to meet the armies' needs. Farther west, the Brittany peninsula promised fine ports but was too distant from the English airfields. So logistical and air support restrictions dictated that the planners choose to land in western Normandy, adjacent to Brittany and possessing the excellent port of Cherbourg. Plans called for an early capture of Cherbourg and then making Brittany's ports the main objective.

Since the available ports in Normandy were garrisoned and fortified, the landing would have to take place on beaches rather than docks, and beaches likely to be defended by German soldiers. Yet success in seizing beaches could not fully solve the problem of supply until the armies had captured ports and the quartermasters had made them ready for cargo landing and handling. This meant that initially the armies would have to supply themselves by using the beaches as ports.

To facilitate this, the planners had provided two artificial harbors, parts of which tugs could tow across the English Channel and engineers would erect them. Altogether the invasion utilized over 6,000 vessels from large and small freighters to battleships, whose guns would give artillery support, to small boats, specially built for landing soldiers and their equipment on the beaches.

The Allies had the objective of liberating France from the Germans and then proceeding with the persisting strategy of invading Germany itself if necessary to attain the war aim of Germany's unconditional surrender. A persisting strategy differed from raiding in its logistic requirements, because the armies could not depend on a single base area, as German submarines did when they returned to their French ports or the Eighth Air Force and Bomber Command did on their air bases. As armies advanced, their bases had to keep pace with them. Although they could obtain some food and other supplies in France and Germany, the Allies had to get most of their fuel, ammunition, and replacement soldiers and weapons from increasingly distant base areas (i.e., the United States, the United Kingdom, and Canada). Thus, for a persisting strategy, logistic considerations would condition movements in a way quite foreign to raiding strategy.

In the operational strategy to implement a persisting strategy, maneuver conformed to the tactics of land combat. This meant the same set of alternatives, to go forward, either directly ahead or around the antagonist, to remain in or to defend a position; to move laterally either right or left; and to withdraw. The choice depended on the forces engaged and on the strategic situation and objectives, an interaction amply illustrated in the 1944–1945 campaign to liberate France and invade Germany.

GERMAN DEFENSIVE PREPARATIONS

As the British and Americans advanced their preparations for their well-known plan to conduct an amphibious invasion of western Europe, the Germans accelerated their creation of a fortified defense to repel the attack. Emphasizing the coast nearest Britain, they fortified the shoreline by placing impediments along all the beaches that were suitable for landing troops. These included iron obstructions in the water, to check or impale landing craft, and beaches covered with steel posts and land mines to halt tanks and infantry. In addition to building barriers and fortifications to prevent egress from the beaches, the Germans placed concrete bunkers on the ends of the potential landing beaches. From these the defenders could direct crossfire at the flanks of landing troops and vehicles while the invaders also were confronting defenders entrenched ahead of them.

The Germans had many suitable weapons available because they could use guns no longer fully effective in the field. For example, the excellent 50-mm antitank guns, deadly against tanks in 1940, could no longer cope with the larger, more heavily armored tanks of 1944. But, mounted on the flanks of the beaches, they could direct a deadly crossfire against small landing craft, amphibious tanks, and the armor on the sides of even the largest tanks disembarking on the beaches. On one beach, four miles long, on which the Allies landed, the Germans had emplaced approximately one gun every 100 yards for the length of the beach. To supplement these defenses and the usual complement of field artillery, there were heavy guns protected by concrete.

Behind this fortified coast, the engineers established a system of camouflaged strong points of earth and concrete to give protection to infantry, antitank guns, and field artillery. For three miles inland they reinforced natural obstacles with antitank barriers and a liberal use of mines and barbed wire.

In addition to this fairly elaborate fortified defense, the troops landing on the beaches and facing it would also have to cope with a German specialty, the counterattack. Suffering from fewer disadvantages than other tactically offensive actions, the counterattack gained its peculiar strength because it could frequently catch the attackers unready to defend. This lack of preparedness often resulted because troops on the offensive, not expecting an assault, had the wrong dispositions for a defense or were so disorganized by their own attack as to permit only a feeble defense. The counterattack received special emphasis in German defensive doctrine.

Thus, by fortifying themselves so thoroughly, the Germans had made a very traditional response, concentrating to counter an adversary's concentration. The war had already illustrated this use of concentration as the counter to concentration. When the Royal Navy had concentrated its merchant vessels and warships in convoys, Admiral Doenitz responded by concentrating his U-boats in wolf packs. When Air Marshal Harris concentrated his bombing campaign on Berlin, the Germans responded by concentrating antiaircraft guns, fire fighters and engines, and fighter planes to counter his repeated raids on Berlin.

This consistent behavior in warfare suggests an analogy with Sir Isaac Newton's third law of motion, that every action has an equal and opposite reaction. Although warfare is not like classical physics and astronomy in its susceptibility to laws, military events tend strongly to conform to this model because one antagonist does quite consistently seek to act to counter the moves of the other.

THE ALLIED DISTRACTION PLAN

The Allies expected German defensive preparations as a reaction to their well-publicized intention to invade but viewed the problem of an amphibious attack as more serious than the German fortifications. To help carry out this combined logistical and tactical operation, the British and Americans provided 229 specially built ships of four thousand tons for landing tanks and other heavy vehicles on beaches and 1,145 smaller vessels specialized for landing men and lighter equipment on beaches.

Yet Allied planners knew that the German army in France had more men than they would be able to have ashore for some time after the initial landing. But command of the sea gave the initiative to the Allies while denying it to the Germans. So the British, not needing to post troops to defend their ports or beaches from invasion, could commit all of their forces to the assault on the continent. Moreover, this sea power made any part of the adversary's coast vulnerable to a sudden attack and landing by seaborne forces. Hence the Germans had the impossible assignment of being strong everywhere.

Yet, since the Allies had made their choice on the basis of the two most obvious needs, air support and ports for supply, the Germans could make the same calculations of the Allied needs and establish their strongest defenses just where the invading forces planned to land. Even so, there were two possible Allied lines of operation on which the fighters could cover an invasion. One was in Normandy and the other at the Channel's narrowest at Calais.

Because the Germans did reason that the high value of air support and protection from air attack would govern the Allied choice of landing area, they concentrated their defensive preparations on the coastal areas within fighter plane range of British airfields. Further, they naturally felt that the most likely landing area would be near Calais at the narrowest part of the English Channel and closest to British air bases and nearest to Germany. Because the Germans gave inadequate consideration to the low capacity of Calais and adjacent ports, they had picked the wrong line of operation for their concentration. The Allies knew this through their intelligence but could not know the degree to which the German command had become committed to the view that the invasion would come in the Calais area.

Of course the Allied planners knew that to overcome the superiority of the fortified defense, the forces on the offensive must assail weakness, and usually defenders were weak only when surprised.

Consequently the planners resorted to distractions to draw their adversary's attention to some place other than the objective of the attack. In doing so they had the aid of the Germans' belief that the invasion would likely occur near Calais across the narrowest part of the Channel.

One of their most effective distractions was creating in Britain, opposite Calais, a fictitious U.S. army group, which encouraged the German supposition as to the invasion's line of operations. Because the Allies placed radio transmitters in southeastern England to simulate the radio net and traffic of an army group, German communication intelligence heard this radio activity that confirmed what their spies had told them. Dummy camps, counterfeit headquarters, mock roads and railroad sidings, and phony troop movements enabled German aerial reconnaissance to corroborate the presence and great size of this bogus force.

The flamboyant and well-known American General George S. Patton, Jr., commanded this fraudulent army group. He had the military reputation to make him the logical commander of such an invasion force, and it helped the deception that he was the kind of man who called attention to himself by, for example, riding in a huge automobile covered with stars and flags. German spies reported his activities and other evidence of the army's existence. The British could assure the dispatch of these reports to Germany because they had identified all the German spies in the United Kingdom and kept them at work sending to Germany British-devised reports designed to mislead the Germans.

The Germans responded to this elaborate sham and other deceptions by seeing it as confirmation of their thesis and the wisdom of their decision to place their most powerful defenses in the Calais vicinity and hold in that region the bulk of their best troops. So distraction could use Newton's third law to cause a concentration in the wrong place and thus aid the offensive by helping gain surprise and so enable the attackers to find the defenders weak.

THE OPPOSING FORCES

In 1944 the Allies enjoyed a great superiority of land force over the Germans, but, in view of the immense difficulties of attacking a fortified defense while making an amphibious landing, certainly no surplus. Initially they had 39 divisions for immediate commitment, of which five infantry and three airborne divisions would land the first day. By the end of the ofirst week, they would have 16 divisions ashore. The Germans had only six weak divisions in the Normandy area. But nearby, to the northeast guarding the Calais area, the German Fifteenth Army had twenty divisions. In spite of their defensive concentration near Calais, these troops also constituted a reserve, that is, a force that, because it was not engaged with the enemy, could move to conduct or reinforce an attack or assist a defense elsewhere. Often commanders held back units in reserve for just this purpose, and this the Germans did by keeping all ten of their armored and motorized divisions in France in reserve. But, since any force not irrevocably committed to combat with the enemy could function as a reserve, the German command could employ many of the divisions posted near Calais as a reserve and use them to reinforce the defense or conduct a major counterattack in Normandy. The possible use of this force as a reserve was one of the many reasons why the Allied command used the spring to employ its air power in a way that would, among other effects, restrict the German use of strategic reserves.

THE AIR CAMPAIGN AGAINST GERMAN STRATEGIC MOBILITY

Beginning in April, the Royal Air Force's Bomber Command and the U.S. Eighth Air Force diverted a major part of their effort away from bombing Germany in order to carry out raids to cripple the French and Belgian railroads that moved and supplied the German troops in the Calais and Normandy areas. They bombed seventy rail centers and progressively disabled French and Belgian railroads. Because the railroads carried Belgian coal to fuel French steam locomotives, by the beginning of June coal shortages, breakdowns, and damage had disabled 1,500 of the 2,000 locomotives serving northern France. This, and the smashing of bridges, tracks, and yards, had reduced traffic by 87 percent. In order not to compromise the deception that the main effort would take place in the Calais area, the bombers flew two missions against it for every one directed at Normandy.

Yet even the Eighth Air Force daylight strategic bombers could not hit the bridges over the Seine River, essential to both rail and road travel. Bridges had always proved as difficult to hit as they were important to disable. Even the very accurate German Stuka dive bomber performed poorly against these narrow, rugged objectives. So the bridges and the moving targets, trains and trucks, became the special provinces of the armies' air forces, their raiding cavalry of the air.

And the armies had available a large number of the aircraft best suited for these missions, the fighter bomber, the growth in size of fighters having made them ideal for this purpose. A comparison of the British Hawker company's fighters illustrates the change. The Hurricane of 1940 had a 12-cylinder, 1,030 horsepower engine; the Tempest of 1944 had a 24-cylinder engine of 2,400 horsepower and four 20-mm (.79-in.) cannon instead of eight .303-inch machine guns. The Tempest, twice as heavy and over 100 miles per hour faster than the Hurricane, comfortably carried 2,000 pounds of bombs and eight rockets.

The rockets added much versatile firepower, coming in two sorts, a 60-pound high explosive for most targets and an armor-piercing model for tanks and other armored vehicles. The U.S. P-47 Thunderbolt fighter made an equally formidable fighter bomber, and the U.S. forces also used the A-20 and the B-26 light bomber.

Together, the two air forces destroyed the 20 rail and highway bridges over the Seine River between Paris and the coast, the task requiring an average of 220 tons of bombs per bridge, an average of over 100 sorties per bridge. The bombers also returned to disrupt efforts to ferry freight across a river where the bridge was down, to interrupt repair work, and to wreck the bridge just as the engineers were completing their repairs. The same kind of unremitting air campaign also made it necessary for the Germans to make all troop movements at night, a procedure that could slow motor movements to a horse's pace.

THE LANDINGS AND MONTGOMERY'S DISTRACTION

The landings on the coast worked well, though not, naturally, quite according to plan. The British and Canadians had a comparatively easy time, but the Americans faced serious difficulties. Their veteran troops performed effectively and enough green men displayed courage and initiative that they too managed to infiltrate between the German strong points and so control the beaches and permit reinforcements to land. The landing of the three divisions of parachute troops behind the German front lines helped disrupt the defense. This, like the good performance of the infantry, the effectiveness of the artillery support from the warships, and the ability of the air forces to hinder the movement of even local reserves, contributed to the tactical success of the landing.

In the Calais area the German Fifteenth Army remained in position, held there by the German command's conviction that the Calais coast would be the scene of the main effort, one reinforced by the bogus army across the strait in England. Thus it thought that the distraction was the genuine threat and was sure that the real invasion was only a ruse. But these troops had another reason for remaining in position, the almost insuperable obstacle Allied bombing had placed in the way of their rapid movement.

Nevertheless, except for the capture of the port of Cherbourg, the Allies were not meeting their expectations for steadily expanding their bridgehead. Although the Germans brought four infantry divisions from Brittany and three armored or motorized divisions from the reserves, they had not augmented their forces enough to make a threatening counterattack. Still they were strong enough to contain the Allies, achieving this in spite of an earnest effort by the British to capture the town of Caen and so increase the opportunity for advancing eastward toward Paris or Germany.

The effort to seize Caen followed the original plan, one made under the supervision of General Sir Bernard Montgomery, commander of the British and Canadian forces, who had operational control of U.S. General Omar N. Bradley's First Army. According to the plan, the supreme Allied commander, U.S. General Dwight D. Eisenhower, left control of operations to General Montgomery. When more troops had landed and the scope of operations had expanded, General Eisenhower would assume personal command with Montgomery heading the Anglo-Canadian army group and Bradley the U.S. Army group. The capable General Montgomery had the advantage of ample command experience in North Africa and Italy, a penchant for thorough preparations, and an often difficult personality. Far less seasoned, the apparently diffident Bradley proved himself a wise and decisive commander. Eisenhower shared Bradley's competence and decisiveness but also had some charisma and the temperament to be at the focal point where military, political, and personality forces met.

Montgomery's efforts to push eastward had naturally attracted German reserves until, by the end of June, there was the equivalent of one German division for every three and two-thirds miles of front facing the Anglo-Canadian forces, whereas each division of those opposing Bradley's Americans held almost eight miles of front. And the British general became increasingly aware of what a fine distraction his offensives were making for General Bradley.

Montgomery's distraction thus gave aid to Bradley in carrying out the plan's objective of advancing south to Avranches and gaining access to Brittany. Though facing terrain made ideal for the defense by many earthen embankments, he nevertheless pushed doggedly forward to gain a position from which he could break through the German line and exploit his superior strategic mobility.

BRADLEY'S ST. LÔ BREAKTHROUGH AND PURSUIT

The generals of World War I had perfected the technique of the breakthrough but had lacked the armored divisions to exploit it. Bradley knew the method and had the armored divisions. Success depended on surprise in order to concentrate against weakness, and the attacker gained surprise by a secret concentration of men, artillery, and ammunition. Then, when a short, accurate, and intensive barrage had flattened defenses and stunned defenders, the attack began.

Bradley had only one deficiency. Lacking the heavy and super-heavy artillery that had played so important a part in the barrages of the First World War, he could not deliver as heavy or as deep a barrage as needed. But he had the air forces. Although they lacked the artillery's accuracy, they could reach as deep as needed and not only did they have the ability to deliver more high explosives in as short a time as a World War I barrage, they could do it anywhere. The airplanes' ability to concentrate quickly at any point gave a much better assurance of the surprise necessary to find the Germans weak and unprepared.

Yet the bombers lacked the pinpoint accuracy of calibrated guns, firing under known meteorological conditions, from positions established by survey, and at targets equally well located. Bombers could compensate for the inaccuracy of their aim by saturating the target area with far more explosives than the artillery, but they had great difficulty telling the friendly troops from the enemy.

General Bradley's remedy for this included pushing forward until he had his forces lined up along a major lateral highway, a line clearly visible to the aircrafts' pilots. Further, he planned to use the accurate bombing of the low-flying fighter bombers to attack the first 250 yards beyond the road, the heavier and less precise planes bombing beyond, to a total depth of 2,500 yards.

By the end of the third week of July, Bradley had completed his well-concealed preparations and was in position along the highway, with three infantry divisions packed along a four-mile front and backed with 1,000 artillery pieces. Behind he had a motorized and two armored divisions to exploit the breakthrough of the German front made by the infantry divisions, artillery, and aerial bombardment. The 1,500 heavy and 380 medium bombers dropped 3,437 tons of bombs, and 559 fighter bombers hit the frontal zone with 212 tons plus quantities of flame-thrower fuel, jellied gasoline called napalm.

The plan worked. Montgomery's distraction ensured strategic surprise, and good security, including that intrinsic to the use of an air bombardment, assured tactical surprise. The offensive broke through at St. Lô and drove 40 miles in the week after it began on 25 July. That carried it beyond Avranches, which opened the way to Brittany and the capture of its fine ports, a conquest that the planners expected would finally place the invasion on a firm logistical foundation. In making this advance, the U.S. forces pursued the Germans, who made adroit night withdrawals, left plenty of land mines to impede pursuers, and fought effective delaying actions.

Inevitably chasing the enemy generated much confusion, well illustrated by the experience of an American armored column pursuing at night. An impatient half-tracked carrier kept insisting on passing vehicles during the night until it at last passed the column's lead vehicle, the commander's tank. This irritated the commander until he realized that it was a German half-track that, in the dark, had assumed that it was in a German column; the commander's tank then opened fire and wrecked the German vehicle.

Naturally the aircraft made the most effective pursuers, just as had the horse cavalry of old. The P-47s, for example, discovered a big concentration of German vehicles in daylight and were able to carry out a series of attacks for six hours. The planes, with the help of some artillery fire, destroyed 180 tanks, other vehicles, and guns.

The fighter bombers patrolled the sky, responding to calls from air support parties on the ground, as well as making their own searches for the enemy. So that aircraft would not confuse them with fleeing Germans, armored forces far in the lead would identify themselves by laying distinctive colored panels on the ground. With incomparable mobility and an unfettered facility for rapid concentration, the cavalry of the air made a perfect offensive combination with the armored cavalry on the ground.

In much of European warfare, pursuit had lagged behind retreat. The ability of those running away to impede those following took many forms: burning or breaking bridges, sinking boats, and felling trees across roads. Having a few retreating soldiers halt and deploy for combat would impose a considerable delay on far more numerous pursuers, because they had to change from march to combat formation in order to drive even a feeble detachment from their path. The gradual decline of cavalry had further handicapped pursuit.

When World War II brought to full flower the new cavalry of the air and the tracked and armored cavalry on the ground, it restored many of the capabilities and much of the old power of pursuit. Even so, retreat as skilled as that of the Germans retained an ascendancy over pursuit.

In the course of this offensive, a long-planned reorganization of the U.S. forces took place smoothly. General Bradley divided his army into the Third Army under the able and experienced General George S. Patton, Jr., and the First under his deputy, General Courtney Hodges. Bradley then headed both of them as commanding general of the new Twelfth Army Group.

EXPLOITATION OF THE BREAKTHROUGH AND THE GERMAN COUNTERATTACK

In spite of having gone as far in one week as the American World War I Meuse-Argonne offensive had in six, the commanders continued to think in terms of World War I, which they had studied so thoroughly. So, instead of a strategic breakthrough, they envisioned slowly pushing back an adversary who made maximum use of the fortified defense. The planners had used this assumption in making their timetable for reaching the German frontier.

Although students at the Command and General Staff College devoted considerable time to military history, their instruction often tended to stress battles rather than campaigns. This resulted in an emphasis on pursuit as the outcome of a victorious battle rather than its role in creating or clinching a strategic gain. Thus Bradley had become thoroughly imbued with this outlook and saw his breakthrough as an opportunity for a destructive pursuit and as strategically significant because it would enable his forces to follow the plan to enter Brittany and capture its vital ports. Then the armies would turn eastward and resume the task of methodically pushing the Germans backward through France. This was how the Allied commander, Marshal Foch, had had to conduct the final campaign in France in 1918, successive offensives driving the Germans back bit by bit. Even Bradley's colleague, General Patton, whom Bradley regarded as precipitate, even reckless, expected to use "1918 methods" in operations in France.

But, as the leading units approached Avranches, General Montgomery, still in charge of operations, saw a different potential in the situation. He envisioned turning the German armies in Normandy and trapping them either by reaching their rear or pressing them against the bridgeless Seine River. The maneuver, which Montgomery ordered with Eisenhower's enthusiastic support, is called a turning movement, and it formed the core of three of Napoleon's most successful campaigns. In these he passed around his adversaries' flanks and, by blocking their retreats, inflicted serious losses in men or territory. If General Montgomery needed an example of a turning movement with motorized troops, he would have found it when he had commanded a division of British troops in France in the spring of 1940. There the Germans had succeeded in turning the French and British and winning the war with the campaign. So, following Montgomery's order, Bradley used his motorized forces, his strategically offensive troops, to turn the Germans facing the Allied armies in Normandy.

When the Germans at last committed their final reserve, the troops from the Calais area's Fifteenth Army, it was not to halt Patton's turning forces but to strike at the narrow neck near Avranches through which moved the ammunition and fuel supplies essential to Patton's army. Early on 7 August the German attack, with a motorized and four armored divisions, achieved tactical surprise when it dispensed with any preparatory artillery bombardment. The German attack failed, the two U.S. divisions holding the line receiving timely reinforcements. General Patton had held one of the reinforcing divisions in reserve and diverted an armored division and part of another as they passed Avranches on their way to join the advance. The fighter bombers also showed that their mobility made them a fine reserve by promptly assailing the German attackers.

The availability of reserves defeated the German counterattack, and the diverse sources of these reserves illustrated their essential character. General Patton had held one of the divisions out of any combat, ready to commit it when needed to repulse a German counterattack. This unit was a reserve in the usual sense. Nevertheless the passing armored divisions were also reserves, because, not being inextricably committed to combat, General Patton could divert them to reinforce the defenders. The fighter bombers could easily function as a reserve while engaged in combat because, as raiders and never having any commitment beyond the few hours of their raid, they could easily change their objective to the attacking Germans. Consequently, on the first day of the attack, British fighter bombers were able to fly 294 sorties to help the defenders.

At the outset, Patton's men had an easy task in exploiting German weakness, driving forward through a friendly country where the local French resistance often had more strength than the few remaining Germans. But in its drive south to link with Patton, the Canadian First Army faced old adversaries in deep positions. Although about half of the German forces slipped between the converging Allies, they left behind 50,000 prisoners, 10,000 dead, 420 tanks and other combat vehicles, 5,000 other motor vehicles, and 830 field guns.

FROM NORMANDY TO THE GERMAN FRONTIER AREA

With the Germans who had long resisted Montgomery near Caen now also retreating eastward toward the Seine, the Americans had the initiative and saw an opportunity to make the most of it by cutting off retreating Germans with another turning movement. But this failed because U.S. forces did not drive deep enough eastward before making their turn into their opponent's rear.

The succeeding eastward pursuit through France of the fleeing remnants of the German armies soon taxed Allied logistical resources and ingenuity. In spite of a delay in making Cherbourg an operational port and the German garrisons still holding the ports of Brittany, total supplies landed were adequate, thanks to the quantity of cargo coming over the beaches far exceeding expectations.

In the general advance behind the fleeing Germans, the British then combined the pursuer's initiative with the familiar device of concentration to make a 200-mile advance from the Seine in eight days. The commander of the British Second Army achieved this by giving all of his transportation to one corps, which then dashed ahead, capturing Brussels, the Belgian capital, on the afternoon of 3 September and the following morning capturing Antwerp, one of Europe's largest ports. Fortuitously, this feat facilitated a third Allied effort to turn the Germans, 25,000 fatigued and disheartened Germans, surrendering.

ALLIED STRATEGIC CHOICES

But, when the advancing armies extended themselves 300 miles from their bases at Cherbourg and the beaches, they reached the limit of the ability of trucks to provide for the armies even with France's good roads and helpful population. The capture of Antwerp would have solved the problem had German troops not continued to block Antwerp's access to the sea. A better situation would have to await the restoration of service on the French railroads.

General Eisenhower, now controlling the operations of the Anglo-Canadian and U.S. army groups, made decisions in late summer about concentration, not of units in time or space but of logistic resources in space in support of one, the other, or both of two offensives on two different lines of operation, in the north toward the Ruhr, south toward the Rhine.

While logistic constraints slowed General Eisenhower's forces, the Germans were reforming their lines, refurbishing fortifications, and bringing reinforcements of seasoned units as well as those created for this emergency. The force of 63 weak divisions for a 350-mile front contained large numbers of green men, many from the bottom of the manpower barrel. For example, the Germans called to military duty deaf men, putting them together in their own battalions. They functioned surprisingly well, but did encounter difficulties: For example, it was dangerous for a messenger, staff officer, or other visitor to approach one of these units when it was near the front. Unable to hear a visitor's approach, the deaf soldiers were easily startled and likely to shoot without asking any questions.

Before the onset of the logistically induced lull, a second invasion completed the operations to liberate France from the Germans. The Allies had planned this, a landing on the French Mediterranean coast, to occur simultaneously with the landing in Normandy. Such coordinated landings would have confronted the Germans with the concentration in time. A numerical example clearly shows its capacity to cope with a concentration in space on interior lines. If a force of 100,000 is between two of 50,000 each, it can use concentration in space to direct 75,000 against one adversary while keeping the other at bay with 25,000. Yet, if the opponent on exterior lines used the concentration in time of simultaneous advances, the one force of 50,000 would have the two-to-one advantage of assailing the 25,000 while the other of 50,000 defended against an attack by 75,000, only a three-to-two superiority. Thus concentration in time could prove superior to concentration in space.

But, since the supply of landing craft could not support two simultaneous invasions, the Mediterranean landing did not occur until the middle of August. The landing of the Seventh Army, with the equivalent of seven divisions of U.S. and French troops, had immediate success, advancing north to complete the continuous front from the sea to Switzerland.

THE ALLIED ADVANCES: LOGISTIC AND COMBAT STRATEGY

The strongest effort of the Allied broad-front push in the fall came first when Montgomery's forces on the northern line of operations made an effort to reach the Ruhr industrial region. The plan involved linking a ground attack with the landing of an airborne army of three divisions along the 60-mile path of the planned ground advance. But the difficult terrain, the presence of German armored forces, and the weakness of parachute troops in artillery and antitank weapons contributed to the failure. Still, it ultimately gained some ground and, with other efforts, liberated some of the southern Netherlands.

Montgomery's forces also devoted much effort to clearing Germans from Antwerp's access to the sea, resulting, when successful in November, in a daily tonnage unloaded there that almost equalled the rate coming through the beaches and ports of Normandy.

Attacking next to the south in support of Montgomery's offensive, the Americans crossed the German border, captured the industrial town of Aachen, pierced the adjacent frontier fortifications, and began a slow, dogged push toward the Rhine. Farther south, Patton, after coping with German counterattacks in September, made some progress attacking toward the east, as did the Sixth Army Group south of him, which reached the imposing barrier of the Vosges mountains in early November.

When, in November 1944, General Eisenhower ordered simultaneous offensives by all forces, he did so as a continuation of his strategy since September. He had chosen this concentration in time after rejecting new proposals for concentration in space, with the objective of the Ruhr, Germany's essential industrial area just across the Rhine from Montgomery's armies. Eisenhower had dismissed this as a "geographical objective", and asserted that the "real objective was to kill Germans," regardless of where they were.

In choosing killing Germans in combat as the method to defeat the German army, General Eisenhower had selected a difficult means, particularly when it meant doing so against a fortified defense. Taking the Germans prisoner, as the operational strategy of turning movements had done, damaged the enemy just as much as killing them.

Certainly tactical conditions gave little hope for another breakthrough. The area ahead contained permanent fortifications built or modernized before 1914 and those of the West Wall built in the 1930s; the masonry buildings of villages and towns of a densely populated region; as well as such traditional obstacles as field fortifications; forests; hills; rivers; and short, overcast winter days that severely limited the fighter bombers.

The strategy of concentration in time did have the merit of tending to immobilize the enemy's forces, making it very hard for any forces that were engaged to move to reinforce another sector either for offense or defense. On the other hand, it did nothing to enhance the ability of the attackers to overcome the obstacles they faced. Without an offensive concentration of men and weapons, the obstacles assumed a proportionately larger role in the balance of power between attack and defense. In fact, if General Eisenhower thought that his offensive were giving him the initiative, Hitler demonstrated otherwise when he prepared a disconcerting blow that aimed at piercing the American line and carrying out a turning movement.

THE GERMAN COUNTEROFFENSIVE AND THE FINAL ALLIED OFFENSIVE

Although the German commander in the West, Field Marshal von Runstedt, a veteran of many victories, believed his force inadequate for an offensive, Hitler insisted. The plan was a virtual duplicate of the campaign of 1940, aiming to pierce the Allied line in the Ardennes Forest and then turn north into the rear of the British forces in Belgium, cutting them off just as in 1940. The Germans were able to attempt this because the strategic situation gave them both the initiative and a weak point at which to strike.

By mid-December most of General Eisenhower's simultaneous advances had reached the German frontier and so confronted either the Rhine or the German frontier fortifications. Only in the difficult Hurtgen Forest sector, east of Aachen, had Allied forces pierced the fortified zone, but now they faced flooding from enemy control of upstream dams on the Roer River. Thus, seeming strong everywhere, the Germans had accumulated a reserve that they could use for an offensive to exploit the initiative. Further, the cloudy winter weather would severely restrict the use of the Allied cavalry of the air and did ground most planes for the first week of the offensive.

Believing the enemy too weak, too short of fuel, and too wise to attempt an offensive, Allied intelligence officers discounted any indications of an attack. In addition, they assumed that the difficult terrain of the Ardennes Forest region and the barrier presented by the Meuse River would make impossible a large-scale attack there. This had long been an established French and German view of the Ardennes, and in 1940, the French had made the mistake of acting on this judgment when they had held the Meuse largely with divisions composed mostly of reservists with very few regular officers and noncommissioned officers. In 1944 the United States had four divisions on a 90-mile front, less than half the number the French had on the Meuse in 1940. Two of these U.S. divisions were new and without combat experience and the other two had left the front to rest, having— together—suffered 9,000 casualties while on the offensive. On the front for the offensive, the Germans had a powerful force, 19 divisions of varying strength, seven of them armored.

Beginning their attack on 16 December, the Germans gained tactical as well as strategic surprise, but they had much more difficulty than in 1940. Then they had made a well-planned march through the neutral Belgian and Luxembourg territory of the Ardennes and did not meet the main line of French resistance until they were out of the rugged Ardennes and had reached the Meuse River and beyond. In 1944 they had to fight their way through the area's hills, trees, and poor roads, making it very difficult for the Germans to deploy their large mechanized forces and easy for the American soldiers to offer a resistance that constantly imposed delays. Although the Germans captured more than half of one of the green divisions, all American soldiers fought hard, and the two U.S. recuperating veteran divisions displayed exemplary skill and determination.

Also a lack of fuel handicapped the Germans. They captured some, but not as much as they needed. One spearhead in the north pushed way ahead early in the advance, halting for the night after a day of dazzling progress. In the morning, when Allied reinforcements blocked its way, it tried unavailingly to turn the position and then waited for reinforcements, which never came. It had run out of fuel, but its advance had, at one moment, carried it within a quarter of a mile of a fuel depot containing two and a half million gallons. Less than a week later, this spearhead began its retreat, on foot.

Failure to make an immediate breakthrough confronted the Germans with the arrival of enemy reserves while still in the Ardennes. And the Allies, confident that the German attack was not merely a distraction, were free to make a counter concentration against the German offensive. Moreover, the highly motorized Allies rolled rapidly on good French and Belgian roads. As in 1918, the defender could move his reserves faster than the attacker could exploit his success.

On the day after the offensive began, Eisenhower ordered forward his two divisions held back in reserve, one to the north side of German penetration and the other to the south, to the communication center of Bastogne. The American ability to hold this town, even though surrounded, did much to retard the German advance while other reserves deployed and entered the action. On that day the general also ordered south an armored division held in reserve near Aachen.

Two days later Eisenhower ordered the Third Army to go on the offensive northward into the German flank. This General Patton did by forming a corps of three uncommitted divisions and ordering another corps from his southern flank, the neighboring Sixth Army Group using its uncommitted troops, to take over the vacated sector. Soon these two corps were counterattacking north into the flank of the advancing Germans, who had made a deep bulge into the Allied line, a shape that gave the Battle of the Bulge its name.

Meanwhile, Eisenhower had given Montgomery control of the north side of the bulge. He responded by stationing his reserve, the capable 30th

Corps, which had captured Brussels and Antwerp, near the tip of the bulge to make certain that the Germans would not cross the Meuse. He then used more of his troops to replace in the line north of the bulge the redoubtable U.S. 7th Corps, which had made the breakthrough at St. Lô. This corps he used to complete the forces needed to contain the north face of the Bulge.

But, unlike Patton, Montgomery did not counterattack, preferring to let the Germans wear themselves out in a futile effort to go ahead against 19 Allied divisions, superior in numbers of men, artillery, and tanks. When, at that time, Field Marshal von Rundstedt recommended discontinuing the offensive, he made the same estimate of the situation as Montgomery; still, Hitler continued the attack. But soon counterattacks began, aided by clear weather and the cavalry of the air. And the Germans were back to their starting point within a month of their beginning.

The immediate Allied commitment of troops held in reserve and the conversion into reserves of troops not inextricably engaged with the enemy created an ample reserve, and their high degree of mobility assured their timely arrival. So the prompt and effective working of Newton's third law of the opposite reaction doomed the German offensive.

During January the Americans coped with another German attack, straightened their line, and readied a series of successive offensives to advance to the Rhine. Beginning on 8 February, the first of these, in the north by Montgomery's army group, proved so threatening, and thus so distracting, that it drew enough German reserves to enable the adjacent U.S. forces to break through to the Rhine in the last week of February. Then on 6 March Patton, farther south, surged forward to the Rhine, captured a major bridge at Remagen, and converted it into a bridgehead over the formidable river obstacle. A day later the Sixth Army Group in the south began its offensive and in ten days had reached the Rhine on most of its front. Without conscious imitation of Marshal Foch's 1918 campaign, these three successive offensives had hurt the enemy as much and gained more territory.

On 22 March the well-seasoned and fully supplied Allied armies, elated at victory and full of confidence, crossed the Rhine against an enfeebled foe. In a week they had made three deep penetrations, which, when the advances met each other in another week, enveloped two large groups of German troops, completing the depletion of the combat capabilities of the German armed forces in the west. What remained was to occupy the country, a task performed with wariness of sporadic, and sometimes determined, resistance.

Just as tactics serves different purposes for operational strategy, so operational strategy itself uses concentration of force in space and time for turning movements and attack or defense against hostile armed forces. This is equally applicable to the two stategic methods, the raiding and persisting strategies. Land, sea, and air forces all use raiding strategy, usually a quick blow at an adversary's weakness. Unlike the raid, which is transitory, persisting strategy seeks to acquire, control, and defend the surface. The 1944 contest for the control of France exemplfies persisting strategy on land.

From the beginning of the war, German aircraft and submarines had pursued a raiding logistic strategy against Allied commerce at sea, and Allied aircraft had also employed a raiding logistic strategy when they had bombed German industrial and transportation facilities. In addition, from the war's outset the Allied navies had employed the persisting logistic strategy of blockade against Germany and Italy. On the other hand, the German conquest of France, as well as the Allied reconquest, illustrates the operation of a persisting logistic strategy on land, one implemented by the combat strategy.

The initial conquest of France gave Germany well-positioned submarine and air bases for pursuing their raids against Allied commerce. But France made a far greater contribution to Germany's war effort by the logistic support that it unwillingly provided.

As a part of the armistice agreement in 1940, France had to pay—stated as a cost of occupation—an annual sum approximately equal to 25 percent of its gross national product. In this way the Germans could purchase huge, continuing quantities of such products as grain, meat, woolen clothing, and shoes. The exports to Germany so depleted France's leather supplies that shoes for French domestic consumption had wooden soles. Germany also received valuable industrial products and raw materials, particularly iron ore and bauxite for making aluminum.

In taking enough weapons to arm 88 of their own and allied divisions, the Germans acquired H-35 tanks for their armored divisions, S-35 tanks for Italy's, 400-mm (15.75-in.) howitzers for their siege of Leningrad, and 105-mm guns for Romania's army. France had to furnish its enemy with a variety of other military goods, including trucks and assorted airplanes and engines. The Germans also acquired naval and antiaircraft range finders, self-propelled gun carriages, and electronic equipment, including military radios and the radar detectors used by German submarines.

Yet an increasing number of French people recovered from the shock of the 1940 disaster, and in many subtle ways they sought to sabotage Germany's successful attempt to make France an adjunct to its war effort. For example, the Germans took to Russia a French 520-mm (20.47-in.) howitzer. With a carriage more than 100 feet long, this railway-mounted weapon weighed 265 tons. The French did not tell them that they had never fired the gun, that it was one of two completed at the end World War I, and that the other had burst when fired. Its ultimate fate remains uncertain, but it helped the Germans not at all. According to one account, it went to aid the siege of Sevastopol and burst when it fired its first shot as the French had expected; according to another, when it arrived to support the siege of Leningrad, the U.S.S.R. forces captured it before it could fire.

The experience with the cannon illustrates the problem of defective products made for export to Germany. This happened when workers sabotaged the product during manufacture or management deliberately used an incorrect design. The Germans sought to solve this problem—sabotage, production delays, and Allied air raids—by moving plants to Germany. These included arsenals, an automobile factory, oil refineries, and machine tool works. They also brought one million French workers to Germany, joining more than a million prisoners of war whom they had put to work rather than released at the end of hostilities in 1940. With their own supervision, the Germans expected to have higher production and fewer defects.

Of course this immense contribution to the German war effort did cost something. The Germans employed 30 divisions to occupy France and Belgium, both to control the countries and to protect against Allied raids. Yet these divisions were small and contained many unwilling soldiers, such as Polish conscripts. From 1943, French guerrilla resistance also constituted a cost to the Germans. Beginning slowly, these forces increasingly interrupted communications in France. At the time of the Allied landing in Normandy, 200,000 guerrillas took the field, attacking German convoys. A German division, for instance, required only eight days to move from the Russian front to the French frontier at Strasbourg, but due to Allied bombing and French sabotage, it required 23 days to reach Caen. And gradually the guerrillas took control of substantial areas of France. Nevertheless, French aid was a bargain, and when the Allies liberated France, they removed Germany's largest single external logistical prop.

Furthermore, the Allies also gained, just as had the Germans, because a persisting logistic strategy on land can have a positive aspect. Their first and very tangible gain had come almost two years earlier, when they had invaded French North Africa and quickly conquered most of it after a brief resistance. Here they found an army of 175,000 men, plus reserves, whom the commander had kept at a high level of proficiency in anticipation of the day that they could fight against Germany. Fully rearmed and given logistical support by the Allies, this force took the field as five infantry and three armored divisions, some of whom fought the Germans in Italy and all of whom became part of the French First Army, fighting on the southern end of the Allied line in late 1944 and in 1945.

Yet, the Allies made little further effort to mobilize France's manpower reserves, many of whom had received military training. The need to supply them with weapons and logistical support proved a serious obstacle to a large-scale mobilization. So the French combat effort amounted to providing replacements for the existing units, forming two additional divisions to fight the Germans, deploying 30,000 men to guard the Italian frontier against the German and Italian forces in northern Italy, contributing 30,000 men to the forces besieging the French ports still held by the Germans, guarding German prisoners, and assuring security within France.

Thus French forces consisted of barely a fifth of the troops based in France and deployed against Germany in 1945. Yet this number is a strong testimonial to the positive effect of a persisting logistic strategy. Moreover, this is only the most visible part of the French effort, because the French economy contributed much besides its land, buildings, hospitals, ports, railroads, canals, and highways to support the Allied armies in France and Germany.

Yet the Allies were not able to gain as much as the Germans from their conquest of France. This was true because the Germans had so thoroughly looted the country and because Allied bombers, French guerrillas, and retreating Germans had damaged so much, particularly railroads and bridges. Also the Allies lacked facilities that could use large quantities of iron ore and bauxite, nor, when the end of the war was so clearly in sight, did they see any point in trying to couple French production to their needs or begin the creation and equipment of significantly larger French armed forces.

The example of France shows the advantage of a persisting logistic strategy on land over a raiding strategy, long predominant in Europe until the seventeenth century when Western European armies and states became powerful enough to pursue a persisting strategy. It had the advantage of being more thorough, because occupation completely deprived the enemy of the area's resources and could have, as in the case of France, the positive effect of harnessing the conquered area to the victor's war effort. Of course, this does not compare the costs of the raiding and persisting methods, and both strategies—raids by bombers and conquest of territory—had political objectives and results as well as the aims of a military logistic strategy.

The growth in the size of military forces increased the significance of logistics just as did the emergence of the modern industrial economy and its dependence on distant markets. This significantly enhanced the role of logistics in war, and nothing more vividly demonstrates this than the place of the remote base area in the strategy of World War II in Europe.

The sea, air, and land strategies of the European theater centered on this remoteness of the base areas. The German submarine logistic raiding strategy endeavored to cut Europe off from its North American base area; the Allies' sea blockade isolated Germany from important imports, and their logistic raiding campaign by air attacked the German base area directly. On the operational level the raids against communications endeavored to cut German armies off from their base area.

Operational strategy also depended on exploiting the remoteness of the adversary's base area. The partially successful turning movement from the St. Lô breakthrough illustrates this, as did the successful turning movement near the Belgian border. Likewise, Hitler's Ardennes offensive aimed to turn the Allies by reaching their rear, taking Antwerp, and so interrupting their communications with their overseas base areas.

Chapter 7

The United States in the Pacific in World War II

In the war against Japan, 1941–1945, the United States played the largest
role but did so as part of a widespread alliance. Yet in the Pacific it had
the dominant part, and this chapter will concentrate on that. The war and
most of its campaigns have the distinction of a complete integration of land,
sea, and air power, and this feature gives the war its special strategic interest.

LOGISTICS

Unlike the forces in northern Europe, those in the Pacific had a far longer
supply line but one not molested by hostile raiders. The prevalence of water
communication in the Pacific and adjacent seas and the adversary's dependence on a remote base area offered unequaled opportunities for strategic maneuver by land, sea, and air forces.

TACTICS

As wooden sailing ships gave way to iron steamers in the nineteenth
century, navies built battleships with thick armor plate and big guns to
contend for the mastery of the seas. The long range and great accuracy of
the new rifled cannon enabled ships to fight at great distances. Because a
gunner's eye over a sight no longer sufficed for shooting at thousands of
yards, the range finder became an essential aid to aiming. One range-
determining device had the gunner look at the target separately with each
eye through different telescopes several feet apart. Thus he saw two images,
one with each eye. But the mechanism allowed him to move the telescopes

until he had superimposed the images, and the adjustment would make a triangle with the range finder as its base and the target at its apex. By measuring the angles and using trigonometry, the gunner could calculate the distance to the target.

In the early twentieth century ships began controlling the aiming of all the big guns from a central station with a large range finder. Since both the ship and its target ship moved, navies developed computers to calculate speed and correct the aim so that the shell would intercept the enemy ship at its predicted position at the end of the time it would take the shell to travel to the target.

Naval architects placed the ships' big gun positions so that most could fire on either side of the ship, and the admirals formed their ships for battle in a line for the same purpose as forming infantry in line, to develop maximum firepower. They also increased firepower and improved fire control by doubling, or more, the number of big guns on the new battleships. After 1908 navies built only this type, called *Dreadnoughts*.

THE BATTLE OF JUTLAND AS A PRECEDENT

In World War I a battle in the North Sea between the British and the Germans illustrates the tactics of combat between the armored big-gun ships. This did not happen early in the war because Germany's fleet, seriously overmatched by Britain's, did not challenge the British blockade. Finally, toward the end of the second year of the war, the German fleet, not expecting to meet the main British force, put to sea, steaming north along the coast of the peninsula of Jutland in late May 1916. The British fleet, also at sea, steamed to intercept the smaller, slower German force. The British had 28 modern *Dreadnought* battleships mounting eight or more big guns, the Germans 16, plus six pre-*Dreadnought* ships with only four big guns each. The antagonists were evenly matched in quality, the British ships having bigger guns, the Germans thicker armor, and the British having better-quality armor, the Germans better ammunition.

When the scouting forces of cruisers and battle cruisers found and fought each other, the weaker Germans fell back until their battleships hove in sight. The British then turned back toward their own fleet. This meant that the British knew the position and course of the German battleships, but the German admiral was ignorant even of the proximity of hostile battleships. And the Germans were steaming to disaster, because British Admiral Jellicoe had formed his ships into a column and was leading it across the path of the German fleet where it would form a line within good gun range. The British could thus carry out naval warfare's principal tactical maneuver, crossing the enemy's T. This gave the same advantage as an attack on land in which one force assailed the flank of the other, forcing it to fight in one direction when it was arrayed to fight in another.

When the British crossed the German line, the Germans resorted to a well-practiced maneuver, the fleet making a sudden retreat by having all ships turn 180 degrees and flee. When the Germans again blundered into the British, they once more saved themselves by rapid retreat and escaped in the dark.

The outcome of the battle illustrates the difference between tactical and strategic results. Tactically the Germans seemed to have won because the British suffered greater losses in terms of the tonnage of the ships sunk. But, since the British fleet was nearly twice as large, the losses were in about the same proportion as their strengths. This made the depletion, the tactical result, even. Further, in terms of total naval forces available for any subsequent engagement, the British had far more resources than they had committed at Jutland. The navy had 22 pre-*Dreadnought* ships completed after 1900, averaging 13,950 tons. The Germans had 14 such ships, averaging 12,500 tons. If the British had encountered really severe losses at Jutland, they could also have had an additional reinforcement of not just 12 older French battleships, averaging 16,465 tons, but seven *Dreadnoughts* as well. So the Allies possessed such an overwhelming superiority in available battleships that it more than compensated for any potential German victory of depletion at the Battle of Jutland.

Like most land battles, this naval battle did not alter the strategic situation. German sea communications outside of the Baltic remained interdicted by the Allied blockade.

The Battle of Jutland, which conformed to the admirals' presumptions, remained the basis for naval thinking during the interwar years. As the ranges at which ships fought had exceeded expectations, battleship design required serious modifications. Since the greater the distance between ships, the more arched became a shell's trajectory, shells fired from a long range were not only more likely to strike a ship's deck but would do so at a sharper angle, one likely to enable a shell to pierce the thin decks adequate for close-range combat. So, during the 1920s and 1930s, when navies modernized their old battleships and built new ones, they included much more thickly armored decks. As mines and torpedoes had proved a bigger threat than anticipated, these ships also had enhanced protection against underwater explosions.

These changes automatically gave the ships excellent defenses against bombs, including the effects of near misses exploding, like a mine, in the water next to a ship. The new battleships had high speed, 27 to 31 knots, and cruisers and destroyers had speeds of three and six knots, respectively, faster than the battleships and a comparable improvement in underwater and deck protection. For the most part the battle cruiser type blended with the battleship and the armored and protected cruisers merged also. All ships had strong antiaircraft armaments, 4- or 5-inch guns for high-altitude defense and to protect against torpedo boat and destroyer attacks and 40-

and 20-millimeter guns for defense against low-flying aircraft. During the war, ships added many more of these small guns. Early in World War II, ships gained much-improved fire control against airplanes and other ships through the use of radar. Radar sets emitted radio waves and, by receiving them when reflected back, could give the distance and direction of movement of the object from which the waves reflected. Thus fire-control equipment not only acquired more accurate range and direction finding but could function easily at night.

THE EMERGENCE OF THE AIRCRAFT CARRIER

The earliest impact of airplanes and dirigibles on warfare at sea resembled that on land, but to a lesser degree. Air reconnaissance lacked the importance that it had on the World War I land fronts, especially on the western front, because navies still had their usual means, scouting by cruisers. Sailors were able to take planes to sea with them because, equipped with pontoons, they could take off and land on water.

The Russian navy had used airplanes for aiding gunners in the spring of 1915 in their bombardment of the Turkish coast near Constantinople. Also in 1915, aircraft played a crucial role in the destruction of the German protected cruiser *Konigsburg,* which had taken refuge in the Rufiji River in German East Africa. Well up the river, it was almost invisible between jungle-lined banks. Two British seaplanes and two monitors mounting 6-inch guns had come from Britain to attack the cruiser. The first offensive action, an attempt by the aircraft to bomb the ship, failed when the Germans shot down one of the planes. The two monitors then moved up the river to take the cruiser under fire. But this attack failed too when the salvos from the cruiser's 105-mm (4.13-in.) guns, very accurate because directed by a concealed observer on the river bank, drove the monitors back. The next effort, which employed bombardment at 9,500 yards, beyond the range of the cruiser's guns, had success. With the remaining seaplane spotting the fall of the shot, the monitors' 6-inch guns made appropriate corrections and hit the anchored ship with the eighth salvo. Rapid fire then reduced the *Konigsburg* to a flaming wreck.

Fleets naturally wanted to carry with them aircraft for the same purposes armies used them: reconnaissance and assistance in fire direction. Early attempts to do this involved seaplane carriers that could set the pontoon planes in the water for takeoff and pick them up after landing. As early as December 1914 the British sent three such carriers on a raid against German naval bases, and the next year a plane from a seaplane carrier sank a Turkish transport by flying low over the water toward it and dropping a torpedo. This was the first success for torpedo bombing, which the navy had only just tried the year before.

Realizing the value of a ship on which aircraft could land, the British first made unsuccessful experiments with separate spaces for takeoff and landing. Finally, in October 1918, the *Argus,* with a single, dual-purpose flight deck, became the first operational aircraft carrier for land planes to join Britain's fleet. Entirely flat, with funnels, bridge, and all facilities usual in a superstructure located along the ship's side, the 14,500-ton, 20-knot ship could operate 20 land planes. Since the earliest airplane used, the Sopwith Pup, could take off if it could taxi for 20 feet into a 20-knot wind, the *Argus* could create the wind needed for the Pup to take off by steaming at full speed. Further, the plane could land easily, often hovering above the deck when flying into a 20-knot wind with the *Argus* steaming at 20 knots beneath it.

With more-advanced aircraft that could not fly so slowly, carriers needed arresting gear, cables stretched across the deck that would catch a hook dangled from a landing plane. By World War II most carriers were bigger than the *Argus* and could steam at 30 knots to keep up with cruisers and facilitate the takeoff of larger planes from a longer deck steaming into the wind at 30 knots. Usually carrying antiaircraft guns only, the vulnerable and virtually unarmored aircraft carrier required protection from other ships.

In 1939 only the British, American, Japanese, and French navies possessed carriers, the French having only one. Yet the three principal navies had come to attach great significance to their carriers. When the British began to modernize their navy in the 1930s, they showed the value placed on carriers by authorizing five battleships and five carriers, but quickly added two more carriers. The United States and Japan gave a similar emphasis to air power at sea.

Navies intended that carriers should have three types of aircraft: torpedo planes, bombers, and fighters. The fighter had the function of protecting the carrier and escorting the torpedo planes and bombers during their attacks. The torpedo planes had the mission of assailing ships, particularly armored ships, which were very resistant to bombs. The navies wanted to exploit the accuracy of dive bombers to cope with the problem of hitting a moving target by diving toward it and releasing their bombs only when very close. Bombing not only lacked the accuracy of artillery fire with sophisticated fire control, but, unlike the gunners, bombardiers could not make corrections on the basis of where the first and subsequent bombs had landed; for them every bomb dropped was like the initial shot with a cannon.

In the first engagement between fleets in which an aircraft carrier participated, a British force of cruisers, a battleship, and a carrier met an Italian squadron with two battleships and the support of land-based aircraft. In spite of the Navy's stress on torpedo bombing and training for it, the carrier's torpedo plane attacks twice failed to hit large Italian cruisers. Fortunately for the airplanes, the Italian antiaircraft gunners had no better aim.

Nor had it been a good day for Italian aviation either. Numerous Italian bombers, attacking for three hours from a high altitude, failed to hit any ships, though they scored many near misses on their favorite targets, the carrier and the battleship. The Italian bombers also did not hit their own fleet, in spite of bombing it through error for two hours. Happily for the Italian aviators, the British antiaircraft guns failed to hit them, as did the guns on the Italian ships, which defended themselves against their own air force.

In the fall of 1940, carrier aircraft gave an astounding demonstration of what they could do when they attacked the Italian fleet in its base at Taranto. A single modern British carrier came at night within 170 miles of Taranto and launched ten torpedo planes and eight dive bombers, which made their attacks by the light of flares. The torpedo planes disabled three of the six Italian battleships in the harbor and crippled two cruisers. The raid, which immediately reduced the Italian fleet to inferiority in the Mediterranean, cost only two planes.

Carrier aircraft, so important in the Mediterranean Sea, had a smaller role in the North Atlantic because overcast conditions and big waves often restricted flying. Yet carriers and their torpedo bombers had a critical part in the sinking of the German battleship *Bismarck*. This occurred when it sortied into the Atlantic to raid convoys and then fled from a hunt by the British fleet for five days in 1941.

As the fleeing *Bismarck* came within a half day's steaming of German bases on the French coast, the aircraft of the carrier *Ark Royal,* coming north to intercept it, found their quarry. A flight of 15 torpedo bombers managed to fly off and return to the carrier, in spite of the surging of its deck in a very heavy sea. At least two torpedoes struck the *Bismarck,* reducing its speed, disabling its steering, and leaving it unable to escape the two British battleships that soon arrived and promptly overwhelmed it.

Virtually without armor, the fragile, vulnerable airplane wrought a major change in sea warfare by adding range and versatility. Just as it provided reconnaissance for the armies and observation to aid their guns, the airplane could reach beyond the range of the guns. This meant that the aircraft at sea had extended the range of the fleet's armament as far as the plane could search, find, attack with bomb or torpedo, and return.

Against other ships, even battleships, the aircraft carrier was an intrinsically superior weapons system, able to attack its antagonist without itself being vulnerable. Yet, as the experience of the British carrier *Glorious* showed early in the war, this dominance depended on the aircraft carrier being at a safe distance from the ships it attacked. The *Glorious,* en route from Norwegian waters to Britain, suddenly encountered two fast German battleships. Both the carrier and the battleships could steam at 30 knots, but the Germans increased their speed faster, opened fire and sank the carrier without any of its aircraft even leaving the deck. At that range the battleship was the dominant weapon system; at 100 miles the carrier had superiority.

Yet the fragile carrier itself was an air attack's most attractive and vulnerable target. This situation brought to naval warfare the need for a combination of arms comparable to that on land. Just as armies had to combine antitank and antiaircraft guns to protect each other, and the infantry, from aircraft and tanks, so the carrier had to have other ships near it for its protection. Not only could battleships and cruisers give protection from surface vessels, but their powerful antiaircraft armaments could help fend off air attacks. To protect carriers and other ships in a fleet, the British and American navies built a total of 27 antiaircraft cruisers, and the British converted 9 old crusers to antiaircraft duty. These 36 ships mounted from eight to 16 heavy antiaircraft guns and many more smaller guns.

In the Atlantic and the Mediterranean the combination of the carrier and the battleship constituted the capital ship of the naval war. But, with the clear weather of the vast Pacific, the carrier alone was the ascendant weapon system.

LAND-BASED AIRCRAFT AGAINST SHIPS: GENERAL MITCHELL'S TESTS

The American apostle of air power, General William Mitchell, paid much attention to control of the sea. He saw there scope for the airplane, not as a weapon system that would become the collaborator of the ship but as one that would supersede navies. The thin-walled bomb impressed him with how much more explosives it could carry than an equally heavy artillery shell with its thick sides to withstand firing from a cannon and a strong point to penetrate armor. He believed that a near miss by a big bomb would sink a ship by the water pressure against its hull generated by the immensely powerful explosion. He also believed that a hit on the ship itself, even a battleship, would disable it by breaking every light bulb in the ship. Early he had an opportunity to experiment with the power of bombs against some captured German warships.

In 1921 General Mitchell, with the cooperation of the navy, used a German cruiser and battleship for his test of the efficacy of bombs. Many naval officers, aware of the failure of light bombs to hurt ships in World War I, were skeptical of the ability of aircraft to harm armored ships. Others had doubts about the ability of bombardiers to hit ships. After all, when a German battle cruiser had run aground for six days, British seaplanes had flown over 200 bombing sorties (separate flights) against it and scored only one hit, an ineffectual one on a smokestack.

But Mitchell prepared well for the test, having fabricated special 2,000-pound bombs and readied his force of 250 aircraft by months of training.

With the assistance of naval observers, he conducted his first test against a 5,100-ton German protected cruiser. Sixty planes with 100-, 250-, and 300-pound bombs made the first attack against the anchored ship. Inspection then revealed that the bombs had done considerable damage to the upper deck and killed the goats placed in cages on the deck. But there was no damage below the protective deck. The second phase consisted of six aircraft carrying 600-pound bombs. After a few bombs had fallen, the observers signaled a halt for an inspection. But the planes continued, dropping all of their bombs, sinking the ship, and precluding an investigation of the condition of the light bulbs or any other effects of bombs, as large as any used in World War I.

The test on the well-armored 22,400-ton battleship was a special occasion, attended by celebrities, the secretaries of War, Navy, and Agriculture. After two hours of bombing with 250-pound bombs, the six planes with 600-pound bombs made their attack, with two bombs hitting the water close to the side of the ship and three on the deck. Inspection showed a slight list and the stern lower.

The test continued the next morning with planes dropping 1,100-pound bombs, scoring three hits, damaging the superstructure, and causing the ship to sink lower. Then came the final act, eight planes, each carrying a 2,000-pound bomb. After six bombs, one hit and five near misses, the ship sank.

General Mitchell saw this as a demonstration of the end of surface navies. But it had only the more limited significance that aircraft could sink anchored battleships. And this happened in World War II on a notable occasion when bombers attacking in level flight sank a stationary battleship. This occurred in 1944 when British four-engine bombers flew over a Norwegian fjord to attack the anchored German battleship *Tirpitz,* modern and twice the size of the ship Mitchell's bombers had sunk. But each British bomber carried a single 12,000-pound bomb, six times the weight of those Mitchell had used. These proved effective enough to capsize the ship, making it a total loss.

But, in his enthusiasm, General Mitchell failed to note the limited significance of his tests and tended to assume that aircraft in level flight could sink moving as well as anchored ships. In World War II such bombing tactics against ships in motion enjoyed little success. They usually failed as dismally as did the attack by Italian bombers on their own and British squadrons. In the German invasion of the island of Crete in 1941, perhaps air power's most notable contest with sea power, the German air force inflicted serious damage on the British fleet. Without the unremitting air attacks, the ships could easily have interdicted German troop movements by sea; and without them and their heavy equipment, the airborne troops might well have failed to capture the island.

In this contest, the British had 12 cruisers and about the same number of destroyers. The cruisers had good antiaircraft capabilities, but the destroyers could defend against low-level attacks only. The Gemans had 280 twin-engine bombers for high-level attack and 150 dive bombers.

For their high-level bombing, the experienced German aviators dropped sticks, or sequences, of bombs, seeking to have the stick intersect the course of the ship. This meant the bombs were small and the hits few. The Germans had no torpedo bombers; the British had used these at Taranto, and experts regarded them as the most effective airborne weapon system against ships. But the dive bombers did their part well, dropping 1,100-pound bombs, dangerous to cruisers and fatal to destroyers. That the British lost three cruisers and six destroyers is a testimony to the effectiveness of the dive bombers and their seasoned pilots.

STRATEGY

The strategy of the Pacific war unfolded in an initial Japanese offensive that took the Dutch East Indies and the British and U.S. Asiatic colonies. A series of costly naval battles halted the Japanese advance south and east and laid the foundation for Allied advances. These took place along two major Pacific lines of operation: from the Hawaiian Islands westward through several island groups to the Philippine Islands and north from Australia and then westward to the Philippines via the north coast of New Guinea.

These operations combined land and sea forces working together with the tactical power of each enhanced and their sphere of combat operations immensely enlarged by land- and sea-based aircraft. The airplanes used machine guns, small cannon, and bombs to attack targets on land and these and air-launched torpedoes to assail surface ships. This profound tactical change from earlier wars meant that airplanes from carriers could range over the land, their raids implementing combat and logistic strategies by attacking troops and their transports and supplies. At the same time, the land-based aircraft could reach out over the sea to implement the same two strategies by assailing war and merchant ships.

The distinctive overlapping of land, sea, and air warfare created an exceptional tactical, logistic, and operational collaboration between land, sea, and air forces. These joint operations reached their apogee in landings on Pacific islands by troops carried on transports while the carrier planes protected the ships from land-based aircraft and also added to the support given troops ashore by naval gunfire. Often, aircraft based on adjacent land areas assisted, or substituted for, the carriers and big warships in controlling the sea, protecting the transports, and giving support to the troops.

Using efficient sea communications and often replenishing warships at sea, the Allies pushed their offensives toward Japan by a sequence of conquests until they reached the Philippines and then moved closer. All the while they sought bases from which to subject Japan to a close blockade and to prepare for an invasion. At the same time, they extended the area of combat even more when submarines raided under all the seas whose surface Japan controlled, and the big, new B-29 bombers raided Japanese cities and laid mines in the nearby seas to tighten the blockade so well begun by the systematic raids of the submarines.

THE INITIAL JAPANESE ADVANCE

In 1931 Japan had begun a new phase of territorial expansion when, by a brief, decisive land campaign, it took Manchuria, a large province in northeastern China. It continued in 1937 with a more extensive military compaign to conquer more Chinese territory and to bring the whole vast empire under its control. But, though often defeated, China continued its resistance until this opposition, and the vast size of the country, stalled the Japanese advance. Thus the attempt to subjugate China had proved an embarrassing failure for Japan.

Unable to acknowledge this, the Japanese compensated by seeking a more fruitful field for conquest. So, when Japan began war with the United States and Great Britain in December 1941, it did so with clearly formulated objectives and a military and political strategy well adapted to achieve it. It aimed to acquire the Dutch East Indies, now the nation of Indonesia, and gain control of its huge petroleum production, its rubber, and its other valuable resources. Since the Germans had overrun the Netherlands, the colonial administration could have no support from its homeland.

The war of Germany and Italy against Britain and the Union of Soviet Socialist Republics had disrupted world trade and made Japan dependent on the United States for oil and other products. As the United States was using its position to pressure Japan to withdraw from China, the possession of the East Indies would give the Japanese political as well as economic independence and an empire susceptible to further economic exploitation.

Although the Dutch colonies constituted virtually the whole of Japan's war aims, the Japanese knew that neither Britain nor the United States would countenance such a drastic change in the balance of power in the Far East. Yet, with Britain involved in war with Germany and Italy and the United States absorbed with this struggle and the potential threat it presented, Japan, bolstered by an alliance with Germany and Italy, felt that this constituted a propitious time to take the valuable colonies.

So Japanese strategy foresaw eventual war with the two nations possessing the world's most powerful navies; but the strategy anticipated this naval conflict by planning to seize the colonies that could have provided enemies' bases for an offensive by their naval and air forces. Thus the Japanese projected the creation of a barrier of land possessions to aid their fleet in its defense of their conquests. This military strategy of a persisting offensive on a grand scale fit the political strategy, for these conquests comprised the limit of their war aims; Japan had neither the motive nor the power to assail Britain or the United States. Yet it expected to be in such a strong defensive position that the cost of the reconquest of all of these colonies would be greater in time and material and human resources than the colonies would be worth to the British and the Americans.

The military strategy to secure their acquisitions involved gaining protection on the east by taking the Philippine Islands from the United States; on the west by conquering Britain's possessions, the Malay States and Burma; and on the south by acquiring much of the Dutch and Australian colony of New Guinea and some of the adjacent islands.

The Japanese, who had already absorbed the French colony of Indochina and secured the cooperation of Thailand, correctly concluded that they had the power to make these vast conquests in only a few months. The task would be so easy because, with the exception of the British in the Malay Peninsula, the colonial powers had relatively small military forces in their possessions. Further, these powers typically equipped their colonial forces with inferior weapons such as obsolete aircraft and the oldest ships. This policy had no effect when, for example, the British and Italian colonial forces fought each other with outmoded biplanes, but would be disastrous when confronting the Japanese who had monoplanes and otherwise well-equipped and highly proficient land, sea, and air forces. With this superiority and the advantage of beginning the war, the Japanese could exploit the initiative to strike at weakness.

With its commitments in China and elsewhere, Japan allocated only 11 of its 55 divisions to the conquest of such an immense empire. They proved ample. The army and navy divided responsibilities for the various campaigns. Both the army and the navy had air forces—the navy's, which was twice the size of the army's, having substantial land as well as carrier-based aircraft. Thus air power easily functioned as parts of the army and navy, and the Japanese had no independent mission for air power.

The navy saw one potential difficulty with the plan of campaign, the intervention of the U.S. Pacific fleet at Pearl Harbor in the Hawaiian Islands. Based there, the fleet had about half of the United States' major ships, eight battleships, three aircraft carriers, and a good complement of cruisers, destroyers, and submarines. To prevent the intervention of this force, the Japanese planned a surprise attack to cripple the fleet at Pearl Harbor. Because of the heavy guns and powerful fortifications of the base, only aircraft could possibly make the attack on the fleet.

When the British had disabled three Italian battleships by a night attack at Taranto, they used only one carrier and 18 airplanes. But, for their attack against the U.S. fleet, the Japanese had concentrated overwhelming force: their six biggest carriers, together carrying 450 airplanes, most of the entire fleet's carrier aircraft. On the day of the attack, 40 were not operational, 50 remained to protect the carriers, and 360 made the attack: 40 torpedo bombers, 135 dive bombers, 104 horizontal bombers, and 81 fighters for protection and to attack aircraft on the ground. The morning attack in peacetime gained surprise and was so effective that there was no counter-attack.

The raid ruined one battleship, capsized another, sunk one, and severely damaged four. One, in dry dock, received only a single bomb hit. In addition, other ships, except the absent carriers, suffered severely. Yet the raid failed to accomplish its mission of preventing a trans-Pacific intervention by the U.S. fleet. This was true because the fleet never possessed the capability: The United States lacked the bases from which to supply and support such an intervention across thousands of miles of ocean peppered with Japanese bases.

Still, the raid had a profound military effect. It immediately showed that the aircraft carrier, not the battleship, was the capital ship in the Pacific. Though battleships would be a part of fleets formed around carriers, none would be like those at Pearl Harbor. Their thick armor and big guns made them completely modern, but their 1914 speed of 21 knots made them unable to keep up with the carriers, cruisers, and destroyers, all capable of operating at sustained speeds of 30 knots. New, fast battleships would perform that role. So the Pearl Harbor raid, in missing the carriers, had sunk no capital ships at all.

The realization of the revolution in naval war came with essentially the same clarity to both Japanese and American admirals. Both had remained fully committed to the supremacy of the battleship, with the carrier as an auxiliary, but almost instantly they saw the change and sought means to increase the number of carriers in their fleets just as the war began. The United States was fortunate to have as its central Pacific commander Admiral Chester W. Nimitz. Intelligent and well prepared for his task by the navy's relentless study of all aspects of a war in the Pacific, he encountered little difficulty in adapting the navy's long-matured Pacific strategy to the age of land- and sea-based air power. He proved to be a prescient, flexible, and decisive commander of the fleet and marine team.

In using all six of their large fleet carriers for the Pearl Harbor raid, the Japanese had made a concentration in space. But, also on the same day, 8 December west of the international date line, the Japanese army used concentration in time to gain the most advantages from the initiative conferred on it by taking the offensive unexpectedly. It attacked the British colonies of Hong Kong on the coast of China and advanced into the Malay States, simultaneously crossing the British colony's northern border from Thailand and landing on its east coast. The campaign against the Philippines also began later on the same day with air raids that destroyed on the ground about half of the U.S. planes. Two days later troops landed on the north end of Luzon, the archipelago's largest and most northern island. Other operations followed in quick succession: northern Borneo on 16 December;

Burma on 23 December; islands near New Guinea on 23 January; and Dutch Islands—Sumatra on 14 February, Timor on 19 February, and Java on 28 February.

The sequence of operations permitted the Japanese to concentrate against successive objectives. Realizing the virtual dominance of aircraft's long-range firepower, the Japanese placed control of the air and its exploitation at the center of their strategy. Thus they directed their operations against air bases, of which the colonial powers had built many but lacked adequate air forces to defend.

The Japanese depended primarily on land-based aircraft, including those of the navy, and made the first step in each of their operations' air attacks against air fields until they had destroyed the local air forces. Usually these could expect no reinforcement or replacement. Having thus made the sea-invasion route secure from air attack from the land, they sent the landing force, often accompanied by carriers to give close support to the troops. Making the airfield their immediate objective and repairing it as soon as captured, the invaders shortly had their own land-based planes as their cavalry of the air and also could begin strikes at the air bases and aircraft of the next objective. So they relied almost exclusively on land-based air power, thus diminishing the exposure of their carriers to the risk of air attack.

And the Japanese had shown how formidable such an attack could be, not only against anchored battleships but against modern armored ships at sea. The day after the Japanese began their offensive into the Malay States, two British ships sortied from their base at Singapore under the protection of an overcast sky. These were the 32,000-ton battle cruiser *Repulse*, with 30-knot speed and six 15-inch guns, and the new 38,000-ton battleship *Prince of Wales*, with 27-knot speed and ten 14-inch guns. They aimed to intercept a Japanese invasion convoy. Instead, 80 shore-based enemy bombers and torpedo planes found them when the weather cleared. The first attack by bombers flying at 12,000 feet gained only an inconsequential hit on the *Repulse*, but it did distract the antiaircraft gunners from the almost-simultaneous assault of the torpedo bombers. Within fifteen minutes four torpedoes had sunk the *Prince of Wales* and five sank the *Repulse*, in spite of skillful, high-speed evasive maneuvers.

While the campaigns to conquer the new empire exploited concentration in time, the navy used its large fleet carriers to take advantage of the initiative conferred by its preponderance and exploit its interior lines of operation between its adversaries. Having first concentrated in the east against Pearl Harbor, the carriers then turned south to support the landings and make a destructive raid against the major north Australian port of Darwin. The raid so damaged the base that much time would elapse before Darwin could again serve as a sea and air base.

Then, with five of the big carriers, the fleet turned west and entered the

Bay of Bengal and the Indian Ocean, where it could expect to meet the British fleet. The carriers' planes sank three British cruisers and a small carrier and struck naval and air bases on Ceylon where they met effective opposition in the air. With only two big carriers, the hopelessly over-matched main British fleet kept its distance and based itself on the African coast. So the central position enabled the Japanese navy to strike in over-whelming force in east, south, and west, each time inflicting much damage but suffering comparatively small losses in planes and pilots.

The Japanese army did as well as the navy, sometimes carrying out suc-cessful conquests against overwhelmingly superior numbers. In the Malay States, in a peninsula two-thirds covered with jungle, the defenders out-numbered the Japanese invaders by two to one. But the Japanese resolutely and skillfully took the offensive, their soldiers proving adaptable enough to fight in the jungle and find their way along its trails. Suitably equipped, they had handcarts and bicycles for transport and depended heavily on machine guns and light trench mortars. They also secured much of their food locally, making it partly a base area by living on the country in the old-fashioned way.

On the other hand, their adversary was completely road-bound, one In-dian division being completely motorized, a distinct advantage, but in other terrain. The road dependence of the British forces made their movements, their lines of operation, and points of concentration completely predictable and those of the Japanese, who did not always eschew the roads and moved tanks on them, completely unpredictable. The measure of Japanese opera-tional success in conquering the Malay Peninsula and the port of Singapore is shown by the casualties: British, including a huge number of prisoners—137,000; Japanese—less than 10,000.

Against superior numbers the Japanese also prevailed on the large Phil-ippine island of Luzon. In 1941 the United States had combined the Phil-ippine forces under former U.S. Army Chief of Staff, Philippine Field Marshal Douglas MacArthur. The army also recalled MacArthur to active duty as a general so that he could also command the U.S. troops. He had over 20,000 U.S. and Filipino regular ground troops and 100,000 newly mobilized Filipino forces. With this large army Field Marshal and General MacArthur planned to defend the whole island of Luzon.

The Japanese gained immediate air superiority but brought only two divisions to cope with this big force. Nevertheless, when veteran Japanese troops and commanders displayed exemplary tactical and operational skill, they easily overwhelmed the huge army of newly mobilized Philippine ci-vilians. Soon the defenders retreated to the Bataan Peninsula, the planned site of a final defense; but they were without the necessary food stock, much of which remained in the evacuated city of Manila.

With the advantage of the fortified defense, General MacArthur's forces compelled the Japanese to await reinforcements. But on 3 April, when the reinforced Japanese resumed their attack, their ill-supplied adversaries soon surrendered. Having evacuated with his staff before the capitulation, MacArthur assumed command of forces in Australia.

The main Allied naval resistance endeavored to protect the Dutch East Indies and, therefore, Australia farther to the south. For this they had six cruisers, two each from the United States, Britain, and the Netherlands. They faced double their number of Japanese cruisers, some of which were half again the size of the largest Allied ships. In several hard-fought encounters, the Allies lost all of their cruisers and many of their destroyers without seriously impeding the Japanese advance.

High operational and tactical proficiency as well as superior force made the Japanese navy successful. The Japanese army did at least as well. Adding to the advantage of so many troops with combat experience in China, the Japanese army displayed an exceptional degree of tactical and operational prowess. The Japanese took advantage of the poor visibility in the jungles to make the most of infiltration tactics, pushing through gaps to take positions in the rear and penetrate deeper into, or entirely through, the defense. When necessary, they made good use of the frontal attack as a distraction for a turning movement. In their operational strategy, they displayed the same mastery of concentration against weakness. Exploiting the low ratio of force to space and often widely and confusingly dispersed, they readily turned defenders, blocking their retreats and capturing some forces and precipitating the hasty retreat of others.

Such excellence in traditional tactical and operational methods, even in the jungle, dazzled their opponents, making the Japanese appear invincible military wizards. Later, the hardy Japanese soldier, imbued with the doctrine of his distinctive military ethos, would prove equally dauntless on the defense.

THE FURTHER JAPANESE OFFENSIVE AND THE BATTLES OF THE CORAL SEA AND MIDWAY

Although the Japanese had reached their planned defensive perimeter, their easy successes urged them to improve their position by gaining a stronger hold on New Guinea and by taking islands to its east in order to sever the communications between Australia and the United States. This involved preparing for an army campaign against Port Moresby, the Australian base on New Guinea's south coast. To do this, army troops landed at the villages of Lae and Salamaua on the north coast, preparatory to a drive over the high intervening mountains to capture the key port and its airfield. At this point a Japanese offensive first met American navy carriers.

A month and a half after the defeat at Pearl Harbor, the American navy took the offensive, using a new organization, flotillas called task forces. A carrier provided the nucleus for each of these, supported by cruisers and destroyers. Without old battleships to slow it down, a task force could steam at 30 knots, its speed protecting it against enemy battleships, its destroyers alert for submarines, and the antiaircraft armament of the cruisers and destroyers aiding that of the carrier in repelling any attack by aircraft. From Pearl Harbor the navy sent two of these task forces, one comprising the 20,000-ton carrier *Enterprise* and the other her sister the *Yorktown*. They made attacks on the Japanese Marshall Islands in January and another, by the *Enterprise,* against the captured U.S. Wake Island. These three raids harmed the Japanese little but benefited the United States much because they gave the task forces crucial experience in flight operations and conducting attacks under real, rather than simulated, combat conditions.

The U.S. carriers met the Japanese when U.S. intelligence deciphered Japanese messages and learned that the Japanese were sending an expedition by sea around the eastern end of New Guinea to attack Port Moresby. This intelligence enabled the Allied forces to seize the initiative. This they did by again sending the carrier *Lexington* back from Pearl Harbor to join the *Yorktown* and, when they returned from a raid, by ordering south the remaining two carriers, the *Enterprise* and the 20,000-ton *Hornet,* which, however, did not arrive until after the battle. But the naval forces would at least have parity in carriers.

Most of the major sea battles in the Pacific would be between carriers, and, in the absence of overwhelming force, the factor of chance had an enhanced importance compared with such engagements as the Falkland Islands and Jutland.

Though capital ships, carriers were, unlike battleships, lightly armored, comparatively fragile, and thus very vulnerable to bombs as well as torpedoes; a lucky bomb hit, for example, could disable a carrier but only cripple a turret on a battleship. Also, unlike gun ships, they had only an intermittent offensive capability; when they had launched their aircraft for an attack, they could make no other until their planes had returned and received a new supply of munitions and fuel. To try to have a constant offensive capability by sending out a series of small sorties would sacrifice concentration in time when attacking a target and give enemy antiaircraft weapons a particular advantage. Luck would play a major part in whether the time and target chosen for an attack would prove the best one. Admirals on both sides grasped these special variables of the new sea warfare, which they would inaugurate at the Battle of the Coral Sea.

The *Lexington* and *Yorktown* moved westward and closer to New Guinea, groping for the convoy bound for Port Moresby. Meanwhile, the two Japanese carriers to their east searched south and west for the single carrier they expected. Then each antagonist thought they had found the other, 61 Japanese planes sinking a tanker and a destroyer, believing them to be a carrier and a cruiser. Ninety-three U.S. planes set out to attack little gunboats and old cruisers, erroneously reported as two carriers and four modern cruisers. Instead they discovered a carrier accompanying the landing force, the *Shoho,* converted from a fast tanker. When they hit the little ship with seven torpedoes and 15 bombs, it promptly plunged to the bottom.

Japanese aircraft losses in this stage of the battle also showed the effect of chance. A group of twenty-seven planes seeking the U.S. carriers unexpectedly lost one third of its planes when it encountered not a carrier but its fighter planes. Then, seeking to return to their carrier, some planes became lost in the darkness, some crashed into the sea, and one was shot down when it, one of several, tried to land on a U.S. carrier, having mistaken the ship for its own. Only six of the 27 planes on the futile mission returned to their carrier.

The next day the carriers found each other, 99 U.S. aircraft severely damaging the big carrier *Shokaku,* and 69 Japanese planes raining bombs, and lacing the water with torpedo wakes around the U.S. carriers. The 20,000-ton *Yorktown* avoided all but one bomb, and the stoutly built, 36,000-ton *Lexington* readily weathered several bomb hits and three by torpedoes. But then a series of explosions from gasoline vapors, released by the jarring of the torpedo explosions, started uncontrollable fires, which destroyed the *Lexington.*

The smaller and comparatively fragile *Yorktown,* however, had only the easily controlled damage from its one bomb hit. Critically weakened by the loss of half of their carriers, the Americans withdrew, as did the Japanese admiral, pleased with a victory even greater than that attained, his pilots having reported sinking two carriers. In one respect he had lost more heavily, half of his pilots, highly skilled veterans of the Pearl Harbor raid. Weakened by the withdrawal of the big Japanese carriers, the Port Moresby invasion force withdrew. Tactically a defeat because of the loss of the *Lexington,* the Battle of the Coral Sea was a strategic victory for the Allies because it achieved its objective of protecting Port Moresby.

Then the Japanese revised their strategic plan as a result of a U.S. tour de force, a political raid on Tokyo by Army Air Forces planes launched from a carrier. This militarily insignificant event aroused the Japanese to an exceptional degree. They instituted a retaliatory program of sending up small, unmanned balloons carrying explosives to drift with the prevailing westerly winds to the United States. This scheme had a measure of success when some of the balloons reached the United States where they fell to earth and often exploded. The balloons caused more alarm than harm.

More immediately, this raid on Tokyo induced the Japanese command to extend the defensive perimeter by capturing Midway Island, a small but important base 1,300 miles northwest of Pearl Harbor. Simultaneous with the Midway expedition, another would establish a base in the Aleutian Islands west of Alaska. This operation and its troop ships would have the support of two 25-knot carriers, the converted liner *Junyo* with 48 planes, and the old, small *Ryujo* with 30. The assault on the Aleutians had the dual objective of confusing the U.S. command at the time of the Midway attack and securing an air base for reconnaissance.

The Japanese planned the Midway operation on the assumption of their superior operational skill, confirmed by the Battle of the Coral Sea in which they had suffered the *Shokaku* damaged but believed they had sunk both U.S. carriers. But they had lost their edge in skill.

The Japanese fleet carriers had lost 29 planes in the Pearl Harbor raid and 57 in the Battle of the Coral Sea. In between they had used up aircraft and, more critically, pilots in operations to support the landings in the Dutch East Indies and Rabaul, the raid on Darwin in Australia, and the cruise in the Indian Ocean and the air combat at Ceylon. Accidents as well as enemy action also wore down the air strength of such a busy fleet. No longer could it embark 450 aircraft, even if the *Shokaku* were fit for action. So only four carriers set sail for Midway, and these were carrying only 272 planes, not even their full complement, and had many pilots not only inexperienced but having only an attenuated training program. So the fleet no longer had the quantitative and qualitative superiority that would have virtually assured it of victory.

Since the U.S. Navy had intercepted and deciphered the Japanese operations order, the initiative passed to the U.S. command. It chose to exercise it by concentrating to defend Midway. In addition to three available carriers, *Yorktown, Enterprise,* and *Hornet,* it augmented the defenses and air strength of the tiny island itself.

Still, the three U.S. carriers also lacked their full complement of planes, but had 235, and the 121 assorted planes on Midway gave the defenders the equivalent of another carrier, making the odds even at four against four.

The Japanese had not planned with their customary strategic acumen. Believing they had sunk two U.S. carriers in the Battle of the Coral Sea, they expected to encounter no more than two U.S. carriers at Midway. Counting Midway as a third carrier, they expected to have a four to three superiority. Deeming this adequate, they displayed their overconfidence in their carriers' airmen, now of diminished quality, by failing to concentrate. The Midway invasion fleet, separate from and behind the carriers, included the small light fleet carrier *Zuiho*. With a speed of 28 knots, it could have kept up with the fleet carriers and added its 30 planes to the battle force.

Moreover, the Japanese navy could have embarked the 78 aircraft on the slow carriers with the Aleutian expedition in the 34-knot *Zuikaku*, left behind for lack of aircraft. This measure of concentration would have added 108 planes, a 40 percent augmentation of the battle force. Thus the American navy had concentrated for the battle, and the Japanese had not.

While the attackers expected to surprise them, good U.S. communications and cryptographic intelligence had made the defenders ready, and air reconnaissance from Midway had found the Japanese armada when 400 miles away while the three carriers waited in ambush northeast of Midway.

On the morning of 4 June the admiral of the Japanese carriers, unaware of the lurking American carriers, sent half his force to attack Midway, losing 38 planes and doing little damage. Midway's first counterattack failed with heavy loss, defeated by the Japanese fighter defense and the failure of Flying Fortresses at high altitude to hit the moving ships.

Then the Japanese admiral refueled and rearmed his planes to launch all of his forces at the U.S. task force his reconnaissance had finally found. But, as he was thus preparing, 118 airplanes from two U.S. carriers made a disorganized attack. While the Japanese fighters concentrated on wiping out the hapless torpedo bombers at a low level, the dive bombers arrived in full force at a high altitude. From them three carriers received four, three, and two bombs each. These set off explosions of the bombs and torpedoes prepared for rearming the Japanese planes, and all three ships sank. The fourth carrier, separated from the other three, launched its aircraft, which sank the *Yorktown,* but 24 dive bombers from the carrier *Enterprise* then sank the last Japanese carrier.

Though the Japanese invasion force still pushed forward with its large force of cruisers and battleships, the commander soon realized that the Battle of Midway had decided who controlled the sea around that island. This gave the battle an exceptional quality of decisiveness, but the strategic context and the balance of forces would determine its strategic significance.

THE STRATEGIC SITUATION IN 1942, POLITICAL AND MILITARY

The defeat of the Japanese force who had endeavored to take Midway threw the Japanese back on their original defensive line. This situation fully harmonized with their strategy of quickly attaining their war aims—the seizing of the European and U.S. colonies and the defending of their acquisitions against the inevitable counterattacks. They based this strategy on the assumption that Britain and the United States would eventually conclude that the cost of recovering these possessions would exceed their value. This would be particularly true of the United States because most of the lost colonies were British and Dutch, and it had planned soon to divest itself of the Philippines. So they had expected that Britain and the United States would make peace by conceding to Japan the essential parts of its conquests.

But the Japanese raid on Pearl Harbor had inadvertently destroyed the basis of this policy. As a military raid, its disabling of seven obsolete battleships had little effect. But the attack had immense political significance. It had come an hour before, rather than the planned hour after, the notification of the Japanese declaration of war on the United States. This made it even more clearly a surprise attack made in peacetime, something dishonorable and a violation of international law. Of equal significance, it had inflicted a humiliating defeat on the United States. This attack made the war not one merely to recover the Philippines and European colonies, but a war to avenge the defeat and punish Japan. The war's objective for the United States became the unconditional surrender of Japan.

To carry out a war against an island empire, the U.S. Navy had long foreseen the necessity of a prolonged naval campaign to establish bases near Japan. This meant capturing a number of the many island bases through which Japan controlled the central Pacific. The Marine Corps had prepared for this campaign by developing the doctrine and equipment to conduct the amphibious landings necessary to seize some of these islands and convert them into American bases.

The marines would be able to land because the navy's control of the sea would protect the troop and supply ships bringing them. In the plan the key to the control of the sea rested on battleships, in which the United States possessed a clear superiority over Japan, 15 to 10. To intercept and sink the convoys of marines and supplies, the Japanese would have to defeat the American battleships that would be covering the convoys.

But the Pearl Harbor raid overthrew the presumptions of that strategy. Independent of the loss of the battleships that had conferred that naval superiority, the principal supposition that underlay the navy's plans had ceased to be true. The sea had always controlled the land; now the airplane based on land enabled the land to control the sea. In the past the land had dominated the sea only in protecting harbors from naval attack and closing such narrow straits as the Dardenelles, which ranged from one-half mile to four miles wide. Here in 1915 Turkish defenses had demonstrated the traditional dominance of land defenses by turning back an attack by 16 British and French battleships, sinking three.

The 16-inch gun, the biggest generally used on battleships and for coast defense, could maintain an accurate fire at a range of 20 miles, making this the limit at which land's gunfire could control the sea. But single-engine bombers could reach out more than 200 miles and twin-engine planes over twice as far. The Japanese sinking of the *Prince of Wales* and *Repulse* had shown how vulnerable, even at high speed, well-armored ships were to torpedo bombers.

Further, when airplanes superseded guns, the traditional superiority of land-based guns over warships continued in a new form. Just as coast defense gunfire could more easily damage or disable ships than their shells could hurt coast defenses, so aircraft could more readily harm aircraft carriers than sea-based planes could damage air fields, a truth demonstrated at the Battle of Midway. Air fields could create a fortified defense to preserve parked aircraft with low walls of earth or concrete. And coast defenses and air fields were much less expensive to build and far easier to repair than ships.

In addition, in favorable weather, land-based aircraft could find ships more easily than carrier planes could find land targets. Although hills, forests, buildings, and cities created obstacles on land, the comparatively smooth sea made ships easy to find through visual and radar observation. So, with anything like equal terms in aircraft strength, navies had serious disadvantages in assailing land targets. And, because aircraft could concentrate so rapidly, a land objective could expect quick reinforcement.

The United States had begun the war with six powerful fleet carriers, each faster than 30 knots and able to operate 70 or more planes. The Japanese had the same number. In addition they had two light fleet carriers of about 10,000 tons. Half the size and with half the airplanes of the fleet carriers, they were also slower, one capable of 28 knots and the other 25 knots. In addition the Japanese had converted two 25-knot liners into carriers, each capable of operating almost 50 planes. But they had only used their six big, fast fleet carriers for the Pearl Harbor raid and only four for Midway.

The battles of the Coral Sea and Midway had changed the relative strengths. The United States had lost two of its best, the *Lexington* and the *Yorktown*, but the Japanese had lost four, leaving the navy with only the *Shokaku* and *Zuikaku*, its newest fleet carriers, and the four smaller, slower vessels. Since the Japanese navy had long calculated that it needed 70 percent of the American strength to fight successfully on the defensive, it still had ample sea-based air power even if the whole force together steamed less rapidly than the Americans'. Clearly the United States had no margin in a sea fight and certainly none to try to substitute carrier aviation for land-based. But, since the United States had prepared well for a war with Japan, this need not always be true.

THE STRATEGIC SITUATION IN LIGHT OF THE RELATIVE PREPAREDNESS OF THE BELLIGERENTS

The initial quick successes of the Japanese had given the impression that the United States was inadequately prepared for the war. Of course, all of the belligerents had deficiencies in their readiness for World War II, but a comparison with the quality of Japan's preparation clearly exhibits the thoroughness of America's.

Its huge size, lack of powerful or hostile neighbors, and the security from invasion also provided by the oceans had meant that U.S. defense had required no army beyond a militia and a small but competent professional force as a basis for expansion. Its Philippine colony, occasional friction with Japan, and concern for the balance of power in the Pacific and the Far East had dictated that the United States maintain a navy considerably stronger than Japan's. A satisfactory balance of power in the Atlantic and Europe seemed adequately guaranteed by the British fleet, the world's largest, and the French army, considered the world's best and regarded by most authorities, including the German General Staff, as clearly invincible on the defensive.

The German defeat of the French in May and June of 1940 totally transformed America's security situation. Suddenly Britain seemed beleaguered by Germany's air and submarine forces, now based on the French coast. Americans now had fears of what would happen not only to the excellent French fleet but even Britain's fleet if the United Kingdom made peace with Germany. Many suddenly feared that Germany had the potential to control the Atlantic.

The transformation of the world situation and these security fears gave rise to the launching of a gigantic defense program in the summer of 1940. This included building a "two-ocean navy" capable of guarding the Atlantic as well as the Pacific and an enlargement of the army air corps sufficient to have the world's largest air force as well as largest navy. Plans included giving the army the capability to make a powerful overseas commitment. So by September 1940, the United States was preparing for war and had ordered a general mobilization by calling up the national guard and the organized reserve corps and introducing conscription to fill the ranks of the rapidly expanding armed services. The mobilized forces had guidance from plans made in the decades after World War I and an army and navy whose officers had prepared themselves for just such a contingency.

The 1940 naval building program defined the significance of the mutual depletion of the American and Japanese navies' carrier forces in 1942. In addition to more battleships and a huge number of cruisers, the 1940 program provided for 11 *Essex*-class carriers, with more ordered later. These displaced 27,100 tons compared with 19,900 of the *Enterprise, Yorktown,* and *Hornet* and even less for the *Wasp.* Appropriations also provided for a naval air service of 15,000 planes to go with these carriers and provide the other aircraft needed by the colossal navy projected. To accomplish this, the navy set on foot a huge pilot- and crew-training program.

On New Year's Eve, 1942, the navy commissioned the *Essex,* the first of its class. It would require about six months to make the ship, and its successors, battle worthy by remedying defects and training the crew and aviators. Thereafter the construction yards completed a new *Essex*-class carrier on the average of every other month in 1943 and continued at a higher rate until, by the end of the war, the navy had commissioned 22.

But the experience at Pearl Harbor showed that the 1940 building program still had not made adequate provision for aircraft carriers. The navy remedied this with a measure that made it irrelevant whether the Japanese had lost four or no carriers at the Battle of Midway. It quickly used the resources of the 1940 building program, by ordering the completion as light fleet carriers of nine of the planned 30 fast, 10,000-ton cruisers then under construction. The yards finished all nine in 1943, the first in January, the *Independence,* giving its name to the class. Displacing only 11,000 tons, able to operate 35 planes (less than half an *Essex*), and having only a modest antiaircraft armament, their 100,000 horsepower and 32-knot speed enabled them to keep up with the *Saratoga, Enterprise,* and the *Essex* class. Together they added more than 300 operational aircraft to the fleet's carrier air strength. So the navy added more than a carrier a month in 1943.

Moreover, in June 1941 the navy had commissioned its first escort carrier. It used merchant ship hulls, converting a few from already-completed merchant ships but laying down as carriers most of the over 70 built. With the low speed of 16 to 18 knots, they could not steam with the fleet but specialized in providing air cover for convoys and amphibious landings and air support for the troops landed. They carried from 20 to 35 aircraft.

The Japanese found themselves in an entirely different situation. With the *Shokaku* and *Zuiho* repaired, their carriers had the capacity to operate almost 300 planes in the fall of 1942. But the Japanese then had only 100 operational carrier planes, having no more than 100 trained pilots remaining. This situation exhibits how poorly, compared with the United States, Japan had prepared for the war. They had completed perfect preparations for one campaign, but for none thereafter. The force Japan took to the Battle of Midway used some replacement pilots, but they had only 100 flying hours, compared with the 700 that constituted the Japanese standard before Pearl Harbor and the 300 then provided by the American navy. When the Japanese used up their elite force of elaborately trained and widely experienced pilots, the navy had few to replace them and those quite inadequately prepared.

If the Japanese had completed training more pilots and building more airplanes, they would then have faced a bottleneck of carriers. In addition to the *Zuikaku* and *Shokaku,* fleet carriers like the *Essex,* and the small *Zuiho,* Japan had the two 25-knot converted liners. Their preparedness for war included converting three more, but these were too slow to operate with the fleet. In 1942 Japan had only three fleet carriers under construction and commissioned none until 1944. These were the forerunners of a program for 21 fleet carriers, a carrier building plan that matched that of the United States but that was begun two years after the American program. By not beginning to prepare for a long war until well after the war had begun, Japan could not hope to compete with the United States.

In addition to the carriers, the American navy surpassed the Japanese in all other classes of ships. Already having superiority in cruisers, it completed 11 big cruisers with nine 8-inch guns, doubling the tonnage of such ships and, with 36 smaller cruisers, tripled the tonnage of these. It also repaired and renovated the old, slow battleships and completed by the end

Table 7.1
Aircraft Production

	Japan	Germany	Britain	France	U.S.
1939	4,467	8,295	7,942	2,700	2,141
1940	4,768	10,826	15,043	7,000*	6,086
1941	5,088	11,776	20,094		19,433
1942	8,861	15,556	23,672		49,445
1943	16,693	25,527	26,213		92,196
1944	28,181	39,807	26,461		100,752

*Annual rate as of May 1940; production was still increasing rapidly.

of the war 10 new battleships with nine 16-inch guns, two with a top speed of 27 knots, four that fell short of their designed speed of 30 knots, and four that surpassed their projected 33 knots. Since all carried 20 5-inch and 68 or more 40-mm antiaircraft guns, each contributed almost as much to the air defense of a carrier they accompanied as two antiaircraft cruisers.

At the beginning of the war the American navy had 5,260 aircraft, Japan's 3,202. But each had about the same number of operational combat aircraft, the difference indicating the large American commitment to training. This is reflected in Japan having 7,000 flying personnel, pilots, navigators, gunners, etc., compared with 6,750 pilots alone for the United States. This number also showed the large number in training.

The Army Air Forces had also provided for the pilots to go with their enormous number of new airplanes. Figures on aircraft production, given in Table 7.1, exhibit preparedness in the air and also show the curious fact that the countries attacked were much better prepared for war in the air than the aggressors, Germany and Japan.

The French had postponed large-scale production so as to produce the most-modern designs possible. The U.S.S.R. produced about 25,000 aircraft in 1942, 37,000 in 1943, and 40,000 in 1944. Because both the U.S.S.R. and Germany stressed single-engine planes, they produced fewer engines and less total weight of aircraft than the British, who emphasized multi-engine bombers. For example, counting air frames, essentially the aircraft without its engines, in 1944 the British produced 208 million pounds and Germany only 175 million pounds. These production choices reflected the British on the offensive with bombers and the Germans on the defensive with fighters. This is also reflected in U.S. production. Nineteen forty-four's production, for example, required 256,000 engines, more than two and a half per plane. Of the wartime production, 52,000 constituted specifically navy types. In addition, the navy used Army Air Forces aircraft, such as the B-17 bomber and, particularly, the B-24, its faster companion with a longer range.

TECHNOLOGICAL FACTORS

This ample provision for ships and airplanes and the personnel to use them would have lost much of its significance had the United States not, on the whole, had good designs for its weapons and proper quality in making them. The new carriers, battleships, and cruisers proved equal to those of the enemy except in the Japanese construction of two 64,000-ton battleships. These dwarfed the 45,000 tons of the United States' largest, as did their nine 18.1-inch guns compared to the U.S. ships' 16-inch. But the Japanese ships never fought any U.S. battleships.

The navy made its principal error in just the area where the Japanese had chosen to excel, torpedoes. The U.S. torpedo had an explosive charge of 780 pounds and would run seven and a half miles at 26.5 knots; the larger, better Japanese torpedo carried a half-ton warhead and would run eleven miles at 49 knots.

Design was not the only U.S. torpedo deficiency; during the first year and a half of the war, more than half of the U.S. torpedoes failed on account of one or the other of two defects. They ran deeper than the designed depth by about eight feet, enough to assure that they passed beneath many of the ships at which submarines, aircraft, and surface ships aimed them. And, when they did hit the target, they often failed to explode. The Germans also had a problem with torpedo reliability at the beginning of World War II but solved it quickly. It required 21 months of war to detect and remedy both defects in American torpedoes.

The United States gained its principal technological advantage from operating with radar from the outset. Radar could see the enemy at night, aircraft as well as ships, and in day or night provide far more accurate data than the optical range finders. The quality of the equipment improved rapidly and steadily throughout the war. The Japanese lacked radar until the fall of 1942, and the performance of their equipment usually lagged behind that of the U.S. sets. The U.S. antiaircraft guns gained a significant advantage by the use of radar to make the variable time, or proximity, fuse. A tiny radar set in the shell would detonate it when near a Japanese plane. This gave more accuracy than the old method of using fuses timed to explode after the computed time for the shell to reach the presumed height of the aircraft.

In aircraft, the Japanese began the war with better designs in several categories, but the U.S. aircraft improved and ultimately surpassed the Japanese planes in important respects. The lighter weight of the Japanese airplanes gave them a significantly longer range, but they had achieved the light weight by sacrificing the valuable features of ruggedness, armor protection, and self-sealing gasoline tanks.

The Army Air Forces procured a fine set of modern two- and four-engine bombers. Expecting to be on the offensive and confident of the ability of heavy bombers grouped in formation to defeat attacks by fighter aircraft, the air planners provided no high-performance, high-altitude fighter. So not until 1943 did the U.S. fighter pilots have the P-47 and P-51 aircraft capable of contending with the best airplanes of their antagonists.

THE FIRST ALLIED OFFENSIVE

The United States wanted to take the offensive in the area north of the Coral Sea. Here, where the Japanese were still advancing, there existed a point of contact between the adversaries, and the Japanese drive in New Guinea still threatened Port Moresby, and their push southeastward in the Solomon Islands menaced the sea lane between the United States and Australia. So the navy planned a surprise concentration and offensive to drive the Japanese back by taking Guadalcanal, the island in the Solomon group that represented the farthest Japanese advance. Eight hundred miles east of Port Moresby and even farther from Australia, Guadalcanal was out of reach of Allied land-based air power.

To supply this deficiency and protect against the Japanese fleet, the navy concentrated three of its four carriers to support the August 1942 landing of a reinforced Marine division. This made a pattern in American strategy, successive carrier concentrations between the central and south Pacific. The operation went smoothly, the outnumbered Japanese quickly losing their airfield to the marines, who promptly had it in working order. Soon it provided a land base for some fighters and dive bombers, whereupon the navy withdrew its vulnerable carriers. On the strategic offensive, the Americans now had the advantage of the tactical defensive.

This surprise landing met few Japanese troops but provoked a long struggle for the jungle-covered island, the Japanese bringing in infantry reinforcements at night. Then the Japanese struck to make major reinforcements of their land forces, gain command of the sea, and deprive the Americans on Guadalcanal of their line of supply and reinforcement. The *Zuikaku, Shokaku,* and the small 25-knot *Ryujo* came south with two battleships, 13 cruisers, and reinforcements for the Japanese soldiers fighting to recover the island. The *Ryujo* acted independently to support the landing and, in the expectation that it would function as a distraction, draw the first carrier plane attack and so enable the big carriers to strike the U.S. carriers first, the tactic that had won for the Americans at the Battle of Midway.

When the U.S. fleet moved to intercept, the naval Battle of the Eastern Solomons ensued. When the Americans found and sank the *Ryujo,* they left the big carriers unmolested; the Japanese planes damaged the *Enterprise* at a cost of losing over half of the attacking aircraft to fighters and antiaircraft fire.

Japanese submarines then inflicted serious losses, sending the *Saratoga* home for repairs and sinking the *Wasp*. This left only the *Hornet* and the hurriedly repaired *Enterprise* to meet four enemy carriers in the Battle of the Santa Cruz Islands. Again the carriers assailed each other, sinking the *Hornet* and damaging two of the Japanese carriers. But the Japanese lost over 50 pilots, the U.S. forces only ten.

So by the end of October, the United States possessed only one undamaged carrier, the just-repaired *Saratoga*. Emergency work returned the *Enterprise* to service in November. The Japanese situation differed little, with the fleet carrier *Shokaku* and light fleet carrier *Zuiho* disabled. The *Zuikaku,* the only operational fleet carrier, had help from two 25-knot converted liners. Thus, like the gingham dog and the calico cat that ate each other up, the U.S. and Japanese navies had virtually destroyed each other's carriers.

To help tide the navy over until the *Essex* was ready and to enable the battered *Enterprise* to have an overhaul, the British carrier *Victorious* joined the Pacific fleet and cruised with the *Saratoga*. The two ships' seasoned sailors and aviators, speaking approximately the same language, worked well together, even operating each others' planes. The ships differed in that the *Victorious,* larger than the *Enterprise,* operated only about 60 planes because it devoted so much of its displacement to the heavy armor protecting its flight deck and aircraft hangars. The anomaly of the *Saratoga* bearing the name of a U.S. victory over Britain, hardly suiting the name of its companion, *Victorious,* doubtless received little notice. But two differences between the carriers proved a mutual advantage when the British sailors discovered the vast quantities of ice cream carried by the *Saratoga,* and the American officers found the liquor on board the *Victorious.*

THE BEGINNING OF SUSTAINED OFFENSIVE OPERATIONS: THE SOLOMON ISLANDS

The Guadalcanal landing provoked the major carrier battles of the Eastern Solomons and Santa Cruz. While these battles were accomplishing the mutual depletion of the carriers of both navies, the island itself and the adjacent waters witnessed a long, costly struggle, exemplifying Newton's third law when each side concentrated more force, attacked the other's line of supply and reinforcement, and endeavored to protect its own.

The day after U.S. troops had landed on the island, the Japanese navy showed its virtuosity when a squadron of seven cruisers steamed south to make a night attack on the landing forces and their covering flotilla of destroyers and five large cruisers. More significant than their gun armament were the Japanese navy's emphasis on training for night combat and its exceptionally powerful, fast, long-range, and dependable torpedoes.

The Japanese admiral had scouted the Allies with seaplanes and had one aloft when he approached the Allied squadron of five big cruisers soon after midnight. In spite of the Allies' radar, the attackers took their flotilla by surprise, and in half an hour Japanese gunfire and torpedoes sank four cruisers and disabled the other. Fortunately for the Allied transports and troop ships, the Japanese then withdrew in order to be far north when daylight would make Allied air attack possible.

This Battle of Savo Island was the first of a long series of naval battles and skirmishes that eventually involved even the use of battleships in the confined waters of the Solomon Islands. To avoid air attack, both sides moved at night and used destroyers as transport and supply ships because of the speed with which they could make the nighttime round trip to Guadalcanal. In October the Japanese began using battleships as well as cruisers to bombard the U.S. position. On one night two battleships bombarded the air field with 900 14-inch shells, each weighing 1,400 lbs; but even these did not long disable the airfield.

In November a major attack by the reinforced Japanese land forces failed against the fortified defense of the reinforced U.S. defenders. In the same month, there were two night battles in which ships designed for combat at five to 15 miles fought in the dark at a little over a mile. These gave the Americans control of the sea, the Japanese losing two battleships and the U.S. forces one badly damaged. The failure on sea and land decided the Japanese command to abandon their effort to recapture Guadalcanal; they evacuated early in 1943. Thus the United States had successfully combined the strategic offensive and tactical defensive to acquire an air base and gain its strategic consequences: security for the sea lanes between the United States and Australia and an ability to take the offensive under the umbrella of the 200 aircraft based at Guadalcanal.

Although the navy planned to advance westward across the central Pacific by stepping from one Japanese island base to another, this offensive depended on an overwhelming preponderance of sea-based air power. Until enough new carriers were ready, the navy pushed northwestward in the Solomon Islands toward the big Japanese base of Rabaul. This advance, which also stepped from island to island, relied largely on aircraft, at first based on Guadalcanal and an adjacent island. In this drive the Allies faced an integrated defense in depth of six air fields on five islands, positions able to augment and protect one another with their aircraft and reinforce the air and ground defenses by moving at night. The operational situation resembled that in tactics in which strong points covered one another with crossfire.

In five months the advancing Allied forces concentrated against one island at a time, each supported by aircraft based on previously captured fields. This sustained offensive resulted in skirmishes at sea, often precipitated by Japanese reinforcement activities. Usually, a defensive concentration met one on the offensive.

Although the ability to make strategic concentrations against successive

Japanese bases insured success, this did not lead to quick victories. The attackers encountered reinforcements and fortified defenses, not just of earth and logs but of concrete and steel. Each required a costly siege, making slow progress for this persisting offensive.

Before the offensive could get under way, the Japanese launched a huge preemptive strike. To do this, they concentrated many additional aircraft at Rabaul, using units from their carriers. Here they had the support of four airfields and underground workshops. In early April 1943 they conducted a raid with over 300 planes against the Guadalcanal area, airfields, and ship anchorages. The airmen reported a brilliant success: a cruiser, two destroyers, and 25 transports sunk and 175 airplanes destroyed, all with a loss of only 39 planes. But they had made a very erroneous assessment: The raid actually destroyed only 25 planes, one destroyer, an escort vessel, and three merchant ships. So the sudden concentration for a counterattack failed to halt, or even delay, the Allied offensive.

The Japanese had no monopoly on such egregiously inaccurate and grossly misleading damage assessments. For example, in one unescorted bomber raid against Germany, the crews on U.S. aircraft believed that they had shot down 288 of the 300 fighters that the Germans had employed that day; but the Germans had actually lost only 27 of their fighters.

The erroneous Japanese assessment led to a repetition of this concentration in the fall. This time it resulted in not just negligible damage to the Allies but heavy losses to the Japanese, particularly of 121 carrier planes and 86 of their crews. This again set back the effort to rebuild their strength in carrier pilots. Inadequate training capacity meant that their pilots joined with 100 hours of flight training; the American pilots by then received 500.

As a result of the conquest of an air base 250 miles from Rabaul, Allied land-based aircraft, already attacking from New Guinea, could make such frequent, systematic raids as to destroy Rabaul's offensive capability. Without this it had no strategic significance, and the Allied offensive could ignore it, a happy outcome considering that with its powerful defenses and a garrison of 100,000 men it represented the epitome of the fortified defense.

THE CENTRAL PACIFIC

For the navy, this drive in the Solomons represented a sideshow while awaiting the availability of adequate carrier strength to advance westward across the central Pacific. By August 1943 the central Pacific command had two new fleet carriers and the light fleet carrier *Independence*. As in early 1942, these would train by attacking Japanese-held islands.

The overall plan called for taking the Gilbert Islands as a preparation for the attack on the Marshalls, a larger group of islands 600 miles away to the northwest.

The two days of unmolested raids on the Gilberts had great strategic significance. The local superiority gained by just 150 carrier aircraft would have kept any reinforcing airplanes from flying in safely. Thus the Japanese could not concentrate aircraft on the Gilberts to counter those based on the carriers, even if the bases could have accommodated enough airplanes. The lack of any raid by the twin-engine, torpedo-carrying bombers based in the Marshalls also showed that the Japanese islands did not constitute an interlocking system of bombers and air reinforcements like that encountered in the Solomon Islands. So the navy faced only a series of isolated points, strong only in their fortified defense.

The force supporting the mid-November invasion of the Gilbert Islands consisted of six fleet and five light fleet carriers, having over 600 operational aircraft, ample to overwhelm the defenders and the Japanese fleet should it appear. In addition, the invasion force had nine small, slow escort carriers and seven battleships.

The difficult part occurred on land where the capture of the fortified island of Tarawa required four days and cost 3,000 casualties. Taking the island against a fortified defense could not have happened so quickly without the fleet's bombardment. The old battleship *Maryland,* whose low speed made it obsolete for its original purpose, used its very powerful armament of eight 16-inch guns to give fire support at close range. The bombardment killed about half of the island's garrison even though the strongest fortifications successfully resisted the bombs and shells.

The taking of the Gilbert Islands established the pattern for the central Pacific of successive concentrations against and capture of Japanese bases. In January 1944 the navy and marines took the first of the Marshalls, while the carriers neutralized Truk, the huge Japanese base 800 miles away. By this time the systematized attack on airfields had become routine: Fighters attacked first, flying low to shoot the parked aircraft, followed by bombers to wreck the bases' facilities. At Truk the damage included the destruction of 270 of the 365 aircraft on the base. This easy success made it obvious that Truk was so weak that the westward advance could pass it by.

Then the ships did not have far to go for resupply because the navy had simplified its logistic situation by converting one of the Marshall atolls into a base, 2,000 miles west of Pearl Harbor. Here the fleet could refuel, replenish stores, make some repairs, and give the crews a little rest.

THE LAND-BASED ADVANCE IN NEW GUINEA

The New Guinea operations benefited from the concentration in time of simultaneous Allied offensives northward from Port Moresby on the south coast of New Guinea and the landing in Guadalcanal because it caused the Japanese to concentrate in space at Guadalcanal, making them too weak to resist the Allied descent on to the north coast of New Guinea.

Operations in New Guinea came under the control of an Allied command headed by General Douglas MacArthur. With his principal combat command experience in France during World War I and in Luzon against the Japanese, he lacked a suitable background for conducting operations in New Guinea. Initially, General MacArthur had difficulty seeing how the principles of orthodox operational strategy could apply to the New Guinea theater, and he had failed to understand the full operational significance of air superiority. But, when he had grasped how to campaign in an archipelago with the forces at his disposal, he performed exceptionally well.

In July 1942 the Japanese had taken the village and small port of Buna on the north coast of New Guinea, improved its air field, and begun a drive against the Australian position at the town of Port Moresby on the south coast. Between them lay a dense jungle and mountains with a peak of over 13,000 feet. Using soldiers and natives to carry supplies over jungle trails, the Japanese had approached Port Moresby in September, when the reinforced Australians counterattacked and drove them back half way to Buna.

Support of this offensive fell largely to the U.S. Army Air Forces based in Australia. Even though the airmen had the A-20 attack bomber, the jungle provided so much concealment and cover that it virtually precluded any air support for the ground forces. Still, the airmen provided crucial logistic support. By the end of the fall the air forces had established air bases on New Guinea's north coast, supplied troops through them, and, in a two-day operation, flown in an Australian battalion; this made a grand substitute for a debilitating five-week march over the mountains and through the jungle. Even trucks came by air in the small transports by the expedient of cutting their chassis in half, flying each part separately over the mountains, and welding the halves back together at their destination.

So, in New Guinea, air transport, usually the most expensive, proved not only the cheapest and swiftest but sometimes the only available means. Of course water transportation had the greatest importance because it brought to New Guinea so much equipment and supplies and many men and women from the United States and most of the remainder of the offensive's needs from Australia and New Zealand.

When the Allies besieged Buna, fortified with steel and concrete as well as earth, they lacked siege artillery or the support of naval guns. Air power also failed them because the flyers could not satisfactorily distinguish friend from foe, and a mistaken strike against Allied troops hurt more because they were not as well fortified as the Japanese. But aircraft met most of the Allies' logistic needs through a large airfield built just 15 miles from Buna. When the Australians took the small post of Gona, a few miles west of Buna, they effectively turned and later captured Buna.

While playing this decisive logistic role, the Army Air Forces were improving their tactical technique under the leadership of their tactically oriented new commander, General George C. Kenney. Part of the improvement came from an aircraft modification workshop established in Australia. For attacking airfields, the A-20 had four .5-inch added to its four .3-inch forward-firing machine guns, half of its bomb space filled with tanks for 900 gallons of gas to extend its range, and the remainder adapted so that it could hold forty 23-pound fragmentation bombs for attacking aircraft on the ground.

More important was the change from the ineffectual bombing tactics used at sea. The system of bombing from altitudes rarely lower than 7,000 and as high as 25,000 feet had proven almost futile. In the Battle of Midway, for example, heavy bombers had dropped 92 tons of bombs on the Japanese fleet without doing any damage. In an attack on a convoy, again using the high-level tactics, the aviators claimed that 1 percent of the bombs hit a ship.

General Kenney decided to leave torpedo bombing to the Australians who had a good torpedo plane. Instead, having knowledge of close ground support tactics, he favored the alternative sea-attack method of skip bombing. Tests against a derelict ship in the Port Moresby harbor had shown that an aircraft at low altitude could drop its bomb, have it skip like a stone, and then hit the side of a ship, exploding inside or in the water beside it. While skipping the bomb, the aircraft used its forward-firing machine guns to riddle the ship's superstructure and partially counter its antiaircraft fire.

The B-25 twin-engine bomber proved well adapted to skip bombing, having first eight and later twelve .5-inch machine guns firing forward. Although the bullets were small, the deluge of so many had a devastating effect on the unarmored portion of most ships. One model of the B-25 tried a 75-mm cannon, but its recoil tended to pop the heads off of the aircraft's rivets.

In late February 1943 the new tactics and the effectiveness of the aircraft modifications showed themselves in the Battle of the Bismarck Sea. This occurred when the Japanese responded to the fall of Buna by sending in from Rabaul 6,900 troops in a convoy of eight transports and eight destroyers, hidden by bad weather and expecting to meet fighter protection. By then the Allied air forces had 336 planes, the equivalent of four fleet carriers. The main attack on the convoy came from the skip bombing by the B-25s and A-20s. Of the thirty-seven 500-pound bombs dropped, the airmen believed that 28 hit, a 75 percent rate compared to 1 percent observed for the high-level method. The machine guns also did much damage, on one occasion in an unexpected way: Assuming that they faced an attack by torpedo bombers, Japanese soldiers lined the rails of their transport to use their rifle fire against the torpedo plane; instead, the skip bomber's eight machine guns mowed them down before they could fire. The sinking of all of the transports and half of the destroyers made this a significant victory and showed the air forces using a tactical method at least as effective against such vessels as dive or torpedo bombing. This tactical method would gain command of the seas north of New Guinea.

PACIFIC LINES OF OPERATION

The campaigns leading to the battles of the Coral Sea and Midway Island followed the same pattern as land operations in that they involved concentrations on lines of operation. The Pacific war began with two lines of operation: one in the central Pacific, on which the Japanese operated with their Pearl Harbor raid in December; and one in the southern Pacific on which the Japanese used their carrier forces in January 1942 to support the capture of the port of Rabaul north of New Guinea. Thus the Japanese carriers had first concentrated on the central line in December and on the southern in January. After their fleet returned from its raid into the Bay of Bengal and the Indian Ocean, it sent two of its carriers to support the southern concentration against Port Moresby.

When American cryptographic intelligence learned of this, the United States made a counterconcentration on the southern line; this resulted in the Battle of the Coral Sea and the defeat of the seaborne advance against Port Moresby. After the Japanese again concentrated on the central line against Midway Island, the pattern of accurate intelligence and counterconcentration repeated itself in the campaign of the Battle of Midway. But, though the Japanese continued their Port Moresby offensive in June with a through-the-jungle-and-over-the-mountains offensive from Buna, the Allies took the initiative on the southern line with their landing in Guadalcanal. This move had the defensive objective of protecting the supply line between the United States and Australia.

The surprise attack on Guadalcanal, which found the Japanese weak, created two southern lines of operation 800 miles apart, the Solomons and New Guinea. Both antagonists stood on the defensive in the central Pacific and concentrated in the south. On the two lines in the south the Japanese concentrated in space by committing most of their forces to its Solomon's counterattack. The Allies, on the other hand, concentrated in time, defending stoutly at Guadalcanal but driving to the north coast of New Guinea. Here they advanced, taking Buna on a line of operations almost denuded of hostile forces by the Japanese reinforcement of their offensive in the Solomons. When the fall of Buna coincided with the Japanese decision to withdraw from Guadalcanal, the Allied concentration in time had won a small victory. Yet this success probably owed more to the ability of Allied air forces in New Guinea, unlike the Japanese in the Solomons, to dominate the air and fill many of the campaign's logistic needs.

In the spring of 1943, when the Allies had continued their offensive up the Solomon chain toward Rabaul, they maintained the two lines of operations in the south. Even so, they aimed these simultaneous advances at a common objective, the key Japanese base of Rabaul, whose capture would consolidate Allied dominance in the Solomons and eastern New Guinea.

Then the ascendancy of Allied air power in New Guinea, demonstrated in the Battle of the Bismarck Sea, changed the situation. This dominance of the air, augmented by the new air bases in the Solomons, also gave the Allies control of the seas north of New Guinea. As command of the sea and air gave control of communications, the Allies could bypass Rabaul, a move that worked just as would the turning of a hostile army in land operations. Because Allied control of the air and the sea in daylight made it too expensive for the Japanese to withdraw their troops, the situation clearly resembled a turning movement that had captured an enemy army. The continued air surveillance of Rabaul corresponded to the costs of guarding the prisoners, but the Allies had no other expense because the Japanese housed and fed themselves from the immense stocks accumulated there.

The continued Allied success in northern New Guinea and the completion of the Solomons offensive in November 1943 coincided with the beginning of the U.S. use of the initiative conferred by its command of the sea to make its first offensive on the central line of operations, again employing concentration in time against the Japanese. When the seemingly formidable Gilberts and Marshalls fell in three months and the great base at Truk proved powerless to defend itself, sea-based air power had also secured a major triumph.

THE INITIATION OF THE WESTWARD ADVANCE IN NEW GUINEA

In the summer of 1943 the New Guinea forces prepared by taking two islands adjacent to the north coast to provide sites for additional airfields for the planes to continue the methodical bombing of Rabaul and supporting the drive to the west. A U.S. force on the north coast and an Australian force in the interior attempted to distract the Japanese by advancing toward Salamaua, while preparations went ahead to turn it by taking Lae farther west.

The combination of the combat and logistic ascendancy conferred by the steadily growing air forces enabled the Allies to advance northwestward and, more important, gain bases or places where engineers could build airfields. In one instance, air transport brought in troops and engineers to create an air base from which fighters controlled the adjacent sky and escorted bombers on their missions. In September 1943, Australian forces had moved by water and, aided by U.S. parachute troops, taken the strongpoints of Lae and Salamaua and so had gained control of the Japanese position in eastern New Guinea.

So the Allies had exploited the initiative conferred by their command of the sea north of eastern New Guinea to drive back the enemy, expand their air bases, and thus prepare to extend their persisting strategy offensive westward. A persisting strategy, not possible at sea except through a blockade, was feasible in the archipelago because the islands were situated so that command of the air gave control of these narrow seas and, with it, the ability to occupy islands and use them as air bases to dominate more of the sea. And the role of the B-25s and A-20s over the sea, with their machine guns and skip bombing, paralleled the strategic role of Allied fighter bombers in western Europe when they often nearly paralyzed German strategic mobility by interdicting daylight rail and road movements.

In an archipelago, control of the air gave command of the sea, which, in turn, gave the initiative and control of the land. And, not only did command of the sea bestow superior logistical facility, it gave unrivaled strategic mobility. The campaign in the central Pacific demonstrated how vulnerable islands became to the traditional operational technique of the turning movement. Although aircraft and, often, ships could escape from isolated islands, without control of the sea, the defending garrisons often had much difficulty retreating.

In the central Pacific, the U.S. forces had to contend with the fortified defense in order to capture airfields. Only later did it become clear that the terrain of atolls lent itself to rapid airfield construction. This would have avoided confronting the fortified defense by permitting airport construction on unoccupied atolls. On the New Guinea line of operations, the Allies easily used this method and, after the costly siege of Buna, increasingly avoided Japanese strength by building their own airfields as bases for their superior air strength.

Thus control of the air and the resulting command of the sea enabled the attacker to avoid the fortified defense and other elements of the adversary's strength and, in the archipelagos, could make the strategic offensive stronger than the strategic defensive.

THE OFFENSIVE ALONG THE NEW GUINEA COAST

At the beginning of 1944, compared with two years earlier, the tables had fully turned. The Allies had the experienced pilots and operated good, modern airplanes, including new fighters, the P-47 Thunderbolt and the F6F Hellcat, fully capable of coping with the excellent Japanese fighter, nicknamed the Zero. In the New Guinea area, the Allies had nearly 1,400 land-based aircraft compared to 750 for the Japanese. In keeping pace with this growth, airfield acquisition and construction continued to provide an adequate logistical base.

These advantages enabled them to abandon the step-by-step method of advance used in 1942, 1943, and early 1944. Instead they planned to advance almost 600 miles to Hollandia, thus taking the whole northern coast of New Guinea with a single gigantic turning movement. Not only would this block the retreat of the 40,000 Japanese troops along the intervening coast, but Hollandia's sea and air facilities would make it an Allied base for the development of a new complex of air bases to support a further drive westward.

Still, such a long advance would extend beyond the range of fighter planes, even of the twin-engine P-38. So the air forces used their workshops in Australia to add fuel tanks to the P-38s to give them the range to escort bombers on the 1,200-mile round trip to Hollandia.

Nothwithstanding their range, these P-38s, based so far from Hollandia, could not support the landing by providing the fighter plane cover to protect the ships and landing forces. In order that the landing would have this protection, the naval forces in the central Pacific would provide an air strike and fighter cover by sending fleet carriers to support the landing. Since the navy did not wish to risk its carriers near so many Japanese air bases, the fleet carriers would make only a two-day appearance. So instead of the fleet carriers remaining, the central Pacific forces also provided six little escort carriers to stay until captured or newly built air fields could operate aircraft.

While the modification of the P-38s and other preparations went forward, bombers began systematic air attacks against Wewak, the major Japanese base between the Allied forces and Hollandia. A series of 16 raids in 17 days dropped 3,000 tons of bombs and destroyed 37 Japanese planes in air combat and many more on the ground. The Japanese then withdrew their aircraft from Wewak, just as they had from Rabaul. And the bombing campaign had accomplished its two objectives: eliminating the base from which Japanese fighters could intercept bombers on their way to Hollandia and convincing the Japanese command of what it already presumed, that Wewak was the next Allied objective. Naval bombardments of the coast at Wewak reinforced this distraction.

In spite of the withdrawal of their planes from Wewak, the Japanese were still following Newton's third law: Allied intelligence estimated that the Japanese had concentrated 350 aircraft at Hollandia, ready to assail any forces landing at Wewak. To strike these aircraft and gain the requisite ascendancy in the air, the Allies had 416 assorted bombers and 106 P-38s able to complete the escorting round trips. The daylight raids began at the end of March, and, by mid-April, even sporadic resistance in the air had ended over Hollandia. Yet, to maintain the impression that Wewak was the objective, the Allies continued heavy raids against it.

On 22 April 1944 two U.S. divisions landed at Hollandia, gaining complete surprise and thus encountering virtually no opposition. Even without surprise, the landing would have been easy because the Japanese combat troops were far to the east, deployed to defend Wewak.

Simultaneous with the landing at Hollandia, one regiment surprised and took another airfield at Aitape, a base a little over 100 miles east of Hollandia. Here, by working at night under floodlights, Australian engineers repaired the airfield in only a day and a half; by the afternoon of the second day 25 Australian fighters had landed and were flying patrols the next morning. But they had little to do because the Japanese counteroffensive to the two landings consisted only of night raids by one or two planes. The air forces had done such a thorough job on the surrounding bases that the fighters, and the carrier planes, had nothing to do.

Two divisions of U.S. troops arrived at Aitape and established a defensive line to block the advance of the Japanese 18th army westward along the coast. Trapped by the turning movement, it was going to fight to recover its communications and route of retreat. Because the jungle was so nearly impassable and the only road lay along the coast, the American divisions knew where to prepare their line of defense.

With the U.S. troops in prepared defensive positions, two ill-supplied Japanese divisions tried to drive the U.S. forces from their path with a frontal attack. Failing in this, they attempted to turn the open, southern flank of the U.S. line. Thwarting this maneuver only with hard fighting, the U.S. forces then counterattacked, turning the Japanese by piercing their flank on the coast and threatening their communications with Wewak. Thus, after over three weeks of fighting, the Japanese retreated. The strategically offensive turning movement had advanced the Allies 600 miles and successfully employed the tactical defensive to cut off the enemy army and remove it from the war.

Yet Hollandia's inadequate port and the difficulty of building airfields on its swampy ground meant that, in less than a month, troops landed on the little island of Wakde, about 150 miles west of Hollandia. The feeble Japanese resistance meant that U.S. engineers made the captured airfield operational as quickly as the Australian engineers had at Aitape. Only ten days later, the Allies made their second 150-mile jump, still with the goal of gaining better-and-better-situated bases. But, at the objective, the Island of Biak, they encountered rugged terrain and a powerful fortified defense, garrisoned by 11,000 men who had tanks to support their counterattacks.

The army had not completed the conquest of Biak when a new series of advances began with a landing that overwhelmed the defenders on the little island of Noemfoor, 60 miles to the west, another captured a base on the westernmost tip of New Guinea, and, finally, on 15 September 1944, one more put a base on the undefended island of Morotai, 1,400 miles west of Lae and Salamaua, places the Allies had taken with difficulty just a year earlier. The Allies were now moving ahead as smoothly as the Japanese had in the early months of the war and were using land-based air power in the same way.

Although Morotai was only 300 miles from the Philippines, it was the earlier landing on Biak that had alarmed the Japanese. Its position, 300 miles south of the Palau Islands, would enable bombers with fighter escorts to attack Japanese bases in the Palaus, bases used for ships and aircraft opposing the American navy's drive in the central Pacific. After two small efforts to reinforce Biak failed, the Japanese command concentrated an overwhelming force, one that included troop reinforcements and powerful naval units, including the huge *Yamato* and *Musashi,* the 64,000-ton battleships. This force would have taken command of the sea around Biak and given good fire support to the Japanese defenders and their reinforcements. Skip bombing would have had no effect on the *Yamato*'s and *Musashi*'s armor, 16 inches thick, and the bombers would have found their machine guns overmatched by the battleships' 130 or more 25-mm (.98-in.) machine guns.

But the armada never departed for Biak because the Japanese command learned of the U.S. fleet's advance in the central Pacific toward the Mariana Islands. So Biak fell as the Japanese concentrated instead against the central Pacific fleet.

AIR POWER AND OPERATIONAL STRATEGY

The key to understanding the strategy of the war in the Pacific is the tactical and strategic role of the airplane. Whereas, at sea, the airplane had added a new dimension to tactics, in war on land it had primarily a strategic effect, not just by reconnaissance but by assailing lines of communication and strategic troop movements.

Yet the light cavalry of the air could range over the sea and, in assailing the enemy's communications and his strategic movements over water, it could have a strategic effect similar to that on land. And, though the sea immensely improved the movement of men and their equipment, it made them more vulnerable because it provided no concealment other than bad weather and darkness. Because most of the campaigns took place in archipelagos, the capacity of the army with the dominant cavalry of the air to hinder its opponent's strategic movements by water conferred on the possessor of air superiority three advantages: the initiative, greater facility for concentration in space, and the opportunity for conducting turning movements.

Air power's integration of land and sea operations facilitated the application of operational strategy, as the Hollandia turning movement vividly illustrated. The central Pacific, filled with island groups or archipelagoes, witnessed the same use of superiority in the air. Hence, not only did this intimate interrelation among land, sea, and air power make possible turning movements, it gave lines of operation and concentration in space and time their full potential significance.

The decision presented to the Japanese by the Allied landing on Biak exhibits concentration in space and time working against one another. The Allied advance on two lines of operation, the central Pacific and New Guinea, gave the Japanese the opportunity of concentrating to attack, or to defend against, one or the other. But if the offensives on the two lines of operation were concentrated in time and were truly simultaneous, as the uncoordinated Allied advances adventitiously proved to be, they offered the Japanese the choice of concentrating against one while accepting defeat on the other.

This also illustrates the situation of interior lines of operation: The Japanese were between the two enemy lines of operation, able to concentrate in space against either, and the Allied forces were too far apart to reinforce one another quickly. If the Allied forces had not concentrated in time, that is, had they not moved toward Biak and the Marianas almost simultaneously, the Japanese could have used concentration in space on interior lines first to crush the effort to take Biak and then to protect the Marianas.

In choosing to defend the Marianas, the Japanese command had also elected to concentrate against naval strength; unlike the New Guinea forces, those in the central Pacific were primarily seaborne and fully ready to contend successfully with a concentration of Japanese naval power.

Naturally, the Allied forces could have adopted a single line of operations toward the Philippines and the Japanese sea communications with the East Indies, and this single line would have offered the Japanese no opportunity for concentration in space. On the other hand, an offensive on a single line might not have been able to make as effective use of the U.S. superiority in both the sea-based air power of 900 operational aircraft on fleet carriers in the central Pacific and the 1,400 based on land in the New Guinea theater. Still, if the United States had redundant air power by 1944, would it have mattered if not all of it were used? Of course, the two lines of operation resulted not from an Allied preference for concentration in time but, in major part, to enable the American army and navy each to have major roles in the war against Japan.

THE CONQUEST OF THE MARIANAS AND THE BATTLE OF THE PHILIPPINE SEA

Bypassing the Caroline Islands, the U.S. command moved to capture bases in the Mariana Islands, 1,000 miles west of the Marshalls. As well as providing a base for operations against either the Philippines or to the northwest, these islands could also provide airfields for raids on Japan by the B-29, a huge new bomber with exceptionally long range.

For the Japanese, this threatened their communications with the East Indies. Yet it also presented an opportunity to strike the American fleet while it had to devote much of its attention to protecting the landing forces on one island from air strikes from other islands in the Marianas.

For the attack on the U.S. fleet, the Japanese concentrated all nine of their carriers, a fleet that operated 430 combat planes, about the same number as struck Pearl Harbor on December 7, 1941. Here the similarity with Pearl Harbor ended. The pilots and crews for the Pearl Harbor attack were about ten years older and had ten years' more experience than those who would face the U.S. fleet in June 1944. In fact, most of the Japanese pilots had not progressed beyond learning how to take off and land on a carrier.

The Japanese would meet not only a much larger fleet, but one that had pilots and crews far better trained and vastly more experienced. In addition to the escort carriers for giving close support to the landing force, the American force had seven fleet and eight light fleet carriers, together operating 900 aircraft.

Although the Japanese were well aware of the superior U.S. strength, the capable Japanese fleet commander, Admiral Ozawa, had confidence in the outcome of his planned assault on the American fleet. In part this confidence rested on his failure to appreciate the woeful inadequacy of his pilots' training. He also counted on the 1,600 land-based aircraft he though were stationed in the Marianas. But many of these had not arrived, and losses to combat meant that there were only 50 planes available to support the fleet when it attacked.

Nevertheless, one of the crucial assumptions underlying the admiral's confidence did have a sound basis. Japanese aircraft had a far greater radius of action than American. The design consideration, which kept Japanese planes without pilot armor and self-sealing gasoline tanks to make them lighter and more maneuverable than the American, also gave them a radius of action of 300 miles, 50 percent more than U.S. aircraft. So this difference in aircraft capability gave the Japanese an intrinsically superior weapon system, one able to strike the enemy without exposing its carriers. The astute Admiral Ozawa planned to exploit this to assail the U.S. fleet at so great a range as to make his carriers immune to attack by the shorter-range U.S. carrier planes.

The U.S. forces landed on Saipan in the Marianas on 15 June 1944 to begin the long, difficult task of capturing the island from a Japanese garrison 32,000 strong. The fleet stood by while its planes attacked the airfields on the other islands. The U.S. commander, the wise and careful Admiral Raymond Spruance, knew of the approach of the Japanese fleet. Still, keeping in mind the Japanese penchant for using a distracting force, he did not move west to attack.

Admiral Ozawa made his attack in three waves, too much separated to gain concentration in time. Further, his planes came first upon eight modern battleships, suffered heavily in assailing them, did no significant damage to such well-armed and armored targets, and did not find the carriers.

Incompetent pilots, making inept assaults against the wrong targets, lost over 300 aircraft.

In spite of the loss of two carriers to submarine attack and only 102 planes remaining, Admiral Ozawa did not withdraw because he did not understand the situation. He had accomplished his objective of attacking when out of range of the U.S. planes and was unable to imagine that his attack had failed so completely. Believing the false reports that his planes had damaged five carriers and erroneously expecting aircraft to fly in from Japan to the Marianas airfields, he refueled his carriers the next day and planned to make another strike. Although U.S. planes searched all day, none discovered his fleet until late afternoon and found it in a position at an extreme distance for a strike and too late in the day for the planes to return in daylight. Nevertheless, the Americans sent 236 planes to make an attack in which they sank one and damaged three carriers. They lost 100 planes, mostly to running out of fuel, but rescued all but 16 pilots.

The Japanese fleet steamed to Japan with only 35 operational aircraft. Admiral Ozawa resigned, but the high command declined to accept his resignation. Six carriers remained, and aircraft production had reached 2,000 per month; but there were no pilots, and the navy could not train them as fast as the factories made airplanes. The Battle of the Philippine Sea confirmed that Japan's failure to provide an adequate pilot-training program made the long-range planes and Admiral Ozawa's perceptive strategy useless.

THE LANDING IN THE PHILIPPINES AND THE BATTLE OF LEYTE GULF

In the early fall of 1944 the Allied New Guinea and central Pacific lines of operation joined to assail the Philippine Islands, an archipelago of 7,100 islands with an area half the size of Texas and a population of 16 million. The conquest would begin by landing on the centrally located island of Leyte. The naval forces consisted of many fleet and escort carriers and 12 old and new battleships. Seven hundred thirty-eight ships carried the 160,000 men of the landing force and their equipment and supplies.

The preparations for the landing began with naval air strikes against major Philippine and adjacent air bases. This resulted in days of combat with Japanese land-based aircraft, with two U.S. cruisers crippled and three carriers with minor damage. But the Japanese pilots reported sinking 11 carriers and two battleships; and when it announced the victory, the Japanese navy increased the number of carriers sunk to 19. Soon the Japanese navy's reconnaissance discovered the undiminished state of the American navy, but because there had been a national celebration of the victory, the navy did not announce that news, not even telling the army.

The Japanese navy planned to support the army's defense through depriving the landing force of support by assailing the transports, freighters, and escort carriers in Leyte Gulf. It would divide seven battleships and ten big cruisers into two forces, Admiral Kurita's larger one entering Leyte Gulf from the north and Admiral Nishimura's smaller from the south. If either force got through, it would suffice to sink the vulnerable freighters and carriers, leaving the landing force in a precarious situation.

To prevent the American navy from intercepting these attacking forces, the Japanese plan depended on a third squadron for a distraction to lure the U.S. fleet away from its post of giving protection to the landing. Admiral Ozawa's carrier fleet would make the most effective distraction because, as the most important and vulnerable ships in the Pacific, its carriers were certain to attract the attention of the U.S. fleet under the command of Admiral William F. Halsey, a more intrepid and less calculating and cautious admiral than Spruance. So, while the two surface squadrons made their furtive advance toward the landing area from the west, Ozawa's carrier fleet would approach from the north, luring the American fleet away from the landing area.

On 20 October 1944 the ground forces landed on Leyte and faced only limited opposition on the beaches. And the Japanese fleets began to move.

Yet the first Japanese counterattack came in the air when a few of Ozawa's and 200 land-based planes attacked Halsey's fleet, sinking the light fleet carrier *Princeton*. Instead of spotting and attacking Ozawa's fleet, Halsey found Kurita's battleships and used 259 planes to attack them late in the morning of 24 October. The big raid did less damage than one might have expected because of the amount of attention the flyers devoted to sinking the 64,000-ton *Musashi*. Finally, at the end of the day, it sank, hit by 17 bombs and, more significantly, 19 torpedoes. But, except for severe damage to one cruiser, none of Kurita's other ships suffered seriously.

With U.S. carriers attacking Kurita's force instead of Ozawa's carriers far to the north, the Japanese plan was failing. Realizing this, the shrewd Admiral Ozawa sent his two battleships south to attract Admiral Halsey's attention. This they did, and when further reconnaissance revealed Ozawa's carriers, Halsey turned his fleet north to attack.

So the Japanese plan of distraction and concentration against weakness worked after all. But the Americans had spotted the advance of Admiral Nishimura's battleship force in the south and brought five of the old battleships used for fire support into action against it. With five battleships against two and vastly superior radar, it added little that the U.S. ships also crossed the T of the Japanese squadron in the 15-minute night battle. So the United States won a miniature Battle of Jutland, but one with more-emphatic tactical results.

Early in the morning of 25 October, Admiral Kurita's powerful fleet entered Leyte Gulf and made an unopposed approach to the landing area. The old battleships, which could have stopped it, were three hours hard-steaming away to the south, and Halsey and his battleships were far to the north attacking Ozawa. The only force available, four American destroyers and three slow destroyer escorts, made a vigorous, imaginative, and ineffectual defense. By mistaking the escort carriers for fleet carriers, Admiral Kurita believed that he was attacking Halsey's fleet. Kurita, who had already turned back once and knew of Nishimura's defeat the previous night, withdrew just as his powerful fleet was able to fulfill the campaign's objectives. The distraction had worked, but he did not believe it and so did not exploit his successful concentration against weakness.

Operations in the Philippines continued until the end of the war. The reconquest of the island of Luzon received the most attention, while other forces cooperated with Philippine citizens who had already reconquered much territory from the Japanese.

THE OKINAWA CAMPAIGN

During the Leyte campaign, the Japanese had introduced a new weapon system, one that would reconcile the antithesis of a plentiful supply of airplanes with a lack of pilots competent to fly them. They accomplished this by teaching a pilot to fly well enough to take off and follow a leader to the vicinity of hostile ships and there to dive his bomb-laden aircraft into a ship, bringing destruction to his airplane and death to himself while inflicting serious harm to the ship and its crew. Although pilots in all air forces had occasionally done this and the inadequately trained Japanese pilots had little better chance of survival in combat, systematically applied, this tactic created a powerful weapon system.

The U.S. landing on Okinawa involved over 1,000 ships and a combined army and marine force of 10 divisions with 172,000 combat troops. The Allied fleet had about 200 destroyers, 11 U.S. and 4 British fleet carriers, and 6 U.S. light fleet carriers. Two more U.S. and two more British fleet carriers joined later.

The operation began in March with a three-day effort by the U.S. fleet to neutralize the Japanese air bases on the island of Taiwan and the nearby Japanese island of Kyushu. In the three days, four fleet carriers suffered damage, that to the *Franklin* being so severe that she was still under repair when the war ended.

With the landing on 1 April 1945, there began a long battle with many parts. On land the U.S. forces made slow but sure progress, sustained by naval bombardment, air support, and supplies from ships standing by. This made the operation much like a traditional siege on land, with the troops on shore and their supporting forces on the water besieging the Japanese defenders. Meanwhile, the Allied fleets occupied the traditional role of the covering force, ready to repulse a relieving army trying to end the siege. In this case, the air forces of the Japanese navy and army played the role of the relieving army, and they struck at both the covering fleet and the ships supporting the landing.

The British carriers operated separately, protecting Okinawa from air attacks from Taiwan and the air bases on a nearby island group. They did this in part by attacking airfields, destroying planes on the ground, and making bomb craters in the runways. They also gave protection by attracting Japanese air raiders to themselves rather than to forces closer to Okinawa. Kamikaze planes did score hits on three of the British carriers, but their armored flight decks and hangers meant that they sustained little significant damage.

Although the U.S. carriers provided most of the air power over Okinawa, the more numerous destroyers, also unarmored, bore the brunt of the air attacks. These attained tactical concentration in time by making four separate, major attacks in April, the first on the 6th with 355 kamikaze planes and 341 dive and torpedo bombers and fighters. The U.S. destroyers took positions as much as 50 miles from the Japanese objectives so as to give early warning with their radar and to help guide the interceptors. They also attracted raiders that might have flown on to attack carriers or supply ships. In spite of the distraction of the destroyers and the work of the intercepting fighters, many Japanese planes got through to the landing area and struck 24 ships there.

On 12 April the second assault came, 185 kamikazes and 45 torpedo bombers, protected by 145 fighters. Three days later the besiegers had to cope with still another attack almost as large.

By this time the destroyer pickets had a system of working in pairs with a landing craft. A boat of 350 tons, the landing craft's 1,300 horsepower and 14-knot speed contrasted with a destroyer's 60,000 horsepower and 36 knots; its armament amounted only to a few 40- (1.57-in.) and 20-mm (.79-in.) machine guns. But these craft could help in an emergency as well as rescue downed airmen. When the destroyer *Laffey* shot down nine attacking kamikazes, it nevertheless suffered hits from six planes as well as from four bombs; meanwhile an adjacent landing craft shot down two kamikazes of its own and helped perform the miracle of keeping the *Laffey* afloat. In the sustained offensive of April many destroyers were damaged, but only three sank, and the campaign that began with an attack by 355 kamikazes ended with only 115 in the last April attack. In the final attack, in June, only 45 kamikazes participated.

In defending against such numerous and determined attackers, the antiaircraft defenses of ships had an advantage that armies lacked. The ships could carry a variety of guns, including the 5-inch, as well as radar and the best fire-control systems. These antiaircraft advantages accounted for the success of the air defense at Okinawa and did much to offset the natural vulnerability of ships compared to the protection offered ground forces by such obstacles as vegetation and terrain inequalities.

During the Okinawa campaign the navy 5-inch guns expended over 375,000 shells, almost all firing at aircraft. Since this meant that ships fired almost 70 of these 50-pound projectiles for each Japanese aerial sortie, it gives an indication of what Japanese pilots had to contend with. It also illustrates the magnitude of the logistic task faced by Okinawa's assailants.

The campaign depended upon a logistic system perfected during the Pacific war. The major western Pacific bases at Leyte, Guam, and Ulithi, all 900 miles from Okinawa, could not directly serve a fleet or landing force. For ships to return to these bases for fuel and supplies might mean that there would be as many ships in transit as there would be on station off Okinawa.

But ships could refuel at sea by pumping oil from tankers to warships through hoses between the vessels. The navy extended this method by running lines between ships that could transfer ammunition and everything else from fresh and frozen vegetables to toilet paper. The fleet accomplished this refueling and resupplying by having some ships withdraw from the immediate scene of action to meet the supply ships. This system of bringing the base to the ships went far toward solving a logistical problem as old as war at sea. In the extensive and prolonged blockade in the American Civil War, as many as a third of the ships in a blockading squadron would be absent from their station refueling, even though they had bases nearby.

Not only did bringing the fuel and supplies to the ships keep them near their combat assignments, but it much increased the efficiency of supply. Instead of a warship functioning as a supply ship by steaming hundreds of miles to receive fuel and supplies, a tanker and a supply ship made the same voyage, each carrying enough to supply a dozen or more warships.

In addition to the need for food and ammunition, the forces ashore required water for drinking, which came from four water tankers and two distillation ships. During the campaign, in addition to a variety of food, the men also received 2,700,000 packages of cigarettes and 1,200,000 candy bars.

Although the bases could obtain some supplies in the Pacific, such as much fresh meat from New Zealand, most came from the United States. Okinawa was 6,200 miles from San Francisco, 26 days of steaming at the 10 knots then characteristic of many merchant ships. But supplies first accumulated at western Pacific bases. Ulithi, 400 miles southwest of Guam and important for fuel, had a superb anchorage, a lagoon 19 miles long and 5 to 10 miles wide. Here commercial tankers from the United States delivered oil for the ships and gasoline for the aircraft and land vehicles. Forty navy tankers, with air protection from escort carriers, plied the seas between Ulithi and Okinawa to make refueling rendezvous with groups of warships.

Seventeen escort carriers ferried aircraft from the United States to the western Pacific, and four others then brought them to the battle area. During the whole Okinawa campaign, the U.S. forces received 854 replacement aircraft.

The efficiency of transport by water made it comparatively easy to support hundreds of ships and hundreds of thousands of people 6,000 miles from the base area. Yet, when a Japanese plane sank an ammunition ship and created a shortage of 81-mm mortar shells, air transport quickly made good the deficiency by flying 400 tons of them from Guam.

So the besiegers and their covering force triumphed against the courage and dedication of many Japanese pilots. Japan flew about 5,500 sorties trying to raise the siege of Okinawa, the majority by fighter and dive and torpedo bombers, but 1,900 by kamikaze pilots. Air power at sea, embarked on fleet and escort carriers and supported by land-based aircraft, turned back the offensive by Japan's land-based airplanes. With its aircraft production faltering and its oil supplies ended, Japan had had its last opportunity to assail its powerful coalition of adversaries.

COMPREHENSIVE STRATEGY: JAPAN'S LOGISTIC VULNERABILITY

The operational strategy of concentration and a turning movement, employed in the archipelagoes, implemented a persisting strategy that had the objective of gaining bases from which the navy could blockade and the army invade Japan. Control of Taiwan or the Philippines, particularly the island of Luzon, would achieve the blockade objective, probably to a decisive degree, by making it easy for sea and air power to interdict Japanese sea commerce with the East Indies and southeast Asia. Because most of the Japanese inhabited four large islands and had great dependence on foreign trade, a blockade could defeat it by the logistic strategy of depleting its armed forces by depriving them of their weapons and supplies. Whereas a blockade in the two world wars had handicapped, but not defeated, Germany, Japan was so vulnerable in location and dependence on imports that a blockade would destroy its military power.

Unlike Germany, most of Japan's steel industry depended on imports of iron ore and coal, these coming from occupied China. Its steel production reached 7,800,000 tons in 1943 but, without imports, it could only produce 1,500,000 tons, less than the amount used by the shipbuilding industry alone. And the aluminum industry—and its principal customer, airplane manufacturing—depended entirely on bauxite from the East Indies. Japan also relied wholly on imports for rubber and most of its oil.

The Japanese also had a potential problem with their food supply. Even before the war, they consumed on the average only 2,000 calories a day, compared to 3,400 in the United States and comparable amounts in western European countries. This meant that there was little or no margin for a reduction in consumption. Imports supplied some of the food consumed, but most came from domestic production. Since Japan had a population of 70 million, over half of the United States' in 1941, and a land area the size of California and very mountainous with very little farmland, Japan already relied on an extremely intensive agriculture, the average farm having only two and a half acres. And for their very high productivity these farms relied heavily on fertilizer, much of it imported.

LOGISTIC RAIDING STRATEGY WITH SUBMARINES

While the Allied forces pushed westward to reach a position to implement the persisting logistic strategy of a blockade, the Allied navies used their submarines to pursue an increasingly successful raiding logistic strategy.

Both Japan and the United States had built large forces of submarines under the supposition that they would work with the fleets in battle. Doing their part in a fleet action would include ambushing the approaching hostile fleet and later torpedoing battleships and cruisers made vulnerable by gunfire damage. For this role both Japanese and American submarines had high surface speeds to keep up with the fleets and long ranges to operate in the broad expanse of the Pacific. To have these features, such a submarine would need to displace at least 1,500 tons, double the size of the German U-boats designed for the Atlantic. Yet the Japanese and American submarines turned out to have the proper attributes for raiding Pacific commerce.

The Japanese submarines pursued their original mission of working with the fleet, the submariners disdaining the role of mere commerce raiders. For this reason the United States found convoys unnecessary to protect its Pacific commerce.

After more than a decade of trial and error, the Americans had developed a successful submarine that met their requirements. It displaced 1,525 tons on the surface, had 10 torpedo tubes, and carried 28 torpedoes; diesel engines of 6,500 horsepower gave it a speed of 21 knots on the surface and a range of 10,000 miles. The diesels charged the batteries that gave it a submerged speed of 9 knots and an ability to cruise under water at two and a half knots for 48 hours. The navy standardized this excellent model just before the war and built nothing else from 1940 throughout the war. In 1942 the submarines acquired good radars, both for searching the surface and scanning the sky for aircraft.

The navy immediately implemented the logistic strategy of destroying Japanese commerce, and in 1942 the submarines sank about 725,000 tons of Japanese ships, about 100,000 tons more than Japan built. This construction, and Japanese capture of many foreign ships, reinforced the complacency that had caused the Japanese admiralty to neglect preparation for antisubmarine warfare and long delay introducing convoys. In 1943, submarines sank 296 merchant ships, displacing 1,335,000 tons, double Japanese construction and acquisition for the year. The United States, which had lost 15 submarines, closed the year with 75 operational, 22 more than a year earlier.

Growing numbers, increasing skill, and dependable torpedoes would make the submarines even more effective in the last year and a half of the war. Although not emulating German central control, the navy did radio the results of intercepting and decoding of Japanese messages when they contained convoy routes. On convoy routes submarines used concentration, groups of three or four operating together. They also adopted the effective German technique of operating on the surface at night.

Four submarines, watching the passages between Luzon, Taiwan, and the China coast, illustrated the effectiveness of concentration against convoys by sinking 41,000 tons of ships in five days. But individual boats could do a great deal also, one sinking two merchant ships and a small cruiser in a single brief encounter with a convoy. It then survived an 18-hour depth charge attack. On another occasion one submarine assailed five ships loaded with aircraft and sank three while the captain had the satisfaction of seeing the other two ships collide in their effort to ram his boat. The next night he sank three more merchant ships, but in an attack the following day, his torpedo turned around, hit, and sank his submarine—a rare, but not unknown, event in the submarine warfare of the two world wars.

In June 1945 a squadron of nine submarines entered the sea of Japan, between Japan and the mainland of Asia, and in 11 days sank 27 of the small ships bringing food to Japan. Japanese losses reflect the increase in submarines in 1944, the sinking of 2,700,000 tons of Japanese ships. Until the last months of the war, submarines accounted for 60 percent of Japanese ship losses.

But the submarines were not the only raiders preying on Japanese commerce. Land-based aircraft from Okinawa flew over the sea of Japan and between the work of these raiders above and below the sea and the carrier aircraft, Japan faced an effective and constantly tightening blockade.

THE EFFECTS OF THE LOGISTIC STRATEGY OF INTERRUPTING COMMERCE

Japan had begun the war with 6,000,000 tons of shipping, added 4,100,000 by construction and acquisition, and lost 8,900,000 tons. Most of these losses came from the following sources, as percentages of the total:

submarines	54.7
carrier aircraft	16.3
land-based aircraft	14.5

| mines | 9.3 |
| accidents | 4.0 |

By March 1945 Japan had overseas commerce only with Korea and Manchuria, and this was limited to bringing food and salt to Japan. The narrow focus of this trade made it quite vulnerable to mining. Bombing planes began laying mines and, by the end of the war, had laid 12,000, placing them before harbors on the Sea of Japan, in the Strait of Shimonoseki leading into the important communication artery of the inland sea in the Island of Honshu, and in that sea itself. These mines sank 198,000 tons of Japanese shipping in July alone.

The need for the stress on food imports is reflected in the decrease in the average Japanese calorie intake from 2,000 to 1,900 per day by 1944. During the war, the population had lost an average of 10 pounds per person and school children had become shorter and lighter. This occurred before the average calorie intake dropped to 1,680 in the spring of 1945. Agricultural production, already exceptionally intensive, could not readily increase and faced the effect of a decline in fertilizer production from 3,600,000 tons in 1939 to 1,000,000 in 1943. Imports of phosphate fertilizer fell from 1,000,000 tons before the war to 146,000 tons in 1944. And fish catches had diminished from four and a half to two and a half million tons.

The end of iron ore imports caused the decrease of steel production from its peak of 7,800,000 tons nearly to the 1,500,000-ton level sustainable from domestic sources. In the summer of 1944 the imports of bauxite for aluminum shrunk to 10,000 tons a month and ceased thereafter. The aircraft industry continued production by using scrap aluminum, a rapidly dwindling source of supply. The lack of such minerals as cobalt, chromium, tin, tungsten, nickel, and molybdenum compelled the use of inferior substitutes for the special steels needed in the production of such sophisticated products as airplane engines. The end of oil imports forced Japan to depend on its depleted inventories and domestic production. At less than two million barrels per year, domestic production could make only a meager contribution. The whole output could, for example, provide fuel and lubricants to operate the 30 to 40 thousand civilian and military trucks in Japan, with very little if any left for other purposes, such as flying, heating, illumination, or industrial and farm engines.

All of this meant the successful implementation of the logistic strategy of depleting Japanese armed forces by depriving them of an economy that could support them. But the Japanese had to cope with yet another application of logistic strategy.

THE LOGISTIC RAIDING STRATEGY WITH BOMBERS

The Army Air Forces was using the Marianas and the new B-29 Super-fortress bomber to apply to Japan the same logistic strategy used against Germany. The Superfortress would fly nearly four times as far as the B-17 Flying Fortress and do this faster and with more than triple the bomb load.

The B-29s reached the Marianas in October 1944 and soon began a program of daylight raids from 30,000 feet against steel and, particularly, aircraft production, shipbuilding, and electronics. Although the losses suffered at 30,000 feet were sustainable, the high-altitude flying much reduced bomb loads, and winds as high as 180 miles per hour and clouds on most days limited accuracy. Flying with the wind, the planes moved too fast in relation to the ground and, against the wind, sometimes flew backward in relation to the ground. And despite their great height, the force had lost six percent of its strength to all causes in one month. Moreover, 835 sorties destroyed only four percent of an aircraft engine plant. These results clearly indicated the wisdom of the same shift made by the British in bombing Germany, to adopt area bombing at night.

Raiders at altitudes of 6,000 to 9,000 feet could carry far heavier bomb loads. Further, they encountered little risk because the Japanese lacked good radar antiaircraft fire control and had no radar on their night fighters, and the swift B-29 usually eluded Japanese searchlights. The new approach had great promise because, unlike Germany's masonry buildings, most Japanese houses had wood, and even some paper, used in their construction.

The new strategy made an awesome debut when, on 10 March 1945, 334 B-29s dropped 2,000 tons of incendiary bombs on the huge city of Tokyo. With a population of over six million, it had 50 percent more people than Berlin. The bombs started a fire that made a glow that the airmen could see from 150 miles away. It destroyed an area three by four miles in the densely populated city, killed at least 83,000 people, and wounded 40,000, a toll much surpassing Hamburg in 1943. Because some industrial plants fell within the burned area and the casualties included many industrial workers, the raid implemented the logistic military strategy as well as the political objective, inherent in such raids, of intimidation and discouragement. After the raid, the percentage of Japanese believing that Japan would lose the war increased from 10 percent in December 1944 to 19 percent after the March raid.

This was the first of a series of raids directed against Japan's largest cities, intensified as the number of planes doubled. After the campaign destroyed 105 square miles in Japan's eight largest cities, the raids expanded their objective to include 50 more cities. None of these raids inflicted casualties at all comparable to the first on Tokyo. Bomber losses remained negligible, less than 1 percent per raid. Meanwhile, the program of daylight, high-altitude bombing of industrial targets continued on the rare days when weather permitted. From April through July, weather allowed only 13 days of such bombing. In stating the objective of the bombing campaign, the commander of the B-29s, General Curtis E. LeMay, ignored the political aspect of strategic bombing and clearly enunciated the logistic military strategy of the program of raids when he wrote that it had the objective of the "destruction of Japanese ability to wage war" within six months.

THE DEFEAT OF JAPAN

By the early spring of 1945, Japan was out of contact with all of its overseas forces except those in Manchuria and, in any case, could do little to assist them. The bombing that began then did help to reduce production and morale even more but had no logistic effect on Japan comparable to that on Germany in the last days of the war.

Although the destructive bombing that began in March would do serious damage to many critical industries, this had little practical effect. For example, the destruction of 15 percent of steel production capacity could have little impact when the end of raw material imports had already reduced production by 75 percent. Similarly, reducing shipbuilding capacity by 15 percent had no influence when the steel industry could not supply enough for a 50-percent level of output. Likewise, bombing oil refineries enough to reduce capacity from 90,000 barrels a day to 17,000 would make no impression when the industry was operating at 4 percent of capacity due to the end of oil imports.

Aircraft manufacturing presented an instance of perfect symmetry between blockade and bombing when the bombing reduced airframe productive capacity by 60 percent, but lack of bauxite imports had forced the aluminum industry to rely on scrap and so had reduced the output of raw material for airframes also by 60 percent. Of course, with the depletion of the supply of scrap aluminum, the production would decline further. Moreover, aircraft production would lose any meaning in the absence of fuel for the airplanes.

With a blockade cutting their economy's output by 40 to 50 percent, the Japanese could hardly afford to engage in a war; instead they needed to devote all of their resources to staying alive. A comment made by an American civilian in the late spring of 1945, when Germany had left the war and the navy had bested the kamikazes, seems relevant: The United States should call off the war, bring the troops home, and stop gasoline rationing and other impediments to civilian enjoyment of the wartime prosperity. The navy would continue to blockade Japan, and if the Japanese wanted to remain at war, that would be fine with the Americans, who would be at peace. The United States would always need a navy, and the perpetual blockade of Japan would provide it with realistic training. This remark assumes that the Japanese might accommodate their economy and style of life to no foreign trade, retain independence, and so not have to acknowledge defeat. Thus it could have again become a hermit kingdom, as it had from the seventeenth to nineteenth centuries.

This hypothesis for ending the war thus relied exclusively on the logistic strategy of sea blockade to disarm the Japanese and so render them quite inoffensive militarily. But it overlooked what to do about the large number of Japanese troops in China who would have had a base area in the regions they controlled. Yet an Allied landing and acquisition of a port or ports on the Chinese coast could have provided a base of operations for the more than 30 Allied divisions that such a primary reliance on a logistic strategy would have made available. Well-supplied and with good strategic mobility and a formidable cavalry of the air, this force in its initial operations could have deranged Japanese supply arrangements in China and encouraged the Chinese resistance. The resulting radical alteration in the strategic situation of the Japanese troops in China might well have induced some to enter into conventions to leave China in exchange for transportation to Japan. This the Allies could have cheerfully conceded because additional people in Japan would only have intensified the need to devote more effort to agriculture, a peaceful pursuit.

Actually the United States planned to invade Japan. The assumption of the need for this may have owed something to the strategy necessarily applied to Germany. But without sea or air power Japan could not harm its neighbors. Although the logistic strategy had depleted the offensive power of the Japanese armed forces, the defense of Okinawa had shown that the army had more than ample courage and determination. The mountainous Japanese islands lent themselves to defense, and the 70 inches of annual rainfall would have made the limited level terrain quite difficult for the motorized U.S. forces.

But, seeing no hope of victory, many Japanese leaders had become anxious to end the war, a cabinet with that as an objective having taken office in the summer of 1944. Communication was difficult, especially with the Japanese fruitlessly seeking mediation by the U.S.S.R. The Emperor, who seldom intervened in politics, gave his emphatic and immensely influential support to the partisans of peace. When the Allies modified the demand for unconditional surrender by allowing the Japanese to retain their emperor, this reduced the cost of surrender to one that the Japanese could bear.

Of course, at this point, the United States dropped an atomic bomb on the city of Hiroshima. It had the power of 20,000 tons of explosives, making it the equivalent of several times the power of the biggest raids in Germany. It killed 71,000 people, almost as many as the Tokyo raid, and injured far more than that raid, 68,000. Since it did nothing more than the bombers had been doing with many more aircraft and more men, it amounted to no change in the logistic military and political strategy of strategic bombing. But its gruesome novelty and potential for the future gave it an important psychological impact.

Chapter 8

The Strategy
of the Korean War

Japan had annexed the ancient kingdom of Korea in 1910, and the restoration of its independence had become an Allied objective in World War II. Upon Japan's capitulation in 1945, the Allies occupied Korea—the U.S.S.R. establishing a communist autocracy in the North, and the United States fostering a democratic country in the South. On 25 June 1950 North Korea's well-prepared army invaded South Korea with the aim of uniting the country under its rule.

LOGISTICS

Both antagonists depended on remote base areas, the United Nations' forces having long distances but unmolested sea transport. The enemy drew much from their distant Chinese base areas, to which they had land links subject to incessant raiding by the United Nations' air forces. Though these could halt rail traffic and make road movement very difficult, they never succeeded in interdicting the flow of supplies from China during their more than 200-mile overland journey to the front in Korea. But it raised the cost of transportation to an exorbitant level, as was the cost of the interdiction effort.

TACTICS

North Korea's army of more than 100,000 men was better equipped and trained than South Korea's force of less than 100,000. Yet, in the fighting, the southern forces performed well considering their deficiencies. Although they had light field artillery, they lacked the tanks and antitank guns of the northern army. Further, the North Korean army had many leaders who had gained combat experience while serving in the Chinese army.

The U.S. divisions that early entered combat no longer had the usual nine battalions, being reduced to six, as had been so many German divisions in World War II. The artillery had undergone a comparable reduction, and the units lacked the 32-ton Sherman tank, having instead the 18-ton Chaffee, much inferior to North Korea's 33-ton Russian T-34 tank.

But neither matériel nor numbers would determine the outcome. The U.S. forces had better-trained leaders, including experienced generals, and far more officers and noncommissioned officers with combat experience in World War II. Trained by U.S. advisors, the South Korean army worked harmoniously under the U.S. command, as did the British and Commonwealth forces.

Although jet fighters had superseded the World War II fighters as interceptors and helicopters had become important for carrying small loads and evacuating the wounded, the matériel of the Korean War, like its tactics and strategy, closely resembled that of the Second World War.

STRATEGY

The North had more land and industry than the South but only 9 million people, compared with 21 million people in the South. The South, with 38,000 square miles like Virginia or Kentucky, had mountains dividing the country from northeast to southwest. This feature would make an invasion difficult. But the division of Korea into two countries was too new and artificial for the northerners to meet a determined national resistance. Rather, unpaved roads and heavy summer rains would handicap supply and maneuver.

North Korea aimed to use a sudden attack by its superior army to carry out a persisting offensive by overwhelming the South Korean military and civil forces and achieving this so quickly as to confront the world with a *fait accompli*. Hence it expected to avoid the operation in politics of Newton's third law. Although the South's army resisted, and sometimes well, the North seemed on its way to success had the United States and the United Nations not intervened immediately. The United States thus acted in harmony with its foreign policies of containing communist and U.S.S.R. expansion and with its support for the United Nations and states that faced threats to their independence.

THE NORTH KOREAN INVASION AND THE UNITED NATIONS RESPONSE

The surprise northern persisting offensive had only a few miles to go to capture the capital, Seoul, in three days. Then the North Korean command directed its principal drive southeastward, thus continuing to use the railroad as a line of operations and communications. To occupy the whole country quickly, North Korean army troops also moved down each coast. The United Nations, acting primarily through and at the instance of the United States, promptly resisted this. The United States quickly intervened with air raids and sent a division of troops from their occupation duties in Japan into South Korea through the port of Pusan. This division then moved forward to help the South Korean army defend against the invaders' main effort along the railroad from Seoul to Pusan.

By the end of July, the North Korean coastal and central lines of operations were converging on the port of Pusan and had pushed the U.N. units into a rectangular perimeter of over 100 miles along which the U.S. and South Korean troops defended that port. The North Koreans then devoted August and early September to a series of attacks against this position, held by the 8th Army of United States, South Korean, and other U.N. troops. The northern forces' use of successive attacks enabled the 8th Army commander to exploit his interior lines of operation by moving reserves quickly from point to point to counter each drive. Meanwhile, the U.N. cavalry of the air struck the enemy's logistics with such effect that it had disabled most trucks, and the trains ran only at night.

By this time the U.N. commander, General Douglas MacArthur, had accumulated a reserve in Japan to execute an amphibious turning movement by landing at Inchon, the port near Seoul. This movement would then put the landing force directly on the communications of the North Korean forces assailing the Pusan perimeter. Preparatory to striking such an obvious objective, the U.N. command sought to distract the enemy with air and sea threats against the coast at five different locations. So, when the 10th Corps of army and marine troops landed on 15 September, it found the bulk of the North Korean army still besetting the Pusan position. The difficult landing worked well, the 10th Corps soon cutting the railroad, gaining the airport, and then capturing Seoul.

With the main route of retreat thus closed, the North Koreans, deprived of their fuel supplies, had to leave behind most of their motorized equipment, including tanks and artillery. Because an immediate offensive by the U.N. forces in the Pusan position further complicated its withdrawal, the once so-formidable army retreated by dispersing. Many found their way to North Vietnam by crossing the 100 miles of border between Seoul and the east coast. Others took refuge in the mountains in the South. Thus the victorious turning movement regained South Korea but brought no big bag of prisoners and left a legacy of northern troops in southern mountains from which they harried the country with their raids. This threat occupied the U.S. 9th Corps in October.

THE SEQUELS TO THE VICTORIOUS CAMPAIGN

The U.N. soldiers wanted to pursue the beaten foe into North Korea to destroy those feeble remnants that had escaped northward, thus completing the victory of the combat strategy of the turning movement. Because it could unite Korea under their rule, South Korean political leaders also favored this. For this very reason, the invasion of a *de facto* independent country, it had considerable political significance. Nevertheless, the U.N. sanctioned it, and the U.N. forces pushed north; ahead lay a hostile country the size of the state of New York and the Yalu River, which divided North Korea from China.

So, the U.N. forces planned an offensive with the 8th Army advancing directly north and the 10th Corps making another landing, this time on the east coast. Meanwhile, South Korean troops pushed north at the beginning of October, advancing 15 miles per day in spite of some determined opposition. But late in October they encountered Chinese troops in considerable strength near the Yalu. Then, on 1 November, near the west coast, an 8th Army U.S. regiment suffered heavily from a Chinese attack; the 8th Army immediately went on the defensive. Meanwhile the 10th Corps had landed on the east coast, moved inland, and spread itself widely.

Knowing that the Chinese had concentrated substantial forces just north of the Yalu but convinced that he faced no serious Chinese intervention, General MacArthur decided on a major offensive to end the war. It began on 24 November, but it met a Chinese offensive the next day.

A powerful Chinese attack struck the right flank of the 8th Army, where it joined the 10th Corps. Displaying great tactical skill and a mastery of night fighting, the Chinese turned the 8th Army. The 8th Army commander used his reserve to retard the move enough for the army to extricate itself and fall back 40 miles to a good defensive position. But a Chinese force had pierced that line before the 8th Army arrived. Meanwhile, the Chinese surrounded dispersed units of the 10th Corps. Most escaped, thanks in part to the effective determination of two marine regiments and outstanding logistic and combat assistance from the air forces. The 10th Corps withdrew from two different ports and landed at Pusan.

On account of its thorough motorization and its command of the air, the 8th Army easily demonstrated the superiority of retreat over pursuit. Confronted with broken railways and destroyed bridges and harried by the cavalry of the air, the Chinese pursuers fell well behind the retreating U.N. army. After a halt and some severe combat, the U.N. forces took a position 15 miles south of Seoul, occupying a line across the peninsula. The rugged terrain favored the defense, and heavy Chinese casualties and supply difficulties made them halt.

The U.N. forces then counterattacked, the beginning of a seesaw struggle, with both sides making good use of the fortified defense. This continued until the fall of 1951, when truce negotiations began. The front remained fairly stable until the conclusion of the negotiations in 1953.

The United Nations with its control of the sea and its superiority in air power, artillery, and tanks had success with offensives based upon the methods developed in the First World War. The Chinese also had good offensive power, basing it much on the excellent opportunities that the low ratio of force to space gave to infiltration tactics. Further, though the rugged terrain aided the defense, unless the defender studied it carefully and used it with great care, it could give cover to assailants. Thus Chinese infantry, making the most of these opportunities—the low ratio of force to space, their excellence at night fighting, proficiency at infiltration tactics, and adeptness in cross-country movement—also gained offensive successes. So each army gave a different emphasis to the tactical legacy of the two world wars.

Strategy showed more uniformity than tactics in that each sought to turn their opponent—the United Nations by using sea power to create and exploit an open flank, and the Chinese by using a concentration against weakness to break through a defense and so create two flanks to turn.

The debacle of the U.N. advance in North Korea owed much to its unreadiness to defend. Just as in tactics a counterattack has the advantage of likely catching the adversary in an offensive stance and not properly arrayed for the defensive, so in operational strategy did the Chinese counteroffensive have an inherent advantage, one augmented by surprise. The defeat also had a debt to the failure of the U.N. command to give adequate consideration to the applicability of Newton's third law to the political sphere.

Some responsibility may also belong to the myth of pursuit as the mandatory means of reaping the full harvest of depletion from a combat success. The U.N. advocates of the advance north might well have given some thought to the skepticism about pursuit often expressed by the great captains of old. One of the greatest of these, the sixth-century Roman general Belisarius, expressed thus the disadvantages of the pursuit of a defeated adversary because it could lead to another battle and its attendant risks. In such a battle, he wrote, "we shall win no advantage if we are victorious— for why should one rout a fugitive?—while if we are unfortunate, as may happen, we shall both be deprived of the victory we now have . . . and also abandon the land of the Emperor to lie open to attacks of the enemy without defenders." Thus the wise Roman rather accurately described the result of the U.N. pursuit.

Chapter 9

The Persian Gulf Conflict of 1990–1991

THE ORIGINS

After a long and costly war with Iran in the 1980s, Iraq had accumulated large foreign debts and so stood in particular need of revenues from the export of most of its large oil production. This made it particularly sensitive to oil's world price, one that most of the major oil exporters tried to control through the Organization of Petroleum Exporting Countries (OPEC). In order to sustain a high price, OPEC limited output by assigning each member a quota. No member felt satisfied with its quota, and some sold more than their quota. Kuwait, Iraq's small, vulnerable, and oil-rich neighbor, was one of those that consistently exceeded its quota.

These excess sales, which tended to depress the price of oil, constituted a serious grievance for Iraq, one intensified by a 15-percent decline in the price of oil during the first half of 1990. This, and territorial claims against Kuwait, motivated Iraq's sudden invasion and almost instant conquest of Kuwait on 2 August 1990. In this way it could not only halt Kuwait's overproduction but acquire its output and sell its quota also. But the great powers of Europe and three of the major Arab powers formed a coalition led by the United States. The Coalition responded in an unexpectedly drastic manner, the United Nations quickly voting economic sanctions, which included a trade embargo.

The Coalition powers immediately sent armed forces to Iraq's neighbor, Saudi Arabia. On 6 August, for example, 48 U.S. fighter planes flew to Saudi Arabia without stopping, using aerial refueling and arriving in 16 hours. By 11 August, Egyptian troops were landing with the same objective as the U.S. aircraft: to protect Saudi Arabia from an invasion by Iraq.

Whereas the world could do without the oil exports of Kuwait and Iraq, it could not dispense with those of Saudi Arabia, the world's largest exporter. Thus the Coalition acted quickly to forestall a possible campaign by Iraq's large army to seize the Arabian oil fields.

The powers promptly implemented a blockade of Iraqi ports, which ended seaborne oil exports from Iraq and Kuwait. They also closed the oil pipelines through Arabia, Syria, and Turkey, thus blocking any significant Iraqi oil exports. When Saudi Arabia and other exporters increased their oil production, they filled the void left by the end of exports from Kuwait and Iraq, and world supply again equalled demand. With substantial forces concentrating in Saudi Arabia, the Coalition's political-military strategy of blockade put them in a favorable position. They had not only defeated Iraq's war aim of raising the price of its oil but had deprived it of all of its oil exports. Saudi Arabia's production filled much of the Iraqi and Kuwaiti quotas, yielding additional revenues, which it used to subsidize the Coalition. While squeezing Iraq so drastically, the coalition had nothing to do but blockade Iraq by sea and stand on the defensive on land. In spite of the fiasco of his policy, entailing the loss of all of his oil revenues and his enemies using his quota, Saddam Hussein, Iraq's dictator, formally annexed Kuwait to Iraq.

LOGISTICS

The Coalition's logistics resembled those of the United Nations in the Korean War in its often-long and quite-secure communications and differed in that larger, faster airplanes made air transport of personnel and priority freight commonplace. The supply lines of the Iraqi forces were much more vulnerable than those of the North Koreans and the Chinese.

TACTICS

The tactics employed in the conflict exhibited their lineal descent from World War II. The combatants possessed more and larger tanks than their Second World War ancestors, infantry in fully armored carriers, and more and more powerful self-propelled artillery. In spite of the prominence of the tank, the powerful, cumbersome antitank gun had a diminished role because of the development of the wire-guided antitank rocket. Relying on the shaped charge used with the World War II bazooka antitank rocket, this missile received guidance commands through a wire that it paid out behind for as far as two miles or more as an operator guided it to its target. Its range and accuracy made it formidable, and its velocity of over 900 feet per second made it virtually impossible to intercept or avoid. This was one of several portable rockets available to the infantry. So the infantry had gained a very significant antitank capability, one less dependent on the soldiers' enterprise and courage than the bazooka.

Since the Korean and Second World wars, aircraft had acquired much greater tactical significance, no longer being mostly an adjunct to the artillery in a big barrage or assisting the infantry when the situation made possible a clear delineation between friend and foe. The helicopter provided a principal means for achieving this. Able to hover in the air or, as could the U.S. Huey Cobra, go 140 miles per hour, it could participate in combat with machine guns as powerful as 30 mm (1.18 in.), a gun for the rapid fire of half-pound grenades, and antitank guided missiles. To have these capabilities, it weighed as much as a World War II fighter bomber and had as much horsepower.

With this firepower, the helicopter could assail infantry. And, with its high speed and antitank capability, the helicopter was a weapon system intrinsically superior to the tank because the tank's gun could not hit it, but the helicopter's guided missile was deadly to the tank. Infantry and tanks combined arms by protecting themselves with heat-seeking antiaircraft missiles, potentially deadly to helicopters and a threat to fighter bombers. Even so, the helicopter's maneuverability enabled it to move erratically, take cover behind terrain obstacles, and otherwise elude the formidable missile.

The infantry and tanks in the Persian Gulf conflict also had to contend with fighter bombers that were not only bigger and faster than their World War II antecedents but possessed of enhanced tactical capabilities. Much of this came from more accurate weapons, particularly bombs guided by a variety of means, including lasers. These devices worked by fitting an ordinary bomb with a sensor capable of detecting a specific frequency of infrared light, with guidance fins, and with a computer that enabled the bomb to steer toward a light source detected by the sensor. Just before the aircraft dropped the bomb, a laser beam was shown on the target, either by the plane dropping the bomb, by an accompanying plane, or by ground forces. The target reflected the laser beam, and the bomb homed in on it. In the case of the most modern fighter bomber, the aircraft's laser designator was coupled to its inertial guidance system and automatically tracked the target even when the airplane turned, climbed, or otherwise maneuvered to leave the target area. Bombs could hit as close as two yards from an aiming point.

This increased accuracy, and the ability of ground forces to designate a target, significantly enhanced the tactical value of the fighter bomber. This improved accuracy also augmented its effectiveness in its strategic role of attacking communications, supplies, and troop movements.

So with more tanks and self-propelled artillery, infantry in armored carriers, tactically more significant jet aircraft, and the helicopter, the armies of 1991 had more cavalry and mounted infantry than ever. Thus, against a less thoroughly mounted adversary, the armies had strategically offensive troops.

STRATEGY

The combat, persisting, offensive strategy of the war showed its descent from World War II when the Coalition made full use of the strategically offensive capabilities of its forces and completely exploited its command of the sea and air. But the American and North Atlantic Treaty Organization (NATO) armies had given much thought to fighting a frontal battle and, for this, embraced the World War II strategic role of the fighter bomber within the concept of a battle. So the typical air attacks on enemy forces on the march became tactical and part of the "deep battle."

THE CONCENTRATION OF COALITION FORCES

The Coalition did not feel complacent about the plight of occupied Kuwait, nor did it have any confidence that the serious economic predicament in which it had placed Iraq would soon compel its withdrawal. Saddam Hussein had already demonstrated his obstinacy in his nearly fruitless eight-year war with Iran. He further showed his determination by giving to Iran his small gains from that war in order to keep it neutral in his contest with the Coalition. At the same time, Saddam Hussein endeavored to transform the political situation by representing his conflict with the Coalition as between Arab and Western civilizations, a stand that created a delicate domestic political situation for the Arab members of the Coalition, particularly Egypt and Syria.

So Iraq's adversaries determined to augment their forces in Saudi Arabia until they met the requirements of an offensive to drive Iraq from Kuwait. To counter what they thought to be 540,000 Iraqis deployed in the theater of operations (postwar studies indicate that Iraqi forces may have numbered as few as 340,000 at the commencement of hostilities in January 1991), the Coalition concentrated 800,000 people of all arms. In the air, the 550-strong Iraqi air force, which included many older planes and many ill-trained pilots, faced nearly 1,600 mostly modern combat aircraft flown by the world's best-trained crews and supported by some 600 noncombat airplanes. Iraq had a then-estimated 4,200 tanks (later thought to number only 3,700) of varying vintages and capabilities. These had to contend with 3,600 mostly very modern tanks, supported by some 500 ground-attack helicopters, most equipped with sophisticated antitank missiles and by 144 specialized antitank planes. At sea all the world's premier naval powers deployed ships except the U.S.S.R., which aligned itself diplomatically with the Coalition. Control of the sea ensured that the Coalition's lines of communication remained open. Despite the number of aircraft employed, most of the Coalition's heavy supplies and equipment travelled by ship. Although Iraqi minefields off the Kuwaiti coast did damage two major U.S. warships and slowed down planned offensive naval operations, the Coalition had essentially unimpeded sea communications.

Most of the Coalition's soldiers, sailors, and airmen represented the best of its nations' forces and largely consisted of long-service professionals. The Iraqi ground troops, however, contained a large proportion of conscripts, lacking in both morale and training. On the other hand, Iraq had created within its army a separate, elite organization, the Republican Guard. Better paid, trained, and equipped, these had higher morale, motivation, and loyalty to the regime. The Iraqi army had gained ample combat experience in the war with Iran, and its commanders and staffs had learned lessons difficult to obtain in maneuvers and other simulations of war. Yet they gained this combat experience in mountainous regions or in marshes, a poor preparation for the different conditions of warfare on the desert's open terrain, which permitted large-scale movements and afforded little natural cover.

THE STRATEGIC SITUATION AND THE BELLIGERENTS' PLANS

With a frontier with Saudi Arabia 500 miles long, Iraq seemed to face an extremely difficult operational situation. It appeared as if their well-armed opponents with their immense logistic resources could assail them at any point. Even with a half million well-armed men, Iraq had such a low ratio of force to space that it could not establish a continuous front. A proper defense would have required a distribution in substantial detachments able to defend their locale if assailed and to move rapidly to concentrate in support of other detachments. With mobility comparable to the antagonists', such a defense could expect to confront an advancing enemy force with a concentration having the advantage of the tactical defensive. Yet, to conduct such a defense, the Iraqi command would require good intelligence of the enemy's dispositions and movements, the kind of intelligence traditionally provided by the horse cavalry and now supplied by the cavalry of the air.

But with the coalition having command of the air, the Iraqi army would not have the intelligence of Coalition dispositions and movements to know how to maneuver or where to concentrate to confront an advance. Moreover, as World War II had shown, the Coalition's superb cavalry of the air could so retard strategic troop movements that Iraq's forces could not concentrate in time, even if it knew where. Thus they could not avoid being turned.

So the Iraqi command concentrated on defending Kuwait, necessarily trusting to the enemy to make a direct offensive to recover Kuwait. Because its long war with Iran had given it much successful experience with the fortified defense, Iraq's army made the most of this by preparing elaborate field fortifications to defend the border between Kuwait and Saudi Arabia. The experienced engineers created impressive physical obstacles of ditches and earthen ramparts sewn with a plentiful supply of antipersonnel and antitank mines. These defenses had the protection of indirect fire from powerful artillery. The defenses included entrenched positions for infantry, antitank rockets and artillery, and tanks. Protection for tanks, other vehicles, and guns resembled that used for aircraft, an earthen wall on three sides of the position. Thus, a bomb or a shell had to obtain a direct hit or one immediately before the open side to do any damage.

The fortifications covered the Kuwait border with Saudi Arabia and extended a little westward along Iraq's border with Saudi Arabia. For this long front, they committed only 19 weak divisions, largely composed of conscripts. This provided only about one division for every 10 miles of front, a rather thin coverage. But, behind these, ten additional divisions held positions in Kuwait, with two more posted well to the west of the line. Eight divisions of the Republican Guard remained in southern Iraq, covering the major city of Basra and, presumably, ready to counter a turning movement, reinforce the front, or counterattack.

The Coalition did not have an untrammeled choice of where to attack. The terrain became more difficult the farther west one proceeded along Saudi Arabia's border with Iraq. More important, the Coalition could not supply a powerful advance very far west of their initial position covering Saudi Arabia and its oil-producing region. In fact, only some of the forces making the planned turning movement would go around the west flank of the Iraqi line; the others, more heavily armed, were to drive through the extension of Iraq's defenses along its border with Saudi Arabia.

With their major concentration along the Kuwait border and directly between the Iraqi army and the Arabian oil fields, the Coalition forces, commanded by burly and colorful U.S. General H. N. Schwartzkopf, had little to fear from an enemy attack. So, enjoying the initiative, they could attack when it pleased them. They planned to take advantage of the dependence of the Iraqi army on a remote base area to implement a logistic strategy by assailing Iraq's weapons-related production, petroleum refining, rail and highway bridges, electric power generation and distribution, and communication facilities. Air raids would carry the main burden, using a mixture of old-fashioned and "smart" bombs, guided by lasers, which were almost certain to hit their targets. They had valuable help from cruise missiles, very expensive and requiring the preparation of a radar-intelligible map to the target, but very accurate and virtually proof against interception.

But at the start of the campaign early in the afternoon of 17 January 1991, it began as a combat strategy directed at the Iraqi air force and air defenses. Since Iraq kept its air force on the ground, all attacks against it occurred in the airplanes' well-protected ground positions. Here guided or "smart" bombs could hit them and even pierce overhead cover.

THE AIR CAMPAIGN AND THE BOMBARDMENT OF IRAQI TROOPS

The attack on the air defenses had the help of helicopters that assailed and disabled radar stations, thus giving protection from observation to some of the Coalition's attackers. They also made liberal use of the well-tried means of baffling radars, electronic countermeasures to put decoys into the sky that looked like aircraft on radar and to fill radar screens with static. The most powerful defense proved to be an offensive with a missile that would home in on air defense radars. Soon the threat of such a missile made air defense radar operators use their radars only for brief intervals, thus rendering them almost harmless. So the attackers did their destructive work so well that the Coalition lost only five bombers to the 700 air defense missile launchers and many radar-directed antiaircraft gun batteries. The Coalition also gained much from a few aircraft so designed as to reflect little if any of the radar sets' signals back to its antennas. All together the Coalition dropped 227,000 bombs, of which 17,000 were laser-guided or other types of smart bombs.

The Coalition air forces immobilized the Iraqi planes by disabling their airfields. Even the 500,000-pound B-52 bomber, attacking at the fighter bomber-altitude of 500 feet, participated in this effort. Traditionally a difficult target, the runways proved more vulnerable to the fighter bombers dropping laser-guided bombs or the British "runway busters." These consisted of containers filled with small bombs—some exploded at once to crater the runway, and others contained time fuses to explode later to make repair work hazardous. Apparently the Iraqi air force had planned to withstand the Coalition's attacks in their bomb-proof shelters. When these proved vulnerable to destruction by laser-guided bombs, many of Iraq's aircraft fled the theater of operations and took refuge in Iran.

After the Coalition's air attacks had rapidly neutralized the Iraqi air force, the air forces could devote considerable bombing effort to logistic targets. Since the combat objectives had included communications, the logistic campaign had really started immediately. In the 38-day air and bombardment campaign, the Coalition flew about 3,500 combat sorties against the air defenses; about 1,000 against communications (both a combat and a logistic objective); and 5,500 as part of the logistic strategy, which included cutting the communications between the army in Kuwait and its base area in Iraq.

But a great deal of the air effort went against Iraq's ground forces in largely supplanting artillery in its traditional role in the attack on the fortified defense. It most closely resembled those of World War I, well-exemplified by the British attack against the German defenses near Arras in 1917, in which the British used 2,817 guns along the 12-mile front selected for the attack. In addition to field guns, they used large numbers of heavy guns, including 8-inch and 9.2-inch siege howitzers and railway guns and howitzers, including a 12-inch railway gun that could reach 12 miles into the German rear with a 750-pound shell.

The British barrage began on 9 April 1917 and fired at a steady rate for three weeks when it commenced high-intensity fire for five more days before the attack. At that time the 2,340 Livens projectors joined the barrage. These were trench mortars, which fired a 60-pound shell containing 30 pounds of phosgene gas, one of the war's most effective.

At 38 days, the Coalition bombardment of the Iraqi positions exceeded the Arras shelling in length and did not have one of its major defects. Whereas the bombardment on the 12-mile front near Arras gave ample advance notice of the place on the front of over 300 miles where the attack would take place, the Coalition bombardment covered the entire extent of the nearly 150 miles of fortified front. Further, it took place in much greater depth because it included attacks on the troops posted along the coast and the Republican Guard units far to the rear. Thus, though the bombardment lacked concentration in space, it gave no inkling of where the attack might come. In its lack of concentration in space or time, it differed from the short intense air bombardments in Normandy in 1944 that had supported the St. Lô breakthrough.

Because most of the bombs were far heavier than most of 1917's shells and because they carried, in proportion to their weight, a much larger explosive charge, the unconcentrated bombing of 1991 had essentially the same effect as the shelling in World War I. Thus an observer of a victim of "shell shock" in World War I described a man "alive and unhurt but absolutely incapable of lifting a hand or speaking." In the Iraqi army there were different, but comparable, symptoms after exposure to sustained bombing: Soldiers' "hands shook uncontrollably and they jumped at the slightest sound." Of course, the Iraqis were spared the casualties inflicted on the Germans by the British thoroughness with gas in World War I.

The guided smart bombs gave an accuracy both comparable to and different from artillery's. Whereas the bombers could not hit targets the way artillery observers could adjust a sequence of shells on a target until they struck a preselected target directly, they could deal admirably with targets of opportunity. At night, for example, infrared heat sensors could locate a tank or other vehicle by the difference in its temperature from that of the surrounding ground. The bomber could then use a laser beam to guide a 500-pound bomb directly on the tank from above, defeating the protection offered by the earthen banks around it. Thus the air campaign destroyed an estimated 1,772 Iraqi tanks, 1,477 artillery pieces, and 948 armored personnel carriers.

As the Iraqi defense relied on minefields and other obstacles covered by artillery, the Coalition devoted considerable attention to these Iraqi guns. When Coalition gunners fired to provoke Iraqi return fire, radars determined the Iraqi gun positions and artillery, and air raids quickly silenced the just-located gun batteries. When, during their offensive, the Coalition forces crossed the belt of Iraqi obstacles and encountered only sporadic and inaccurate cannon fire, they reaped the harvest from this effective counter-battery effort.

THE GROUND OFFENSIVE

The Coalition forces planned a powerful turning movement around their adversary's open western flank. To facilitate this, they devoted much effective effort to distractions to draw the attention of the Iraqi command away from such an obvious move. The bombing campaign against the fortified defense and the troops in its rear worked as a distraction, constantly fostering the idea of an attack directly into Kuwait. The presence of large naval and marine forces created a very appropriate concern for an amphibious landing to turn their fortified line on the east. This apprehension led to the preparation of defenses of Kuwait's beaches and of strongpoints along the coast and the posting of six or seven divisions to resist a landing.

When the Coalition moved 100,000 men and 2,000 tanks westward to take a position to execute the turning movement, it took ample security precautions. At the same time, small groups of British and marine personnel with radios simulated forces to create the illusion of undiminished strength on the eastern end of the Coalition line. So, without air reconnaissance, the Iraqi command continued to expect a frontal attack or an amphibious landing. This expectation of their coming across the difficult Gulf coast beach having provided a valuable distraction, the bulk of the Marines, two divisions strong, actually deployed along the Kuwait border.

The offensive plan sent the equivalent of five divisions of the most heavily equipped troops to make the main but shorter turning movement. These drove through the westward extension of the defensive line that covered some of the Iraq-Saudi Arabia border. Considering that the four defending divisions had less than half of their proper strength and that the bombardment had completely demoralized them, there was very little difference between going through the four divisions and around their flank. But three Coalition divisions, less heavily equipped with armored vehicles, did go completely around the flank, going west of the main turning force. Before this began, however, the troops along the Kuwait border began an attack and a Marine amphibious force seemed about to land, both activities designed to keep the attention of the Iraqi command away from its western flank.

The frontal attack northward against the best defenses proved more than merely a distraction. By late on the second day, the joint Arab forces had pierced the two lines of defenses, followed defeated and retreating Iraqi troops, and reached Kuwait city twenty-four hours later. This 60-mile contested advance in less than three days was not confined to the joint Arab force. The whole front, including Marines, Egyptians, and Syrians, surged northward simultaneously, piercing apparently formidable entrenchments and, in the process of routing their well-armed adversary, rendering their units incapable of further effective combat.

Meanwhile, the outflanking force of three divisions marched rapidly north, relying on the satellite-based Global Positioning System to navigate accurately across the featureless desert terrain. The Coalition's ability to coordinate with precision the rapid movement of large forces across the desert took the Iraqis by surprise; it is likely that the Iraqi command considered impossible what the Coalition accomplished with little effort.

One of the outflanking forces' divisions advanced 60 miles by the end of the second day, took an airfield, and established a broad pattern of reconnaissance to detect any hostile force approaching from the north or west. The other two divisions reinforced the northernmost division of the turning force. This placed their north flank near the Shatt-al-Arab River, which passed near Basra and through which the Tigris and Euphrates rivers emptied into the Persian Gulf. There they met the Republican Guard divisions. They had the objective of keeping the Republican Guard from attacking the flank of the main turning force and also preventing the Guard divisions' retreat and inflicting heavy casualties on them.

The main body of the turning movement, composed of U.S. and British armored units, moved north rapidly, then turned east, connected with the divisions touching the Shatt al-Arab, and so had eight divisions arrayed on a line north to south, with their eastward advance directed toward the 80-mile interval between Kuwait City and the Shatt al-Arab. But no turning movement ever took place in the sense of the Coalition forces placing themselves on the Iraqi army's line of retreat north from their positions along Kuwait's southern border. Instead the retreating forces clogged the highway north from Kuwait City, and when air attacks disabled the leading vehicles, the fighter bombers had a field day, destroying the immobilized vehicles and killing their occupants.

The ruins of the Iraqi army fled across the border, not pursued by the victors, who had accomplished their war aim of liberating Kuwait. The Coalition also realized the political objections to having a group of powers dominated by western nations inflicting further defeats on an Arab country.

The overwhelmingly superior tactical and operational skill of the Coalition forces almost rendered strategy irrelevant. When they arrived in the theater of operations, the Coalition troops, mostly picked units of long-service professionals, were well prepared to fight immediately. Then they had as long as four months for additional training for just the type of combat they could expect, knowing also their antagonist and the terrain and weather conditions of combat. With deadly combat almost sure to follow, the Coalition soldiers made the most of their opportunity to prepare themselves. Since the Iraqi command did not use this time so well, the months of preparation widened the already substantial gap between the adversaries in skill and confidence and rendered virtually irrelevant the Iraqi army's long combat experience against the Iranians.

Casualties provide a clear measure of the difference in combat skill between the two armies. Iraq's forces had between 12,000 and 30,000 killed by the long bombardment (more-precise estimates are not available) and 10,000 to 15,000 killed in the four days of ground combat with 86,743 taken prisoner, mostly during the ground offensive. The Coaliton suffered 226 killed in action and 45 taken prisoner.

In its strategy the Gulf conflict ground war much resembled that of the 1944 Normandy campaign. The success of the dummy army in England and Montgomery's pressure around Caen in distracting the Germans had their parallels in the bombardment, the threat of an amphibious landing, and even the simulation by radio of British and marine forces. All of this led to a turning movement in both cases, partially successful in Normandy and almost redundant in Kuwait.

There is a tactical parallel in the aircraft, including the big bombers, playing their 1944 role in substituting for big guns in carrying out a World War I barrage. It differed in being the long barrage typical of 1915–1917 rather than, as in 1944, 1918's concentration in time as well as space.

There is a tactical and strategic comparison in the role of the fighter bomber, so effective in France in cutting German communications and pursuing the retreating foe. A comparison of ground attack aircraft, the World War II A-20 with the Gulf conflict's A-10, exhibits the continuity and change in this type of aircraft. Both had two engines, a broad range of operating speeds, and top speeds of 400 miles per hour for the A-10 and 339 for the A-20. But the A-10 carried 16,000 pounds of bombs, quadruple its predecessor's load. And, instead of the A-20's four 20-mm (.79-in.) and two .5-in. machine guns, the A-10 had only one, a 30-mm (1.18-in.) machine gun, an extraordinary weapon with seven barrels and a rate of fire up to 4,200 rounds per minute. With a bullet as heavy as a 40-mm projectile and a very high muzzle velocity, the gun was exceptionally effective against a tank's comparatively thin top and rear armor. Typically, the A-10 carried special antitank missiles, capable of guiding themselves to their target with their cameras. Some models were sensitive to the infrared spectrum, giving the A-10 the ability to attack at night.

With so much better ground-attack aircraft, the Gulf conflict's cavalry of the air combined another advantage over their predecessors in Normandy. They had largely level and unobstructed terrain over which to operate and did so without the obstacles of northern Europe's often overcast weather.

So in employing aircraft for logistic raids against the enemy's communications with its base area and its strategic movements and in the use of the turning movement, the Gulf conflict's strategy closely followed the best models for attacking an enemy with a remote base area. The tactics, like the strategy, resembled that of World War II, but the armies were more mobile—the Coalition, for example, having mostly self-propelled artillery. Other significant differences, besides the more formidable cavalry of the air, included better and more realistic training. The United States, for example, rotated armored units through a special training facility equipped with sensors, computers, noise generators, and other devices capable of simulating a real battlefield and determining exactly who hit what and when. Also important were improved communications, more information for intelligence purposes, and computers to help cope with this and much else.

Part III

Operations with a Mixture of Base Area Access

As operations from a remote base area became commonplace in the twentieth century, such mixtures of remote and immediate base areas as occurred in Vietnam are likely to be characteristic of many more wars. The United States in Vietnam offers a good example of this blending as well as applications of a variety of strategies.

Chapter 10

The United States in Vietnam

After the conclusion of World War II and the end of the Japanese occupation of French Indochina, France waged a long war against an increasingly capable, Communist-led national insurgency in Vietnam. Following serious military defeats in the North, the French government abandoned the unpopular war to retain its colony. An international settlement made at Geneva in 1954 gave independence to the coastal colonies, the north half of Vietnam going to the Communist insurgents and the southern half gaining independence as a client of the United States. A projected vote to implement union of the two never took place.

LOGISTICS

The relation of the belligerents in Vietnam to their base areas had more than the usual effect, and even the conception and misconception of the location of the antagonist's base area affected operations. Both North and South Vietnam served as base areas for their own forces, but each also depended in part on quite remote base areas—the U.S.S.R. and China for North Vietnam and the United States for South Vietnam. Yet South Vietnam also served as a base area for the South's Viet Cong Communist insurgents who long supplied themselves well enough from that source to threaten the defeat of the South Vietnamese government itself, the titular possessor of their enemy's base area.

Otherwise, the North and South Vietnamese governments had the advantage of sea communications with their remote base areas. But the Viet Cong insurgents and later the North Vietnamese forces campaigning in South Vietnam depended in part on a tenuous line of communications northward. This used trucks over poor-to-mediocre roads and often had considerable reliance on such slow and inefficient means as human beings using bicycles. On the other hand, such transportation methods proved much more difficult for fighter bombers to interdict than trucks moving on highways.

TACTICS

The tactics used by the U.S. forces and taught to the South Vietnamese army derived from those of World War II. They depended on control of dispersed forces by means of an ample allowance of radios and excellent coordination of artillery fire in support of defensive and offensive action.

A distinctive feature of this was the tactical integration of the helicopter. Increasingly well armed with machine guns and rockets, the helicopter functioned as a collaborator with the infantry and also gave mobility to reserves and supplied a fine vehicle for commanders as well as for evacuating casualties.

Another special attribute of U.S. tactics was the degree of support by the fighter bombers; and these were far more formidable than their World War II predecessors. One of the most widely used, the twin-jet F-105, had the same loaded weight as the B-17 Flying Fortress heavy bomber of World War II; a much-higher cruising speed; and, as a fighter, could reach 1,500 miles per hour, five times the B-17's speed.

In spite of its high speed and, consequently, only glimpses of the target and a brief time to decide and act, the jet fighter bombers gave much tactical support to the ground forces. This came as a result of effective coordination, based on long experience, patient and careful study, and thorough preparation.

The tactical participation of the fighter bombers also worked well because many of their tasks did not require precise discrimination between friend and foe. Because the Viet Cong insurgents made use of elaborate fortified defenses, South Vietnamese, U.S., and other associated forces engaged in many operations that resembled the western front of World War I. In most of these the army used the French method of 1915 by relying upon the artillery to conquer the ground so that the infantry could occupy it. And the air force could play much of the artillery's role. In doing this it could substitute quantity of bombs for the accuracy of artillery fire. Compared to artillery shells, bombs were inexpensive and had a simpler mode of delivery. And, in addition to bombing areas identified as hostile fortifications, the ground forces could obtain heavy air bombardments of areas where there were no friendly forces in the expectation that some enemy would be there and harmed by the comparatively cheap attack.

In addition to the fighter bomber, the air force used the B-52 Stratofortress, which had double the speed of the World War II B-17 Flying Fortress and, with 60,000 pounds of bombs, ten times its bomb load. Entering service in 1955 and designed to carry nuclear bombs from one continent to another, it proved its versatility in the Vietnam War and later.

The bigger and faster bombers at high altitude faced a more serious antiaircraft menace than in World War II. Instead of guns firing shells to intersect with the aircraft's computed course and explode near enough to shoot it down, the air defenses could guide a missile to the target. In the U.S. Nike system the search radar found the target, and the target-tracking radar would "lock on" to the aircraft just as with the gun control system of World War II. But then a missile would go up as high as 70,000 feet, tracked by its own missile-tracking radar. The missile battery's computer could then calculate the location of the target and the missile, send commands to the missile to guide it to intercept the target, and then order the missile to explode when very close to the airplane. The missile carried a warhead weighing over 200 pounds whose powerful explosion would send steel fragments in all directions, far more formidable than the explosion of a 23- or 50-pound artillery shell from a 90-mm (3.54-in.) or 120-mm (4.72-in.) antiaircraft gun.

As smaller, shorter-range antiaircraft rockets could use much the same fire control system against lower-flying aircraft and the infantry's homing rockets could reach as high as 5,000 feet, the fighter bombers faced a comparable peril. Further, smaller antiaircraft guns, such as the 57-mm (2.24-in.) and 23-mm (.9-in.) machine guns, had radar guidance, and smaller machine guns still presented a hazard to low-flying planes. The U.S. loss of 1,800 aircraft in the Vietnam War gives an intimation of the effectiveness of an extensive and diligent antiaircraft defense.

STRATEGY

The experience of the Korean War had much influence on U.S. strategy in Vietnam. Thus the military missions sent in the 1950s to create a South Vietnamese army concentrated on preparation to resist a persisting offensive from the North like that launched by North Korea against South Korea. Further, because North Vietnam had a border with China, the experience of China's intervention in Korea made strategists very conscious of Newton's third law and cautious about provoking the active intervention of China or the U.S.S.R. That China had long viewed Vietnam, like Korea, as within its sphere of influence, more than geography and their common communist ideology bound China and Vietnam. Thus, when the United States used bombing against North Vietnam, it was wary of bombing near the Chinese border and was careful not to do anything that could destroy North Vietnam as a state or a society.

So against North Vietnam the United States initially limited itself to a political-military strategy of seeking to raise North Vietnam's cost of the war it supported in the South above what it was willing to pay for the attainment of its political objectives. This put the use of air power against North Vietnam on a tightrope, balancing between action too feeble to create a prohibitive cost and so strenuous as to provoke more formidable Chinese or U.S.S.R. reactions.

The United States initially carried two military strategies with it to South Vietnam. The dominant one, the army's, was to deplete the enemy armed force with a combat strategy. This was in the tradition of General Eisenhower's advocacy of killing Germans rather than depleting them through a logistic strategy. Confident of its skill and plentiful modern weapons, most soldiers viewed this as the best route to a quick victory.

The Marine Corps brought a different strategy, one derived from its experience between the world wars in occupying and combating insurgents in Haiti and Nicaragua. In fact, it had used its experience to develop a manual on this kind of warfare, one that stressed its political aspects. His experience with this kind of warfare helped Marine Corps Commandant General Wallace M. Greene, Jr., to see operations in South Vietnam in a very political light. Thus he early took the position that the primary objective ought to be gaining the support of the Vietnamese people. This different perception of the appropriate strategy led the marines to add a distinctly political dimension to their operations.

THE ORIGIN AND NATURE OF THE CONFLICT IN SOUTH VIETNAM

Although the North Vietnamese government maintained its national objective of creating a united Vietnamese state, it hesitated to pursue this objective aggressively. This deferring of action responded in part to domestic concerns in the new northern state, a desire to avoid a costly unification struggle, and a wish to avoid provoking a deeper involvement by the United States in the affairs of South Vietnam. Further, the U.S.S.R., the leader of the world's Communist nations, then followed a new policy of peaceful coexistence with the non-Communist nations.

The United States subsidized the new government of South Vietnam and helped install Ngo Dinh Diem as its ruler. He proved capable of creating a government and had guidance from U.S. missions, particularly one that supervised the creation and training of an army. But Diem displayed a remarkable degree of political ineptitude, systematically pursuing policies that rapidly estranged an otherwise largely passive and compliant population. Illustrative of the repressive policies of his insensitive autocracy was the abolition of elected village councils and the substitution of appointed officials, many of whom were inept, arbitrary, and often corrupt.

The government also made more enemies among the rural people by its policy toward tenant farmers, the overwhelming majority of the rural people. It did this by the way it overturned the land policy established by the local insurgents against French rule. They had appropriated some of the large landholdings and distributed them to the tenants. The Diem regime returned the land to the owners, and their efforts to collect back rents pushed the landowners' proportion of the tenants' income to and even beyond 50 percent.

Having repealed the insurgent's land redistribution, Diem introduced his own land distribution scheme. But it failed dismally—and not only by affecting merely a few tenants. Even those affected saw little benefit because they had to reimburse the landlord, a compensation the poor peasants had naturally looked to the government to make. So in 1960 in the prime rice-growing region of the Mekong delta, only a quarter of the peasants owned any land, and half of these had but one acre and rented another.

On the other hand, the Diem regime's early and strenuous efforts to root out communism had much success, though also punishing many non-Communists and making many feel hostility toward the new government. And following Newton's third law, its program created a defensive Communist activity, reluctantly sanctioned by the North Vietnamese government, which exercised control over the Communists in the South.

In their campaign against the government, the Communist Viet Cong insurgents relied on raids and used these to assassinate government officials who threatened them. The small groups that carried these out had the traditional advantage of raiders, ambiguity as to the objective and routes of advance and retreat, and thus the opportunity to strike at weakness, often augmenting it by surprise.

They chose some assassination victims because they were competent in their efforts to combat the Viet Cong insurgents and even selected some because they aided the Diem regime by providing good government in their districts. On the other hand, corrupt, oppressive, and incompetent officials were usually exempt from assassination because, by alienating the people, they were the Viet Cong's unwitting allies.

This exploitation of the ascendancy of raiding to make political assassinations had the effect of intimidating many of their adversaries. These political raids, together with the antipathy aroused by the Diem regime, gave the Viet Cong insurgents control of a number of villages. But this provoked a drastic increase in the government's activity, resulting in the arrest of 65,000 suspects and the execution of 2,000 people. Although the government's severity alienated many, it so seriously hurt the Viet Cong organization that it brought about a frantic acceleration in Viet Cong activity and about 700 assassinations in 1958.

Although the government had prepared to defend its villages, the inadequacy of its arrangements made the task of the raiders fairly easy. A militia, numbering 50,000, provided local defense, but in addition to substantial Viet Cong infiltration of its ranks, the force lacked adequate arms. Only two out of three militiamen had rifles, and these were French weapons with ammunition so old that only one in seven cartridges would likely fire. So the regular army had to contribute a large part of its force to guarding key points and patrolling the countryside. This caused the U.S. military mission much anxiety because it interfered with the training of the army to resist an attack from North Vietnam.

In addition to raids to carry out assassinations, the Viet Cong military forces needed raids to capture weapons and to make politically valuable demonstrations to the people of the weakness of the government's military force. When 400 Viet Cong raided a rubber plantation, they gained both objectives by capturing 100 weapons, taking $143,000 in cash, and withdrawing without any effective resistance from the 200 regular troops guarding the plantation.

They also used ambushes of patrols to demonstrate the weakness of the regular forces. On one occasion, they did this easily on a river by concealing themselves on the bank and opening fire on a surprised patrol in boats, causing 75 casualties and capturing 27 rifles and 13 machine guns. Soon after, they ambushed another, sinking two patrol boats and killing over 100 soldiers.

For ambushes on land, they developed a frequently used tactic in which they would dig pits along the side of a road in which a few men would hide. Another man would cover them with bamboo and grass, erase any sign of digging, and then take a position where he could cover their position with machine gun fire. When a government force approached along the road, the concealed soldiers could then surprise it, attacking under the cover of machine gun fire. They also surprised their adversaries with booby traps and mines, and, when lacking mines, used the time-honored pitfall with sharpened bamboo stakes on the bottom.

Viet Cong success exhibited the serious weakness of the newly created South Vietnamese army. In spite of its many failures, the army's commanders consistently reported success in its operations against the Viet Cong. In part they did this because they wished to tell President Diem what he wanted to hear. Many believed a story that when a certain officer took a new assignment and found and reported the Viet Cong very strong and his forces inadequate, the President had promptly relieved him and reduced him to the rank of private.

When the high command claimed that in a three-month period the army had killed 931 insurgents and captured 1,300, the figures looked suspicious because it had captured only 150 enemy weapons. Further, the army had lost over 1,000 of its own rifles, 90 machine guns, and 82 pistols.

Lack of adequate training explained much of the failure. The army offered only eight weeks of basic training, and many soldiers received only some and a few none at all. The units had insufficient commissioned and noncommissioned officers, and these, too, lacked adequate training. The government filled the higher officer ranks on the basis of political reliability rather than military merit, and most officers had no concept of coordination and concerted activity in military operations.

Meanwhile, the Viet Cong was building a military force that drew on the traditions of North Vietnam's successful campaigns against the French and its thoroughly modern military culture. By 1960 the North Vietnamese government had decided that the situation in South Vietnam and the weakness of the Diem government warranted beginning a military campaign by the insurgents to overthrow the Diem government. So the Viet Cong received orders and direction from the experienced leaders in North Vietnam. And with the increase in Viet Cong military power came a diminished emphasis on raiding and the introduction of a persisting strategy.

The Viet Cong already had some sections under its firm control. It had inherited these from the period of combat against the French, and they provided good and reasonably secure base areas. Army penetration of these areas usually resulted in finding a little food but no insurgents. One, on a peninsula in the South China Sea, proved inaccessible to the army because a swamp blocked the only route to the tip of the peninsula. Faced with the alternative of approaching it by water and giving the Viet Cong a clear field of fire, the South Vietnamese commander decided not to press the attack.

Expanding these Viet Cong base areas meant a persisting strategy of taking and holding more territory; and this involved the political task of gaining support and reconciling the inhabitants to the new rulers as well as military victory over the militia and the army. So a team of Viet Cong civilians and soldiers would take a village, with most of the soldiers moving on to the next objective but many of the civilians remaining behind. They then took control of the village, often redistributing land and always creating a local defense force to help hold the community against a counterattack. The Communist military/civilian force thus concentrated against successive villages to conquer and organize new territory and secure it against reconquest.

The Viet Cong soldiers became quite adept; on one occasion they surrounded and captured a company of regular troops and then retained their prisoners as spectators while they ambushed another force coming to rescue the prisoners.

The insurgents' military skill enabled them to accelerate their persisting offensive by seeking to secure territorial control in larger increments than a single village. Once they gained support in and then captured 16 villages in one operation. They quickly established their authority and created a defense that succeeded in holding this substantial new acquisition against the army's counteroffensive.

Another effort to take an even larger area seemed to succeed when Viet

Cong forces captured and began to organize a group of 72 villages. But a week later they failed in defending it against the army and had to withdraw.

THE REACTION TO THE VIET CONG OFFENSIVE

The Diem government responded to the augmented communist insurgency in the summer of 1959 by a program to reorganize the countryside into larger and more-easily defended units, "agrovilles" of 300 to 500 families. These could have defenses and a garrison, and the government made them even more attractive by equipping them with a school, medical service, and electricity. Yet they became still another political fiasco, the peasants objecting to leaving their villages, having to provide the labor to build the agrovilles without compensation, and not receiving enough money to pay for the land they needed to buy. By the summer of 1960, protests had halted the movement into agrovilles.

Meanwhile in 1960 North Vietnam had sent into South Vietnam 2,000 southerners who had moved north in the 1950s but now returned as trained soldiers to provide a cadre for the Viet Cong armed forces. And this year the insurgents assassinated 2,500 officials.

Although the U.S. mission realized that the insurgency problem was political and that Diem's policies caused most of the opposition, they failed completely in their efforts to persuade him to change. He looked only to protect himself from a coup from within and gave little thought to the rapid destruction of the regime in the countryside and the disaffection in the cities.

Thus the U.S. mission could only seek a military solution, recommending increasing the numbers of rural police, expanding the army and giving it helicopters, and once more asking Diem to improve his chain of command and his intelligence organization. It viewed the military problem of combating the Viet Cong as primarily a matter of tactics and did not consider strategy. This is not surprising, considering that in the 1950s the U.S. Army had given little attention to the relevant strategy. The army's experience and strategy for fighting native American raiders had long faded from the institutional memory.

The United States reacted to the deteriorating situation by vastly increasing its military personnel in Vietnam, from 900 in November 1961 to 11,326 by December 1962. These troops advised and helped train the South Vietnam army. The United States also supplied 300 airplanes, among these were helicopters, which provided a dramatic increase in the army's mobility.

But strategy would play a part in the effort to find a military solution to the problem of the success of the insurgents in expanding their area of control. The model for the strategy came from the ten-year British war against Chinese Communist insurgents in Malaya. The strategy, already used in other colonial areas, depended on "strategic hamlets." These resembled agrovilles but used more and smaller towns and created far less rural disturbance.

Based on one of the oldest concepts in war, strategic hamlets employed the fortified defense for protection, just as medieval communities had relied on walls and castles. The plan called for a gradual approach, starting in the areas best disposed toward the regime. Here the government would build defenses and arm and train a village militia to man them. Having secured these villages from communist military and political attack, the program would gradually move into the partially disaffected areas. A part of this would be a thorough screening of the population to root out Viet Cong and their sympathizers. The government could then steadily add more loyal and secure villages to the government's military and political base area. This military and political strategy had the name *pacification.*

This implemented a persisting strategy that resembled that used by the colonists in Virginia and New England. But instead of bringing settlers from abroad, the government had to depend entirely on making secure the existing inhabitants who gave it their allegiance. It had the identical reliance on militia and strongpoints—garrison houses in New England and, in Virginia, the palisading of plantations and even of segments of land demarked by the rivers. In both regions in America the persisting strategy implemented a logistic strategy. As the area of strategic hamlets would gradually spread over the countryside, the Viet Cong insurgents would steadily lose parts of their base area, their source of food and shelter, and their places of refuge for rest and recuperation. So, with the steady loss of their base area, they must gradually abandon their insurgency just as did Opechancanough's Confederacy in 1646 and King Philip's hungry warriors in 1677.

But such a strategy required the patience to proceed slowly and thoroughly. Although one American expert believed that Vietnam could not afford a ten-year pacification campaign, the U.S. advisors advocated the orthodox approach of proceeding slowly, methodically, and certainly. Yet the Diem government did the opposite: It planned to put the whole rural population of 10,000,000 into 10,000 strategic hamlets in 2 years. By coupling a far-too-ambitious program with the usual inept and corrupt administration, it produced something close to a fiasco. Many strategic hamlets consisted of little more than a village with a fence around it; one huge hamlet had a garrison of only old men with swords, a few U.S. rifles, and a flintlock musket.

Nevertheless, the program did establish 1,500 hamlets that met the objective well enough to deprive the Viet Cong of some supplies and disrupt their political communication with the affected villages. They responded to this concern by mounting a campaign that exploited the initiative given them by the passive character of the defensive system.

This meant that the insurgents could make successive surprise concentrations against the most threatening of the successful hamlets. Without strong defenses and well-armed, sufficiently trained, and adequately motivated defenders, a single hamlet must quickly succumb to an attack by a concentration of insurgent regular troops. To survive, the hamlets needed both defensive strength, adequate to make more than a brief resistance, and the support of a mobile reserve of regular troops.

Their situation offers an obvious parallel with the war at sea if one compares the hamlets with convoys, the concentration and assault by regulars with an attack by a group of submarines, and the mobile reserve with a naval support group and its escort carrier. Because the hamlets rarely had adequate defensive strength or prompt enough support from a mobile force, many of them suffered the fate of a weakly escorted, unsupported convoy at the hands of a wolf pack of U-boats. So the Viet Cong's campaign of successive concentration and attack eliminated the bulk of those hamlets most obnoxious to them. A more deliberate and thorough program would likely have had the slow but certain success that would soon reward the Viet Cong's application of the same strategy.

On the heels of the failure of strategic hamlets, the Viet Cong insurgents pushed their persisting offensive to bring more of the countryside under their domination. Nevertheless, the hamlet program inhibited the progress of their persisting offensive as did the increase in the capability of the South Vietnamese regular army. The addition of 8,000 more U.S. advisors had much to do with this progress, as did the increase in mobility given by the advent of helicopters.

Then in the fall of 1963 the Communists suffered a severe blow when a military coup overthrew Diem. Although the resulting government lacked much vigor or consistency in policy, it no longer had Diem's systematic mismanagement or his indifference to the situation in the countryside. These developments, and the failure of its effort to negotiate about a settlement, brought a communist decision to increase their forces and seek a military victory in South Vietnam.

THE COMMUNIST REACTION

North Vietnam had already infiltrated thousands more trained soldiers, equipped the insurgents with modern weapons, and stood ready to send some of their own regular troops to South Vietnam. With this increase in force, they expected to gain a quick victory and believed that when faced with the collapse of South Vietnamese resistance, the United States would withdraw. They based this judgment on the recent historical experience of the United States' withdrawing from China when the Communists defeated the nationalists and its negotiated settlements in Korea and Laos.

The Viet Cong 1964 military persisting offensive fully met their expectations. And they were ready to make the most of their territorial gains, having a well-developed system to organize the countryside and harness its resources to their war effort. Their method combined military and political action and resembled that of many shrewd conquerors in the past.

Having gained control of a village by overwhelming any local militia and thwarting any army intervention, the insurgents took over the local administration. But they made changes very deliberately and with considerable circumspection, taking every precaution to avoid alienating the populace. In villages where the Diem government had returned to the owners land expropriated and distributed during the insurgent war against the French, the Viet Cong regime took this land and gave it back to the peasants who had originally received it. They also took uncultivated and common land as well as some from absent or wealthy landowners to give to the poorest and middle-income peasants. Yet they also encouraged the recipients to make some sort of arrangement to compensate the owners.

By the end of 1964 the Viet Cong had distributed 3,800,000 acres of land to the poorer peasants, an area equal to 10 percent of the land area of South Vietnam and a much greater proportion of the arable land. This distribution had moved so many into the classification of middle peasants that few poor peasants remained.

Thus the insurgents met real needs, created a vested interest in their rule, and sought to mitigate the losses and hostility of those who suffered from the change in regime. In this way, and by tactful behavior and competent and honest administration, they gained the support of most of the rural villagers whom they had conquered as a result of their patiently pursued persisting offensive. They also formed their own militia force for local defense; gained recruits for their regular forces; and introduced voluntary contributions, which soon became taxes. Thus they converted their conquests into very productive base areas.

And they had conquered much, so much that by the end of 1964 they controlled one-half of South Vietnam's population and more than half of its land area. A conquest on this scale vastly increased their base area and contributed much to the growth of their forces by providing more supplies, tax revenues, and recruits for continuing the war against a correspondingly reduced government. As the strength of the government forces changed inversely to those of the Viet Cong, the insurgents would soon have such a preponderance of force as to overwhelm the government troops and take the remainder of the country. The logistic persisting strategy was working to perfection, strengthening the winner as it depleted the loser.

From these added resources and the variety of aid from North Vietnam, they increased their army to 80,000 militia dedicated to the defense of their villages, 35,000 troops effective in conducting raids, and between 30 and 45 regular battalions capable of spearheading the persisting offensive.

But the communists made a political misjudgment in thinking that the

United States would accept this defeat and see the relentless persisting advance of the insurgents engulf South Vietnam.

THE UNITED STATES GROUND FORCES AND THEIR COMBAT RAIDING STRATEGY

The United States made its principal response to the impending Viet Cong conquest of South Vietnam by dispatching substantial ground forces to take a major part in combating the insurgents. By the end of 1965 nearly 200,000 elaborately equipped U.S. troops had arrived, making a force equal in numbers to the Communist forces, including the 35,000 men who had arrived from the north as the Communists, following Newton's third law, began to match the U.S. reinforcement.

This transformation of the South Vietnamese government's combat strength posed a strategic problem for the Communists: Should they continue their persisting offensive in spite of having to meet the superior U.S. forces or should they avoid combat and rely on raids to disconcert and divert the Americans?

The exponents of evading combat looked to avoiding defeat and heavy losses and simply waiting until the United States had exhausted its patience with an indecisive war against an elusive enemy. General Thanh, the Communist military commander in the South, chose to try to continue his offensive to maintain the morale of his men. Further, he feared that a long U.S. occupation might well recover most of the conquests that he had just made. So believing that sending coffins home would make the United States abandon the war more quickly, he gladly faced the U.S. forces in combat.

General Thanh also counted on considerable military success against the green American troops. In fact, the U.S. forces would remain fresh, but comparatively inexperienced, throughout the ground war. This resulted from the practice of limiting the tour of duty in Vietnam to one year and sometimes rotating commanders even more frequently. So General Thanh had a reasonable expectation of matching the Americans with his combat-experienced Viet Cong regulars with their good morale and training.

Still, the Americans' tactical system gave them an advantage in combat in Vietnam. It had its origins with the squad tactics and coordination of indirect fire in World War I, evolved fully with the radio in World War II, and reached maturity in the Korean War and subsequent years with the integration of the helicopter. It had the following five interrelated bases:

1. Combination of arms in which large bombers as well as fighter bombers combined with infantry, armored vehicles, artillery, and helicopters for each to have its own well-understood, interdependent role in ground combat.
2. An excellent communication system and carefully designed and thoroughly understood procedures for using it.

3. Complete methods for coordination of action by ground forces who not only delivered direct and indirect fire where and when needed but employed helicopters and fighter bombers for comparable missions.

4. Ample firepower and a plentiful supply of ammunition.

5. Very good strategic and tactical mobility.

This meant not just moving with motorized and helicopter-carried troops, but that, unlike their adversaries, the U.S. forces carried out their movements promptly, with no delays to have to make night or otherwise furtive movements to avoid air observation or attack.

General Thanh's men experienced this tactical virtuosity early when they endeavored to take advantage of the isolated position of a U.S. battalion in the Ia Drang valley. There in November 1965 the U.S. command had landed an air mobile battalion in an area of great insurgent strength. There they met not Viet Cong but North Vietnamese regular troops, whose commander promptly concentrated three battalions against the lone U.S. battalion. After surviving a night surrounded, the troops faced a concentric attack by the three battalions. Though only one company came by helicopter to reinforce the surrounded battalion, it had the support of aircraft and nearby artillery. After some hand-to-hand fighting, the Americans held the position all day and through another night. Fighter bombers gave assistance as did the very large B-52 bombers, able to carry as many as 84 500-pound bombs. These, and 33,000 accurately directed shells from 105-mm howitzers, decisively defeated the prolonged attack. The U.S. forces suffered 79 killed, the North Vietnamese at least 10 times that number. The U.S. tactical system had demonstrated its formidable defensive capability.

So the Communists, with less sophisticated doctrine and equipment, faced an insuperable tactical difficulty in continuing their offensive persisting strategy. Still, they did not have to cope with a U.S. persisting offensive to reconquer the countryside. Although the American strategy aimed to recover some of the lost territory and to consolidate the South Vietnamese government's hold on the rural areas it still controlled, the main thrust of the U.S. military strategy was to deplete the Viet Cong's regular ground forces. Once it had inflicted crippling depletion on these, the strategy assumed that the South Vietnamese government would be able to control the country.

The American ground commander, General William C. Westmoreland, the architect and advocate of this combat strategy, had a distinctive way of implementing it. Instead of a persisting strategy to compel the Viet Cong to fight to defend the conquests of their persisting strategy, he adopted a raiding strategy, called "search and destroy." Whenever a U.S. unit could determine the location of an insurgent regular unit, it would call for a concentration of force, quickly achieved with helicopters, to attack and try to surround and destroy this enemy unit. This mission accomplished, it would then seek another adversary against whom to make a sudden combat raid.

These operations bore no systematic relation to the South Vietnamese government and army's pacification program. Hence it failed to support this defensive and offensive persisting strategy to give security to the areas they dominated nor their effort to acquire control of villages within the insurgent sphere of control.

By adopting a raiding strategy, General Westmoreland avoided having any significant impact on the enemy's logistics. On the other hand, a persisting strategy, by gradually reconquering the Communists' base area, would have deprived them of supplies and recruits as well as circumscribing their base area in which to maneuver. Yet General Westmoreland did aim at major enemy logistical installations when he could find them.

Knowing the location of an elaborate complex of underground Viet Cong shelters and storage areas, in January 1967 General Westmoreland concentrated 30,000 men against it in an operation called Cedar Falls. After surrounding the base area and having a thorough bombardment by B-52 bombers, the troops moved in. Making no defense against such an overwhelming force, most of the enemy escaped, leaving 700 dead. A week after the completion of the U.S. raid, the Viet Cong had returned. But they found little, the army having carefully ransacked the underground storage areas, finding and taking enough rice to supply a Viet Cong division for a year; this logistical coup recalled the Virginia colonists' destruction of Indian corn fields. Also the troops systematically wrecked the tunnels and chambers, destroyed the surface vegetation, and bulldozed the area.

Nevertheless, General Westmoreland did not have enough of these logistic successes to compensate for the failure of his combat strategy to live up to his expectations. Even if he had switched to a combat persisting strategy, he would have faced disappointment because General Thanh's units maneuvered within their base area. This meant that they had no line of communication to protect and so could move in any direction. So, having no rear, General Westmoreland could not have used the turning movement. Only tactics offered an opportunity for blocking their retreat, made possible by the capability of helicopters to land men in the insurgents' tactical rear.

Nevertheless it proved almost impossible to compel the enemy to fight. Their units often dispersed themselves in jungles, hid in ravines, moved frequently, and rarely presented a large target. Because the mountains or jungle gave the Viet Cong cover, pursuit by air often proved ineffective, even if U.S. forces could determine their antagonist's location or direction of retreat, either of which could change at any time. This meant that most of General Westmoreland's raids found no foe to fight. Just as in the Seminole War, having a battle depended on the Indians' wanting it, and it lasted only as long as they wished.

So only 1 percent of U.S. raids resulted in combat. But because the Viet Cong did want to fight, there were battles, 90 percent initiated by the enemy. Some of these were ambushes and some resulted from invitations by the insurgents to attack them in a thoroughly fortified position. Because, as with the Seminoles, any effort to turn the position would result in an enemy withdrawal, the army had to emulate General Taylor fighting the Seminoles and attack in front. This implementation of the combat strategy resulted in a reenactment of World War I assaults on the fortified defense, with artillery conquering and the infantry occupying. But usually, as with the Seminoles, the Vietnamese would disappear before the U.S. attack had overrun their position.

This economized casualties on both sides but usually favored the Americans because of the destructiveness of their World-War-I-style barrages, often aided by bombers. In one such operation, the U.S. forces inflicted an estimated 1,644 fatalities on the enemy with, in addition to the fire of assorted infantry weapons, 2,096 air strikes and 151,000 rounds of artillery ammunition. Because he could not turn an adversary who could move at will within his base area, General Westmoreland could only deplete the insurgent forces gradually. Thus his strategy properly merited the label attrition. But the destructiveness of the combats, particularly the battles or sieges, often alienated the local inhabitants. This seriously compromised the attainment of the political objective of trying to help reconcile the people to the South Vietnamese government.

So battles came about by mutual consent, each belligerent seeing an advantage. General Westmoreland's military strategy needed combat in which to deplete the enemy forces; and General Thanh's political-military strategy wanted dead soldiers for the United States to ship home in coffins to raise the human cost of the war above what Americans would be willing to pay to gain their war aims. But because the insurgents could refuse to fight, they could control their losses. This meant that they had the power to deny success to General Westmoreland's combat strategy by refusing to suffer a disabling number of combat casualties. Of course, thus protecting themselves from serious military depletion limited the number of politically important fatalities they could inflict on their adversary.

Yet, if the U.S. command had pursued a persisting strategy of systematically conquering territory under the Communists' control, it could have compelled them to fight. Not to have fought would have meant the steady loss of their base area with the consequent diminution of their sources of supplies and recruits and the destruction of their forces by a logistic strategy. Why, then, did General Westmoreland pursue a raiding strategy? It allowed the enemy to limit the effectiveness of his combat strategy, whereas a persisting strategy would have yielded more combat opportunities while simultaneously weakening the enemy with the logistic strategy of conquering his base area.

General Westmoreland seems to have placed a high value upon the possession of the initiative, typically the property of raiders. Yet the elusiveness of the enemy in moving within his base area meant that most raids would fail to find the enemy and so markedly devalued the initiative. Even so, the general could compel the enemy to move to avoid his raids and so disrupt enemy plans and supply arrangements and impose losses of the same kind, if less severe than, Colonel Miles's raids had inflicted on the Sioux on the Missouri and the Yellowstone rivers in 1876–1877.

On the other hand, Westmoreland wished to avoid the broad dispersal of his troops that the pursuit of a persisting strategy would require. Envisioning his forces spread over the country in small detachments, he saw them as vulnerable to a combat raiding strategy in which the insurgents' regulars would use the initiative to make surprise concentrations against his isolated units. But, unused to thinking in terms of the defensive and seeing troops holding the country as occupying an immobile cordon, Westmoreland overlooked the strength of the defensive, the superior mobility of his reserves, and thus the opportunities for inflicting severe casualties that such Communist attacks would have offered him.

THE MARINE CORPS' LOGISTIC PERSISTING STRATEGY

Nevertheless, while the army pursued its distinctive strategy, the U.S. Marine Corps also followed the more traditional politically attuned, logistic persisting strategy and so gave considerable stress to supporting the pacification program. Success against the Virginia Indians, like that against the Sioux, had depended on a logistic strategy. In each case raids could implement the strategy, by destroying the crops or keeping the Sioux on the move during the depths of a severe winter. Though raids could not cripple the Viet Cong's logistics, a persisting strategy could. The marines used a method based not on experience fighting North American Indians but from their recent operations in Haiti and Nicaragua and also more recently developed in expanding European colonies.

In these the campaigning had taken place in the enemy's base area, but in these thickly settled territories the source of supplies lay in every village and cultivated field. So the colonial power had to follow a persisting strategy of slowly conquering the country and reconciling the people to their new rulers. For example, in Morocco, which the French conquered between 1908 and 1934, they acted on behalf of the Sultan and soon did much of their campaigning with locally recruited troops whom they had trained and equipped. So they also pursued a logistic strategy that diminished the base area of those who refused the Sultan's authority and added to the base area of the Sultan and his French protectors.

In their military operations, they took great care to protect civilians from harm and to treat them with marked respect and consideration. They ingratiated themselves with the Moroccans brought under their, and the Sultan's, rule, by providing modern medical care and opening stores that sold popular goods at significantly reduced prices.

So this persisting military operation had a conciliatory political strategy as an integral part, thus having the same basis and method as pacification. This experience, and the application of its concepts in Malaya, had provided the basis for the strategic hamlet program, recommended by the British expert, Sir Robert Thompson, who had commanded in the successful long war in Malaya.

The Vietnamese government also pursued a strategy familiar to the marines, one descended from the strategic hamlet program. So when the marines set out to apply the same principles to their area of responsibility, they established a coordinating committee with Vietnamese civil and military representatives as well as concerned U.S. civilian officials. Thus, within the context of the overall effort, the marines aimed to undermine the insurgents' base area.

In their zone of responsibility the marines faced a situation in which the Viet Cong controlled much of the country and had influence in more. The Communists based their control in some communities on the sympathy, or at least the acquiescence, of the people and in others on intimidation of a disapproving population. Typically, from five to ten Viet Cong agents constituted the effective government of a village, even when the traditional government officials remained in office but not in power. This government made the country the insurgents' base area by providing them with food, recruits, and money. Without this control, the Viet Cong would lack supplies and also that strategic mobility that made its forces so elusive.

The South Vietnamese government attempted to recover communities from Communist control or make them secure against the inroads of the Viet Cong by establishing New Life hamlets, the successor of the strategic hamlet; this failed for the same reason as the earlier program, by proceeding too fast and neglecting to uproot the *sub-rosa* Viet Cong government. Had the South Vietnamese government proceeded slowly and thoroughly enough and then made the areas cleansed of insurgent influence secure, it would have successfully implemented a persisting logistic strategy that would have destroyed the Viet Cong. In their areas, the Marine Corps used its military force in several ways to help forward this government strategy.

In one of these methods, the marines interfered with the Viet Cong tax collecting. Because this took place two or three times a year at harvesttime, the marines would deploy their troops to keep the tax collectors away. Because the insurgents came armed, often in force proportionate to the strength of the marines, a battle usually resulted with the marines having the advantage of the tactical defensive.

For instance, in protecting one harvest, a marine battalion and a detachment of South Vietnamese regular troops had to contend with two insurgent regular battalions who endeavored to enter the rice-growing lowland area to make their usual collection, alleged to be 90 percent of the rice crop. Spread out to block different routes of advance and holding a hill that provided a good observation point, the allies drove back the Viet Cong with heavy losses. They owed their success, as usual, to superior communications facilitating excellent coordination of powerful fire support. In addition to aircraft and field artillery, the defenders had the support of the 30 5-inch guns on five destroyers near the shore. The unmolested harvest brought in 7,000 tons of rice, and the marines believed that the insurgents had suffered 240 fatalities at the cost of one marine killed.

The marines also helped design and make possible sweeps of villages that seemed to have a Viet Cong government. In these the marines would surround the suspect community, while South Vietnamese officials and police screened the population. This included examining identity cards, taking a census, and making a thorough search for anyone in hiding. The marines deployed around the village, apprehending those attempting to escape.

These operations usually required several days, and the marines called them County Fairs. They deserved this name by the effort to make them a pleasant experience for the people being screened. In addition to distributing food and providing candy for the children, the fairs had plays, band concerts, and moving pictures. The marines also had a medical team on hand to give treatment to those requiring it. Although the marines maintained a low profile throughout, their military force prevented interference, and the South Vietnamese government forces usually left with some Communist suspects, trapped by the sudden advent of the County Fair. The marines conducted 88 of these in 1966, screening 46,000 villagers, giving medical attention to 20,000 and killing or capturing 454 Viet Cong.

The marines' highly effective military force could also accomplish other tasks beyond the capability of the government's poorly trained and ineptly led regular forces. On one occasion the marines captured a heavily fortified Viet Cong hamlet, one that government troops had avoided for four years. Having surrounded the village at night, three companies attacked after a heavy air, field artillery, and naval gunfire bombardment. They encountered no resistance but found a supply bonanza, a million daily rations of rice. The government resettled the hamlet's 150 families, using 8,000 laborers to move their possessions and the rice. The marines then blew up the hamlet to prevent its reconversion into a fortified supply depot. In the process, they used 13,500 pounds of explosive to destroy 50 caves, 554 bunkers, and much else. An additional 24 explosions, set off by the effect of the demolition charges, indicated how much of the complex the engineers had failed to penetrate.

To protect each village, the government had organized Popular Force platoons of local citizens. These forces of 20 to 30 men knew the local situation and usually had a commitment to their village; but they lacked much military competence. To remedy this, the marines tried the experiment of the combined action platoon. To create one of these, they secured 14 marine volunteers with at least four months' combat experience. These marines, led by a sergeant and with a medical corpsman added, received a week of training in the Vietnamese language and culture. The marines and the local officials then combined them with a village Popular Force.

The marine sergeant took command, with a Vietnamese as a second in command, and the men in the combined unit commenced training each other. The marines conducted the instruction in squad and platoon tactics and the Vietnamese in language, local customs, and topography. The latter usually had some distinctive features; for example, some villages had land mines and booby traps prepared by the insurgents for government troops who entered the village. But the Popular Force members knew their whereabouts and taught the marines their location and how to recognize them.

The first combined action platoon had duty in a village where, by tacit agreement, the Viet Cong carried on their activities at night and the government officials in the day. After thoroughly training itself, the combined action platoon began patrolling at night and soon ambushed an insurgent unit, suffering no casualties and killing four and capturing one of the enemy. The marines lived in the village and learned enough of the language to conduct rudimentary conversations on a number of subjects. The success of the program led to the creation of 57 platoons by the end of 1966. But the temptation to create so many led to too rapid an expansion and the taking of men not only without combat experience but from logistical rather than combat units. By the end of 1967 there were 79 platoons of fully qualified men, a sustainable level.

The operations of one platoon exhibit the level of morale and motivation possible in such a combined unit. Since the platoon's village served as an insurgent rest and supply point and had its own Viet Cong platoon, the combined action platoon did not live in the village. Instead it established a fortified headquarters on the outskirts in a large house abandoned by an affluent landowner. The Viet Cong met this challenge by assassinating the very effective police chief who had requested the combined action platoon. Both sides then patrolled aggressively at night, and for two months the platoon averaged 11 combats a week, in one of which they ambushed an enemy patrol and killed 21 of them.

But the Communists concentrated 140 men, nearly half of them North Vietnamese regulars, and made a surprise night attack on the fortified house. They killed or wounded the six marines there and five of the 12 Vietnamese but could not capture the house from the remaining seven Vietnamese before a regular Marine company arrived to turn the tables. When the Viet Cong returned two nights later, the combined-action veterans ambushed the unit, pursued it to the river, and kept it under fire as it withdrew in wicker boats. Meanwhile, villagers stood on the bank watching the action and the retreat.

This cheering-section behavior exhibited the degree to which the platoon had become part of the community. On their part, the marines displayed a comparable allegiance to their platoons. So in spite of having three chances in four of being wounded while on duty in one of the platoons, 60 percent of the marines serving in these units volunteered for an additional six months of service in Vietnam to continue with their platoons. The Vietnamese displayed a similar dedication when none deserted the combined action platoons in 1966, compared with the 25 percent desertion rate for the normal Popular Force platoons. Moreover, that no village that had a combined action platoon reverted to Communist control testifies to their effectiveness.

The marine's program to deprive the Viet Cong of their base area also contained a positive political component, an effort to present a favorable image of the South Vietnamese government and its U.S. allies. Controlling highly productive agricultural areas with a population density of more than 1,000 per square mile, the marines sought to follow the injunction of their 1940 manual, to treat people with "tolerance, sympathy, and kindness."

To these they added liberality when they secured from charities in the United States food, soap, and clothing for distribution. Later they could draw on the nationwide campaign of the Junior Chambers of Commerce to supply the means to meet the villagers' needs by alleviating poverty and the effects of war. In addition to distributing food, clothing, and medicine, the medical corpsmen and doctors treated over a million patients in two and a half years and trained 500 Vietnamese in rudimentary health care. Further, the marines provided the raw materials and advice for 1,100 village construction projects. These included windmill pumps for hydraulic projects and, particularly, school buildings erected by villagers for which they had agreed to engage a teacher.

All of these efforts, particularly those to furnish security, supplemented the government's pacification efforts, which had teams, 59 strong, to assist villagers in every way possible. That these teams lacked much military capability made especially valuable the Popular Force platoons, the combined action platoons, and the marine's direct military assistance against the Viet Cong.

The marines conducted this program at the same time that they gave security to the air bases in their northern area of commitment and ultimately participated in a struggle against major North Vietnamese forces. The marines showed their concern about the vulnerability of their dispersed dispositions to a possible enemy concentration and attack. They compensated for this with a fortified defense, beginning with a light outpost line of defensive positions behind which they erected a system of mutually supporting earth and timber strongpoints to man and hold against any serious attack.

While the army pursued a combat raiding strategy and the marines united political and military means to support a logistic persisting strategy, the United States was using air power to conduct a political-military strategy, an operation begun partly as a Newton's-third-law reaction.

THE BOMBING OF NORTH VIETNAM

The first air raid against North Vietnam came as a reaction to the killing of American service men by the Viet Cong and the second as a reaction to a Viet Cong attack in retaliation for the first raid. Yet the bombing program, called Rolling Thunder, was an already-planned exercise in political-military strategy. Believing that North Vietnam directed the Viet Cong insurgency in the south and far-overestimating the aid sent from the North, the United States used a bombing campaign to raise the cost of North Vietnam's involvement to such a level that it would abandon its support for the insurgency in the South.

The bombing began at a modest level, well below the sortie capability of the Air Force and the Navy. The decision for such limited raiding came in part in response to the considerable thought given to the political military strategy of deterrence. In addition to aiming to deter North Vietnam by raising the cost of its policy, the architects of this strategy also wished to discourage the Viet Cong, encourage the South Vietnamese, and demonstrate the United States' determination to dominate the situation in Vietnam. By starting at a low level, the United States could increase its bombing if the political situation indicated.

The bombing also had several constraints. Unlike much of World War II bombing, it aimed to minimize civilian casualties. Remembering the effect of Chinese intervention in the Korean War, the United States would strive to avoid any provocation that might bring intervention by China or the U.S.S.R. This meant that the air campaign could not do things that could lead to the destruction of North Vietnam as a state or a society. This, and diplomatic, domestic-political, and other considerations made the selection of targets for the bombers a highly political task. Although the airmen understood political military strategy, one of Douhet's principal ideas, they found quite maddening a process of target selection that involved the Secretary of Defense reviewing proposed targets with the Secretary of State prior to their presentation at a weekly meeting chaired by the President.

In spite of their political screening, targets for Rolling Thunder had the usual logistic objectives characteristic of World War II. These included the communications with South Vietnam, rail and highway bridges, and the country's small industrial establishment. Petroleum storage facilities were a difficult target because their location in the Hanoi and Haiphong urban area made it hard to bomb them without killing many civilians. Then, careful analysis of intelligence data indicated that North Vietnam had so little dependence on petroleum products as to markedly reduce their significance as an objective. In fact, a thorough study revealed how unrewarding a target North Vietnam was for a World War II logistic strategy. Having essentially a subsistence agricultural economy, North Vietnam offered few of the logistical targets found in Germany and Japan in World War II.

That the country had redundant agricultural labor meant that it rather easily committed 500,000 workers to keeping its communications open. The laborers built alternate roads around intersections, repaired railways and highways and their bridges, and did their part in creating bridge substitutes, ferries, pontoon bridges, and fords. They also moved freight around breaks in roads and railroads, making considerable use of bicycles.

The agricultural nature of the country displayed itself in the results of the bombing of the industrial targets. The destruction of 59 percent of North Vietnam's power plants changed little, in part because of surplus generating capacity and because people were accustomed to using candles and oil lamps. Destroying 65 percent of the oil storage facilities had a small impact on a country that used so little and could operate its railroads with wood or coal. Thus the country proved essentially impervious to a bombing campaign, like those of World War II, that aimed at the industrial and transportation systems.

Moreover, the efforts at interdicting the flow of supplies to South Vietnam failed completely, a result easily understood in terms of the small amount sent there. In the summer of 1967, 55,000 of the 300,000 Communist troops in South Vietnam were North Vietnamese. But even with so many soldiers from the North, the southern base area could supply 89 percent of the needs of the whole 300,000 men. Because the Communist battalions fought, on the average, only one day a month, they had quite modest ammunition requirements. In fact, a little over 1,000 tons per month from the North could supply the unmet needs of the 300,000 combatants in the South. They received these without difficulty.

In three years of the bombing, the large number of raids seemed to produce no political effect, especially when compared with the optimistic expectations of U.S. leaders. As the target restrictions steadily diminished and the number of sorties more than quadrupled to over 13,000 per month, the air raids relentlessly increased the cost of the war to North Vietnam. But even though the bombing killed 59,000 people, this did not raise the price above the value North Vietnam placed on its objective of uniting the whole country under its rule.

The bombing campaign could have striven for a greater political effect by following World War II precedents and incinerating many of the million people dwelling in the Hanoi-Haiphong area. But not only was this sure to cost much diplomatic support and likely to provoke China or the U.S.S.R., it was incompatible with the U.S. Air Force's concept of strategic bombing. The air force believed in the logistic military strategy of destroying an enemy's industries and realized that this would have the desirable by-product of political intimidation; but it opposed bombing solely to kill people in order to cow the survivors or daunt their rulers.

A less drastic form of intimidation would have been to bomb the dikes and dams that controlled water and diverted and regulated its flow to the rice fields. This could have markedly reduced the rice supply but might have lacked effect because China could have made good the deficiency. And such an attack on the food supply would have had many of the political liabilities that would have accompanied singling out civilians as the direct target for bombing.

So the political-military strategy failed because it did not raise the cost of the war above what North Vietnam was willing to pay for its war aim. The bombing also failed as a military logistic strategy because most U.S. strategists were unfamiliar with warfare within a base area. Only having experience with remote base areas, it did not occur to most of them that North Vietnam was not the base area for the forces fighting in the South.

Further, they overestimated the Communists' need for ammunition because they overlooked the sporadic nature of warfare with both antagonists employing raiding, rather than persisting, strategies. Moreover, U.S. strategies also did not note that because the insurgents could avoid battle at will, they could control their ammunition requirements, just as they could govern their casualties, by limiting their combat participation. So the logistic strategy did not have any chance of success because it did not assail the enemy's principal base area.

COMMUNIST CHANGES IN STRATEGY: THE TET OFFENSIVE AND ITS AFTERMATH

In 1967 the North Vietnamese leaders decided to strike a blow at the South Vietnamese government then led by the wiley General Thieu. They believed that this could well cause its collapse, or so weaken it as to make the U.S. policy in Vietnam seem hopeless and prompt a U.S. withdrawal. The plan for attacking cities owed some of its inspiration to a spontaneous popular urban uprising against foreign rule that had occurred early in North Vietnam's struggle for independence from France. So the leaders planned an essentially political-military offensive to try to precipitate many popular uprisings against General Thieu's government.

Unlike a campaign in military strategy, this operation did not have a clear expectation of its outcome. It began in the fall with an effort at distraction, attacks along borders to draw U.S. troops away from the heavily populated areas. Then early in 1968, at the beginning of the Tet holiday, the communist forces would attack at least half of the major and many of the smaller urban areas. This was the task of the Viet Cong, not just the regular troops but the political as well as all military personnel. Widely dispersed in space, the offensive would have concentration in time, all attacks occurring on the same day. That six of these occurred a day prematurely gave little warning to an enemy who already suspected that something was about to happen but had still given many soldiers the customary holiday leaves.

The Tet offensive began on 30 January 1968 and proved to be a military as well as a political fiasco. The Thieu government showed itself to be far stronger than expected: Its soldiers defended it, often with considerable determination; there were practically no popular uprisings in the cities; and the casualties of so many unsuccessful frontal attacks were immense, estimated as high as 40,000 dead and missing. Still there were many spectacular events, such as the capture and holding for over a month of the ancient and honored old capital of Hué. The dramatic assault on the U.S. embassy in Saigon, where the assailants maintained a lodgment for six hours, contributed much to the newsworthiness of the Tet offensive. Except for the destructive siege of the insurgents in Hué, with its house-to-house assaults as well as the besiegers' usual reliance on artillery, the Communist Tet offensive was a relatively brief event.

But it and its aftermath filled the news in the United States where its events clashed harshly with the public's impression of the war as a steady march to victory. The new image of the war received reinforcement from perhaps the war's best-publicized land campaign, the siege of Khe Sanh from January to March 1968.

Adjacent to the border with North Vietnam, the marines held Khe Sanh as a post for patrolling the vicinity and as a base for possible operations into nearby Laos. The North Vietnamese concentrated over three divisions, more than 30,000 and perhaps as many as 40,000 men, to attack one South Vietnamese and four marine battalions, about 6,000 men. Functioning as a part of the distraction effort that preceded the Tet offensive, the concentration against Khe Sanh preceded the offensive by ten days, beginning with an attempt to take a hill that was part of the fortified defense, a system of mutually supporting strongpoints that made up the base's defenses.

In addition to the fortified defense and carefully planned crossfires, the garrison of the base had powerful artillery support from adjacent positions and raids by the big B-52s as well as fighter bombers. Surrounded, but supplied by air, fortified Khe Sanh and its fire support proved impregnable. After several failures to capture any of the fortified hills and an unsuccessful regimental attack against the position held by the South Vietnamese battalion, the North Vietnamese withdrew, having inflicted over 1,000 casualties on the defenders and surely having suffered many more themselves.

The unpromising prospects of the siege are sufficient to explain the withdrawal, as is the change in the strategic context. To the degree that the move against Khe Sanh was to function as a distraction for the Tet offensive, it had served its purpose; and, if the capture of Khe Sanh was to have been the culminating victory of a successful Tet offensive, it could not play that role either. Yet, while it lasted, the apparent uncertainty of whether the marine and South Vietnamese force could hold its seemingly exposed position made it one of the war's most dramatic stories. By having the U.S. forces still on the defensive, it gave support to the Tet offensive's puncture of the U.S. public's optimism.

Because this change in the popular, and also the official, estimate of the situation resulted in an important change in U.S. policy, the Tet offensive became an admirable example of doing the right thing for the wrong reasons. If the Communists had done it for the right reasons, they could have achieved the same effect with far fewer casualties. Nevertheless, in spite of the result, the United States' willingness to begin negotiations and its halting of the bombing of North Vietnam, the severe casualties of the Tet offensive required the Viet Cong and the North Vietnamese army units in South Vietnam to act thereafter on the defensive so as to minimize their casualties and protect their impaired base area.

THE UNITED STATES CHANGES ITS MILITARY STRATEGY AND POLITICAL OBJECTIVE

At the same time in the United States, the change in the apparent prospects for victory led to a reexamination of U.S. strategy and war aims. The U.S. Joint Chiefs of Staff recommended a further increase in the U.S. forces in Vietnam and an amphibious landing on the North Vietnamese coast just north of the demilitarized zone that separated the North and South. They also argued for bombing of new targets in the Hanoi and Haiphong area and, presumably to cut the South off from its assumed remote base area in the North, that an army corps enter neighboring Laos or Cambodia to sever the supply line from North to South called the Ho Chi Minh Trail.

But a new strategy, keyed to a new war aim, evolved in the next year under President Lyndon Johnson, and it became that of his successor in 1969, President Richard Nixon. Instead of the goal of creating a stable, strong, anti-Communist state in South Vietnam, the United States now had the diminished objective of ending its involvement by negotiating a compromise with North Vietnam. It would also create a South Vietnam that, after U.S. withdrawal, would at least have a good change of survival against the insurgents and the ambitions of North Vietnam. This new war aim required strengthening South Vietnam's military forces so that it could eventually assume the full burden of its own defense. As this took place, U.S. forces would make a gradual withdrawal. This program also involved increasing the vigor and competence of General Thieu's government and helping it gain the firm support of its people. This political objective also required a change to give primary emphasis to the strategy of pacification, that is, keeping and expanding control of the countryside.

The army had long given support to the South Vietnamese government's strategy of pacification but never with the enthusiasm of the marines who had made it such an integral part of their strategy in their zone of operations. The army had devoted most of its resources to its raiding strategy, and the South Vietnam army had done little to forward pacification. In fact, its arrogant, insensitive, and sometimes brutal behavior toward citizens often made it effectively an ally of the Viet Cong.

Pacification needed to become the primary strategy for both the South Vietnamese and U.S. forces if General Thieu's regime was ever to be able to stand on its own feet. In his critique of General Westmoreland's raiding strategy, Lieutenant General Phillip B. Davidson called it a strategic defensive implemented by the tactical offensive. By this he presumably meant that it defended South Vietnam against conquest by the Viet Cong regulars and newly arriving North Vietnamese troops. Of course, the raids almost always involved the U.S. forces in tactically offensive operations.

On the other hand, pacification embodied the strategic offensive because it directed its effort at obtaining control of the land and people of South Vietnam, gaining their support for the government, and enabling them to defend themselves. Each displacement of Viet Cong control of a village and the establishment of government control would represent a success for this necessarily patient and thorough logistic strategy. And each such success would deprive the Viet Cong of tax revenues, recruits, food, and a place to or through which it could make an unimpeded retreat. Thus it would implement the very logistic strategy that the bombing of the North was failing to execute because it was not attacking the foe's base area. And, by occupying the enemy's base area, it could not just deprive the Communists of the base area's resources but convert those resources to the government's own use.

The marines' County Fairs exemplified the offensive persisting part of this strategy. Once the government had screened the villagers and organized effective popular forces, it was ready to integrate the village into a system of support and reinforcement by regional forces and the army. Then the defensive would predominate in carrying out pacification.

So the offensive phase typically lacked a significant degree of combat, and much of the burden of defending the conquests fell on popular and regional forces who would man the villages' rudimentary fortifications. These forces also endeavored, by good intelligence, vigilance, and patrolling, to forestall the Viet Cong and keep them at bay. As more villages succumbed to the government's pacification offensive and many contiguous communities came under the government's influence, the task of the defense would become progressively less demanding. This is why one of the modern practitioners of this very old strategy likened it to the gradual spreading of a spot of oil spilled on a piece of cloth or paper.

The exponents of pacification had failed adequately to explain the strategy to U.S. soldiers, who could not easily discern the offensive element in it. Some young soldiers, who understood it well, vitiated their exposition by patronizing their seniors in experience and rank. So some soldiers viewed the strategy as only defensive and saw it as a sacrifice of the initiative that many identified with the offensive.

As a consequence, many officers rejected the offensive persisting strategy of pacification. Yet, in spite of its aggressive image and tactically offensive character, General Westmoreland's combat raiding strategy did sacrifice the initiative. It did this because the Viet Cong's ability to avoid action prevented his raids from being able to hurt them; this meant that they had the initiative to fight, usually on the tactical defensive, when it contributed to the objectives of their strategy. At the same time, they were still on the offensive in the countryside, seeking to expand their base area by bringing more villages under their control; this was an offensive against which General Westmoreland's combat raiding strategy did not offer a good defense.

Moreover, some U.S. soldiers worried that what seemed a passive or cordon defense of the pacification program would give the enemy the initiative and so make the U.S. forces vulnerable to an attack. Because they shared this apprehension, the marines had constructed a fortified line in part of their area of operations. In having concern about being vulnerable on the defensive, many U.S. strategists seem to have overlooked the primacy of the tactical defense even when not aided by field fortifications. They also seemed to have discounted the superb strategic mobility of their own forces. This came not only from the ability to move by motor and helicopter to concentrate at any point to reinforce, but even more rapidly to bring the cavalry of the air into any combat where the terrain and weather permitted its action. In contrast with these strategists' dissatisfaction with this situation, many well-regarded commanders in earlier times would have welcomed the opportunity to fight on the defensive with such great superiority in strategic mobility.

The new U.S. commander, General Creighton W. Abrams, drew on his experience as General Westmoreland's deputy to implement the new emphasis on the pacification strategy. According to the plan, it sought security for the Vietnamese people and the expansion of areas of effective civil authority. To provide this security, the operations of the persisting logistic strategy must insulate the people from the enemy, thus also diminishing the enemy base area, sources of intelligence, and routes for covert movement.

The similarity in the ability of the Seminoles and the Viet Cong commanders to decline battle or accept it on their own terms suggests some differences and parallels. The most notable difference is in population density in the agriculturally productive lowlands where millions lived compared to the few thousand Seminoles and settlers in Florida. Yet the Viet Cong could move through their thickly settled base area with virtually the same ease as the Seminoles in their almost uninhabited space. So the communist insurgents could not only withdraw, as did the Seminoles, by moving in any direction, they also had a resource the Seminoles lacked: They could retreat by blending into the population, becoming indistinguishable from the millions of ostensibly loyal citizens.

Nevertheless, the United States and the South Vietnamese government had one powerful advantage that the generals who fought the Seminoles lacked. Although the densely populated part of Vietnam had about the same area as the Seminole's section of Florida, the U.S. and South Vietnamese forces numbered more than one hundred times as many as the U.S. troops in Florida. This meant that if the government forces concentrated large forces in a given area, they could control it, inhibit Viet Cong movement, and, as in the County Fair operations, winnow out the Viet Cong. Surrounding a village in a surprise movement had a nice parallel with a turning movement because it could trap the Viet Cong and compel them to assume the tactical offensive to fight their way out.

In General Westmoreland's combat strategy, the high population density had proved a distinct liability because the required fighting, with its heavy fire, had inevitably meant civilian casualties, which would alienate the public from the government and its U.S. ally. In fact, the Viet Cong had deliberately provoked fights to create civilian casualties for this purpose. But pacification could turn the large population into an asset. Reconciling them to the government, protecting them from the Viet Cong, giving them arms, training, and village fortifications so that they could protect themselves would change the strategic situation. It did this by increasing the ratio of government force to space and so surrounding and immobilizing every Viet Cong detachment with hostile villages protected by the fortified defense.

In addition to the South Vietnamese government's increasingly relentless offensive to pacify one village after another, General Abrams endeavored to enhance security by persistent patrolling at night as well as in the day. These patrols, like those against the Seminoles, harried the Viet Cong, disrupted their movements, and disturbed their logistic arrangements. They aided security and pacification but did not substitute for the big battle that General Abrams, like his predecessor, wished to have in order to deplete the enemy. The apparently less aggressive war did not appeal to other commanders either. One, quite exasperated with this tame sort of war with its stress on small patrols, exclaimed: "I'll be damned if I permit the U.S. Army, its institutions, its doctrine, and its traditions to be destroyed just to win this lousy war." General Abrams doubtless felt much like the combative General Zachary Taylor in trying to cope with the elusive Seminoles.

On the other hand, the change brought about by the Tet offensive did present opportunities for strategically productive combat. With the insurgents weakened by the heavy casualties of the Tet offensive combats, their base area contracted just as more troops arrived from North Vietnam. Thus the Communist forces in South Vietnam had to rely more and more on supplies from the North. This meant that many regular units moved westward toward or beyond the border with Laos and Cambodia. In these countries, which lacked the power to protect their neutrality, the Communists established depots for all sorts of supplies and kept them filled by overland transport from North Vietnam within the neutral countries over the Ho Chi Minh Trail.

By early 1970 the supply depots had assumed such importance that U.S. and South Vietnamese troops made a large raid into Cambodia against the depots in the areas named the Parrot's Beak and the Fishhook. When the Communist troops retreated rather than defend their supplies, the allies were able to capture much, including 23,000 weapons, 16,700,000 rounds of small arms, and 143,000 rounds of mortar and similar ammunition. In addition, they captured 9,000,000 daily rations, enough to supply 25,000 men for a year. Before withdrawing, the troops and their engineers destroyed the depot's elaborate facilities, including a hospital.

This success for a raiding logistic strategy slightly resembled the English settlers in Virginia raiding the Indians' corn fields and destroying their weirs. Of course, if the Viet Cong had depended on supply depots as conspicuous as cornfields and weirs, they would have lost the war long before 1970. A second such raid, into Laos in 1971, failed dismally when the Communist forces made a determined resistance and drove back the raiding South Vietnamese troops.

With a paucity of such productive logistic objectives available and the Viet Cong's defensive stance, few large combats occurred. So the war more and more focused on the strategic offensive of the pacification program: to provide security to the countryside, exclude the Viet Cong, and gain for General Thieu's government the allegiance of the people in the countryside. The Tet offensive had first given pacification a setback when the South Vietnamese army moved 36 of the 51 battalions in the country to the support of the cities assailed by the insurgents. But soon, with the resulting weakness of the Viet Cong and the return of the battalions sent away, the program made up its losses and forged ahead by the fall of 1968. The rating system used by U.S. officials indicated that three-fourths of the villages were at least relatively secure, compared with two-thirds a year earlier, before the Tet offensive.

When General Thieu took personal control of the pacification program, he gave it perhaps as important an impetus as the shift in U.S. strategy. He improved the village defenses and defenders, held elections, provided training for village administrators, and began a land redistribution program comparable to that of the Viet Cong. The heavy losses of the Tet offensive had reduced not just the numbers of the Viet Cong but their morale, and because their replacement personnel had less competence than those lost, the losses in the offensive diminished the quality also. The Viet Cong also had to rely more and more on coercion, using conscription to fill their ranks and increasing their taxes. This gave the vigorously pursued pacification offensive an opportunity to make significant progress. By the end of 1969, the rating system indicated that nine-tenths of the population lived in at least relatively secure areas. In spite of the flaws inherent in such an estimate of the situation, this represented a marked advance since 1964 and 1965 and a significant reduction in the insurgent base area.

With the contraction of the base area, more regulars had to move westward to be near the Ho Chi Minh Trail and its supplies from the remote base area. But the withdrawal of these powerful forces made the areas of existing Viet Cong control even more vulnerable to the pacification drive. So the offensive persisting logistic strategy was not only working but having a cumulative effect: Conquering the insurgents' territory reduced its base area, which decreased its forces, which diminished its ability to protect its base area, which accelerated its defeat.

THE COMMUNISTS LAUNCH A PERSISTING OFFENSIVE

While pacification was making its significant progress, the negotiations in Paris between the United States and the Communists dragged on inconclusively. Meanwhile the South Vietnamese armed forces increased in size, improved their training, and became more heavily equipped. Coinciding with this rise in strength, the United States reduced its forces in South Vietnam until, in April 1972, it had only 69,000 men remaining, 13 percent of its peak strength.

The progress of pacification and the reduction in U.S. troop strength contributed to North Vietnam's decision to take the offensive with a persisting strategy against South Vietnam. The Communists placed such decisions in the context of the three phases of revolutionary war as expounded by the victorious Chinese Communist leader, Mao Tse-tung. The first phase employed the raiding strategy characteristic of guerrillas; the third utilized a persisting strategy, the most efficient means of conquering and defending territory; and the second phase mixed raiding and persisting. They viewed operations in South Vietnam in 1966 and 1967 as a mixture and now saw the moment propitious for the third phase. In their expectation that victories by their armies might cause the collapse of General Thieu's South Vietnamese government, they envisioned the offensive as a political as well as a military strategy.

The U.S.S.R. had furnished the trucks to move and supply such an offensive and the tanks and artillery needed to match the South Vietnamese army in this respect. Yet these weapons revolutionized the logistics of North Vietnam's army. For example, the new 130-mm gun, a superb weapon that would fire as far as seventeen miles, also weighed 17,000 pounds, 140 times as much as the 82-mm mortar, long the infantry's mainstay. Not only would moving such a weapon be difficult and require much fuel, but each shell weighed 74 pounds, not counting the propelling charge. So, when the campaign began, it is not surprising that the army had not become adept at either the logistics or the use of its unfamiliar new weapons.

The strategy involved three separated offensives, in the North, Center, and South. Having sacrificed concentration in space to attack on exterior lines, the offensives used concentration in time by starting within a few days of each other. General Davidson saw this strategy as essentially political, praising it because if only one of the offensives succeeded in making large gains, it would likely so discredit the South Vietnamese government as to cause its collapse. He did not discuss the merits of concentration in space to make more likely a gain in one place.

As soon as the northern attack began on 30 March, the United States began concentrating additional aircraft to augment those available. In Vietnam and its bases in Thailand the air force had 190 planes and the navy at least that many on its two carriers off the coast. So initially the South Vietnamese air force carried the main burden of acting as the cavalry of the air, flying over 3,000 sorties in April, three quarters of those flown early in the offensive.

By the end of May, the United States had added over 200 air force fighter bombers; for some of these, only 72 hours had elapsed between their departure from the United States and action in Vietnam. Four additional carriers joined, and the number of available B-52 bombers rose from 83 to 171. The number of sorties flown in May was quadruple those of April. Additional support for the ground forces came from the navy's guns, the ships firing over 16,000 tons of shells during the six months of the campaign.

With its heavy equipment easily visible on roads, the North Vietnamese army presented an inviting target for the fighter bombers in their traditional strategic role. In tactical support these made a fine team with the B-52s, which could saturate an area with high explosives. Air action probably accounted for half of the North Vietnamese casualties and half of the tanks destroyed.

The substantial advance by the northern offensive, the first and most threatening, reflected the effect of the still cloudy weather on the cavalry of the air. The invaders tended to advance when they had the protection of clouds and halt when clear weather made them vulnerable to attack. This factor and difficulty with unfamiliar logistics contributed to the sporadic nature of the attackers' advance: four days initially, a halt for six, advance again, and so on. The contending forces were spread thinly, one division for 15 miles of front for the attackers, 19 for the defenders. But their great firepower enabled the defenders to maintain a somewhat continuous front. Thus the attackers encountered many of the difficulties of assailing a fortified defense.

After conquering Quang Tri, the northernmost province, the northern force advanced no farther as it then faced a reinforced defense and a new and very capable general. The central and southern offensives made less progress and also ended in a stalemate as they engaged in one of warfare's most difficult and costly operations, besieging cities. South Vietnamese counterattacks ultimately deprived the invaders of most of their gains.

The good, though uneven, performance of the South Vietnamese forces helps account for North Vietnam's defeat, as does the inability of its army to maintain their usual standard of operational proficiency. The commanders lacked experience with combined arms—advancing tanks, for example, without infantry support. The small units lacked the relevant tactical skill, particularly the infiltration tactics so essential for the offensive against such well-armed adversaries; the ending of the two offensives in sieges of cities deprived them of much hope of success because they encountered the fortified defense, difficult for the assailant and ideal for defenders such as the often-sedentary and indifferently motivated South Vietnamese soldier.

If combined arms on their side caused the North Vietnamese commanders problems, those with the opposing army were a calamity for the invader. The adequately controlled cavalry of the air probably doomed any offensive against South Vietnamese troops performing as well as they did. Clearly the North Vietnamese command underestimated the significance of the enemy air power when operating against heavily equipped forces dependent on a remote base area under the favorable weather conditions that prevailed for most of the campaign's six months.

THE LAST BOMBING CAMPAIGNS

With the beginning of peace negotiations most U.S. and South Vietnamese bombing of North Vietnam had stopped, but air raids continued on the Ho Chi Minh Trail, the main supply route from North to South. With the increasing importance of the remote base, this air activity assumed greater significance. But, conforming to the experience of the Korean War, it did not prove possible to interdict the supply movements with bombing alone. Even so, it did retard the flow of supplies and raised their cost by destroying some and complicating transportation.

When intelligence revealed the accumulation of supplies north of the boundary between North and South that forecast the 1972 spring offensive, U.S. aircraft raided these in December 1971 and again in February 1972. When the offensive began in April, the United States made its main effort in support of the South Vietnamese army, assailing northern troops and trying to disrupt their supplies.

It also raided the North, seeking logistic targets that the diminution of the southern base area had now given much enhanced significance. In addition the bombing had the political objective of exerting pressure to help revive the moribund peace negotiations. Since 1968, serious tensions had developed between the U.S.S.R. and China, and the United States had markedly improved its diplomatic relations with each of the Communist great powers. These consequential world political changes removed many of the earlier constraints on bombing targets in North Vietnam and did so just as they assumed major military importance. The first use of B-52 bombers against northern cities ushered in an attack on Haiphong's oil storage facilities and the accidental damage of four U.S.S.R. ships in the harbor. In early May the U.S. began mining Haiphong harbor and a program of bombing targets throughout North Vietnam.

With the expanded bombing underway and North Vietnam's offensive clearly a failure, the United States received a favorable response when it sought a resumption in the negotiations. Nevertheless, the bombing continued with the political objective of raising the cost of the war for North Vietnam and the military goal of continuing the logistic strategy of diminishing the North's ability to support the armed forces in the South.

New bombs, optically controlled or laser directed toward the target, enhanced the effectiveness of the bombing. The airmen used these "smart bombs" with success at last to assail major railroad and highway bridges. The accurate guidance also permitted the bombing of important targets in thickly populated areas without heavy civilian casualties. Mines having closed the port of Haiphong, aircraft concentrated on the rail and highway links between China and North Vietnam. But the huge inventories of supplies accumulated in North Vietnam limited the immediate effectiveness of this interdiction effort, as did North Vietnam's construction of an oil pipeline from China through Laos to South Vietnam.

The bombing campaign also faced very modern air defenses of over 200 jet fighters and 300 launching positions for high-altitude antiaircraft missiles. Aircraft escorting the bombers used electronic countermeasures to handicap the antiaircraft radar, and other airplanes made attacks against the radars themselves with the assistance of missiles that would home on a radar signal and frequently explode in contact with the radar set. Providing ground control for U.S. aircraft also improved their performance against enemy fighters. With success in the negotiations and an agreement reached by October, President Nixon suspended attacks against Hanoi and adjacent northern areas. By this time, mining the harbor and the bombing had reduced imports by 93 percent, and the flyers no longer had any profitable targets.

But almost immediately the prospects of a settlement diminished when

General Thieu vehemently objected to many parts of the agreement, and the North Vietnamese refused to alter it enough to meet any of his main objections. So in mid-December the United States suspended the negotiations and soon embarked on a bombing program designed to intimidate North Vietnam into a settlement.

To accomplish this, on 18 December B-52 bombers began raiding the Hanoi-Haiphong urban area. They attacked the usual targets and avoided heavy civilian casualties, but they bombed at night to keep civilians awake. On 26 December they raided with 120 planes carrying a bombload equivalent to 800 or 900 World War II B-17 Flying Fortresses. Further, they made this a masterpiece of concentration in time when the airplanes dropped all of their bombs within 15 minutes, thus both saturating the formidable missile defenses and giving the civilians a memorable period of noise and vibration. The attackers lost only 2 percent compared with 6 percent in an earlier raid. Altogether, in a week and a half of raids, the missiles shot down only 15 of the giant aircraft and damaged others.

By 29 December the defenders had expended all of their missiles, and the government had already asked the United States to resume negotiations. With a good basis in the October agreement and a few concessions to General Thieu, the parties easily agreed. Because the United States had not given General Thieu much substance, he received assurances of future support and some additional armaments, including enough airplanes to give South Vietnam the world's fourth largest air force. Further, he could easily see that the April-to-October bombings and the effectiveness of "smart" bombs had much extended the interval before North Vietnam could carry out reconstruction and replenish inventories so as to be able again to take the offensive against the South.

Thus, when Communist operations in the South became dependent on a remote base area, air power could make a more significant military and political contribution to the war. So the United States left Vietnam without, at least superficially, having suffered defeat in its modified objective of leaving behind a non-Communist South Vietnam with a reasonable chance of survival.

SOME OF THE ROLES OF STRATEGY IN THE WAR

At the beginning, the political acumen of the Viet Cong and their military competence had given their persisting strategy success in subduing half of South Vietnam by 1965. Then the insurgents responded to the presence of U.S. troops by adopting the political objective of fighting them to inflict enough casualties to raise the cost of the war above what the United States would pay for victory. Thus the Communists adopted a political-military strategy essentially identical in means and ends with that of the United States in its bombing of North Vietnam.

Since the U.S. forces were searching for insurgents to fight, the Viet Cong found it easy to have the desired combat. Whereas the Viet Cong had typically concentrated to assail weakness, now they took advantage of the U.S. desire to fight to concentrate to defend against strength. Although the defending Viet Cong made the maximum use of the fortified defense, the U.S. barrages made the combats absolutely more costly to the defending Communists than to their assailants. Yet because the Communist put a higher value on their war aim than did the United States on its, these combats forwarded the Communist political goal of trying to raise the cost of victory above what the United States would pay.

When the Communists' erroneous estimate of the political situation persuaded them to make the Tet offensive, they adopted concentration in time. This contrasted with the concentratons in space that had characterized their successful persisting offensive of 1960–1964. Hence concentration in time, made essential by the political rationale behind the Tet campaign, meant that military failure cost many times as much as the defeat of a single offensive based on concentration in space. Hence the losses incurred in so many tactically offensive assaults permanently weakened their military and political resources. When they then reverted to their old raiding strategy, they found their diminished forces pitted against an invigorated South Vietnamese and United States logistic persisting offensive of pacification. Their Tet offensive had brought this about by demonstrating that General Westmoreland's combat raids had failed significantly to deplete the Communists. So the Tet offensive failed twice, once in its goal of at least seriously weakening the South Vietnamese government and further by creating the conditions that induced the United States and South Vietnam to give emphasis to the more effective pacification strategy. Yet, though a military failure, the Tet offensive had the unintended political consequence of helping bring about the modification of the U.S. war aims. When the United States changed to the less ambitious war aim of withdrawal but leaving behind a viable South Vietnam, it became easier for the United States to attain its objective while adopting an objective less antithetical to North Vietnam's goal. So this change led directly to the settlement of January 1973.

With nearly as much irony, the defeat of their persisting offensive of the spring of 1972 and the destructive bombing campaign probably made the North Vietnamese willing to accept a settlement that offered them less than they would otherwise had insisted on. So this hastened the war's end and their eventual triumph over South Vietnam.

These two significant Communist defeats owed something to concentrating in time rather than concentration in space that had given success in their successful persisting offensive of 1960–1964. In 1972 they may have had less, if any, political motivation in concentrating in time, but their logistical skills and resources may not have enabled them to make a greater concentration in space than they did.

The original strategy pursued by the American army resulted from apprehension that the Viet Cong regulars and the newly arrived regiments of North Vietnamese troops could adopt a persisting strategy and finish overrunning the country. To achieve this defensive objective, General Westmoreland chose a combat raiding strategy, rather than deciding to counter the enemy's expected persisting offensive. Thus he rejected the more conventional alternatives of a persisting defense of the government-controlled countryside or a persisting offensive of pacification against the base areas recently taken by the Viet Cong. Thus U.S. strategy responded to that of the enemy—in its original selection and in its change after the Tet offensive.

In Vietnam the United States had an experience consistent with earlier campaigning within a base area, the war displaying all of the characteristics of the English and U.S. wars waged against the Indians. The dense population of some areas of Vietnam, though a marked contrast to the Indian wars, did not change the strategic situation. Rather, the population density offered an additional mode of retreat when insurgent soldiers blended with civilians.

The experience of the English colonists offered a model for success against the ascendancy of the Viet Cong, whether they used a raiding or a persisting strategy. A persisting offensive strategy, consolidated by the fortified defense, would have worked as a logistic strategy by gradually engrossing the insurgents' base area. Just as King Philip's warriors could not subsist in an area of fortified New England villages, so the pacification strategy would defeat the Viet Cong raiders.

One could speculate what the course of the war might have taken had the army followed the Marine example and initially pursued the traditional offensive logistic persisting strategy of pacification. But, if it were a mistake for General Westmoreland not to have adopted pacification, one would be tempted to refight the war mentally with a different strategy. It would then only be fair to delete Communist mistakes also, and this would pretty surely lead to a really impenetrable thicket of what ifs.

Part IV

Some Unifying Elements

Some concepts have proven to be good guides for understanding and evaluating military activity in the past. Because so many seem to have had applicability over more than two millennia in western warfare, it is tempting to view them as immutable and as pertinent to the present, and even the future, as to the past. Yet our understanding of the past changes as research adds to what we know and new questions change the significance of old knowledge. So, in view of the tentativeness of our comprehension of the past, readers should use caution in employing these unifying elements to understand the present or make hypotheses about the future.

Typically military strategists have had at least three considerations in adopting a strategy for a war or campaign. These have included political objectives, opportunities, and constraints; conflict with the hostile forces; and the effect of physical features, including climate and weather. Beyond these three considerations, military strategy has long had a number of ideas that have often guided the decisions of wise commanders. These decisions have usually had one thing in common, the criterion of winning with the least effort.

Since far more warfare has occurred on land than on the sea or in the air, people have had more experience with land warfare and have given it more thought than sea and air warfare. Thus these elements of unity give more attention to land war. Yet, in spite of the differences in tactics and logistics, most of the ideas relevant to land warfare have application to warfare at sea, a point grasped and utilized by one of the fathers of modern naval strategic thought, Alfred Thayer Mahan. And although warfare in the air differs even more from that on land, land war's more ample experience offers elements of strategy applicable to air warfare.

Chapter 11

Political Aspects

Often political or related or comparable objectives have provided Aristotle's final cause of a campaign, war, or battle. This relationship frequently affected the formal cause, the strategy. Among the objectives were religious and economic goals. Even in the absence of a political or comparable final cause, such considerations often exerted an influence on the conduct and, implicitly, the strategy of an operation. So war and politics were usually so intimately involved that adequate attention to the political aspects of military strategy could easily fill another volume. But, rather than ignore the subject entirely, here follow two points that seem to have particular relevance.

POLITICAL-MILITARY STRATEGY

Whereas military strategy sought to accomplish the war's aims by depleting the enemy's military force, political-military strategy made a direct application of military force, usually against the enemy rulers or their subjects.

Since most military actions usually had some direct effect on the hostile rulers, people, property, or morale, it is really difficult to distinguish the two strategies. That victories in the two world wars came through the depletion of the German and Japanese armed forces has made military strategy seem the usual means of ending wars. But because most wars have lacked the military decisiveness of these two as well as such complete military victories, most other wars have had far more military and political interaction.

An example of this is contact with enemy civilians. In this, the armed forces should have known whether the political objectives of the operation dictated the use of intimidation or conciliation. Each had its political advantages and disadvantages. Conciliation, for example, might fail to propitiate the enemy and instead create an impression of weakness, which could encourage an active hostility. Bullying, on the other hand, might also provoke enmity rather than encourage submission.

An incident in the Middle Ages illustrates both effects of intimidation. In 1014 the Byzantine Emperor Basil II defeated the Bulgars in the Battle of Balathista, taking 15,000 prisoners. He released the prisoners; but before he did so, he divided them into groups of 100, blinded all but one in each group, leaving him with vision in one eye so that he could lead the other 99 prisoners home. When they reached home, upon seeing the prisoners, the Bulgarian Tsar Samuel died of dismay.

By sending the prisoners home to their villages, the Emperor broadly advertised the power of the Empire and effectively cowed the Bulgars. Thus they submitted, and their lands became provinces of the Empire. But the Emperor's widely known treatment of the prisoners implanted among the Bulgars two watchwords, patience and revenge. They displayed patience for 168 years, until they gained their independence and had their revenge by attacking the Empire while it was beset by other adversaries. So in choosing intimidation, it was well to recall the possible side effect of a more dangerous hostility.

But the direct application of military force to gain political aims would usually have involved bullying only. For example, the conflict between the Arabs and Israel put the Israeli army in the position of implementing a strategy of daunting its political adversaries. For every Arab terrorist raid, Israel made one, and for every Israeli raid, the Arabs made another. For several decades this has shown the working of Newton's third law, that every action has an equal and opposite reaction.

A cursory examination of the past suggests that when a country employed military force directly for political ends, it should have tried to avoid the tactical offensive and shown wariness of pursuit unless it was clearly superior to retreat. A logistic strategy usually worked better than a combat strategy because it was less likely to provoke an active enmity. The nineteenth century provided many examples of this kind of political strategy when the great powers occupied the ports of debtor nations and collected the customs duties to reimburse their creditor citizens. Once they had seized the port, they had the advantage of fighting on the tactical defensive and usually did not have to fight at all.

The British long used their fleet to implement political-military strategy, a blockade usually proving very effective. Such blockades not only implemented a logistic strategy but were normally nonviolent because merchant ships seldom resisted warships.

Such a political strategy proved its worth in 1962, when the U.S.S.R.

was establishing ballistic missiles in Cuba. The U.S. naval forces intercepted the merchant ships carrying the missiles. This action and the potency of a blockade, together with the potential power of a superior navy against the island nation of Cuba, nullified Cuba as a missile base and facilitated a favorable political settlement.

The Persian Gulf confict of 1990–1991 also illustrates an effective-military political strategy. The military part came through an embargo and a bloodless blockade imposed by the overwhelmingly superior Coalition navies. To counter Iraq's possible response of using its superior military force to seize Saudi Arabia's oil fields, the Coalition landed forces in Arabia and concentrated to protect Saudi Arabia and its oil wealth from an invasion by Iraq. Since Iraq made no attack, the troops did not need to fight, and, if they did, they would have had the advantage of the tactical defensive. This political strategy created a situation that the Coalition, except Kuwait, might have found comfortable, and Iraq uncomfortable, for years, even decades. And, except for the freeing of Kuwait, that was the situation that resumed after the end of active military operations.

Clearly a logistic persisting strategy, particularly at sea, accomplished its objective well, and the tactical defensive posture has worked satisfactorily on land. But raids have traditionally provided the principal means of political intimidation, and those by air still have much appeal because of their simplicity and relatively low cost. Yet they do not have a good record of success. The negligible political results of British and German bombing of each other's cities in World War II illustrates this. So raids also seem to have made easy the operation of Newton's third law more often than has a persisting logistic strategy by sea or land. A recent illustration is that the U.S. air raid on Libya in 1986 could well have provided a motive for planting the bomb that exploded on the U.S. passenger plane that crashed in Lockerbie, Scotland, a few years later.

POLITICAL EFFECTS OF MILITARY OPERATIONS

The course of military operations, including their length and cost, have affected the official and public estimation of the probable length and cost of wars, the likelihood of victory, and the war's other possible results. To illustrate, the prolonged deadlock of World War I affected opinion in various ways. When the expectation of a short war turned into the realization of a long war of unprecedented scale, intensity, and cost, the belligerents compensated themselves by expanding their war aims. For example, in March 1918, in their peace with Russia, Germany and Austria-Hungary took control of eastern Europe, including the Ukraine and Russia's Polish territory. This contrasted with the war's original territorial objective, which included only, at most, Austro-Hungarian annexation of Serbia.

Germany's response to a few days of combat illustrates another reaction

Figure 11.1
Elastic Demand

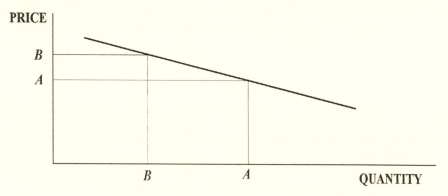

to military events. In August 1918, when British troops made an exceptionally rapid and deep advance at the beginning of Marshal Foch's second
offensive, Germany's principal strategist, General Ludendorff, abruptly
concluded that Germany must make peace.

There is an analogy between consumer demand for goods and services
and popular and official attitudes toward a war, its cost, the desirability of
its objectives, the consequences of defeat, and the likelihood of victory. The
economic concept of elasticity of demand is helpful in making this comparison between views of a war and of products for sale. Graphs are useful
in understanding this. They plot the quantity of the product demanded on
the horizontal axis and the price on the vertical. In this case quantity will
stand for victory and price for the war's human, financial, and other costs.

Elastic demand is very responsive to price. Thus increasing the price will
result in a more than proportionate reduction in demand. Figure 11.1 illustrates a 30 percent price increase from A to B resulting in a 50 percent
fall in demand.

Inelastic demand produces the opposite result. Figure 11.2 illustrates very
inelastic demand where a doubling of the price from A to B results in only
a minute decrease in demand. The demand for salt is the usual illustration
of a product with such an inelastic demand.

A graph of the colonists' demand for victory in 1675–1676 against King
Philip's warriors' raids would surely reveal a quite intelastic demand, reflecting that many felt that the war had put the existence of the colony at
stake. Figure 11.3 provides a graph of the colonists' hypothetical demand.

The natives' demand for victory turned out to be relatively elastic after
the colonists abandoned their policy of killing prisoners or selling them
into slavery. Figure 11.4 graphs the natives' demand for victory after the
colonists had raised the relative price of victory by reducing the cost of
defeat.

Figure 11.2
Inelastic Demand

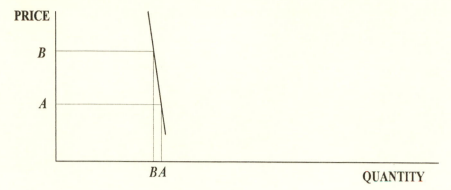

Figure 11.3
Colonists' Demand for Victory

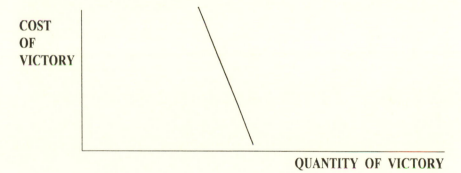

The same graph would reflect the end of the Great Sioux War when the United States gave up its war aim that the Sioux go on a reservation. When the United States amended its demand for unconditional surrender in 1945 by conceding the continuation of the Emperor, it had a similar effect in accelerating the end of the war with Japan.

The United States in its war against Japan in the 1940s doubtless had an inelastic demand curve resembling that of the colonists in King Philip's War. But the United States in the Vietnam War is another example of an elastic demand for victory like King Philip's followers. Expecting an easy victory over a small nation without elaborately equipped armed forces, the United States had a good popular and official consensus in favor of entering the ground war. But this consensus would prove to be a very elastic demand while North Vietnam had a very inelastic commitment to uniting the country under its leadership.

When events disappointed the Americans, who expected an early victory

Figure 11.4
King Philip's Demand for Victory

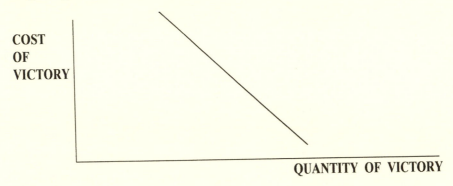

and so increased the price of winning, much opinion turned against the expensive war, not seeing the objective as worth the enhanced cost. At the same time, the extirpation of the Communists in Indonesia reduced the value of victory by undermining the assumption of the vulnerability of Southeast Asian countries to Communists; this so-called domino effect had been the most important presumption upon which the rationale for waging the war had rested. Nor could the United States emulate the belligerents in World War I and add enough to its war aims to compensate for the added costs; there were no new desirable objectives attainable by fighting in Vietnam.

Chapter 12

The Principles of War
and Some Related Ideas

Political considerations entered strategy to harmonize military operations with the aims of the war or campaign, to minimize the number and strength of adversaries, and to gain material and moral support. The principles of war and related ideas had almost exclusively to do with combat operations. Belligerents used combat not just to deplete hostile armed forces directly but to implement logistic as well as persisting and raiding strategies to implement military or political-military strategy.

The principles of war attempted to present in succinct form some of the most effective methods and soundest practices exhibited by a study of the military past. So though the list may seem a miscellany, all identify ideas for the formulation, evaluation, and execution of military or political-military strategy.

THE PRINCIPLES OF WAR

Formal lists of the principles of war, that is, characteristics of well-conducted operations, evolved during the nineteenth century and have existed since early in the twentieth. The U.S. Army currently recognizes nine. Three of these should characterize the management of any enterprise, civil or military. The principle of unity of command enunciates perhaps the oldest concept in management: Someone needs to be in charge. The principle of the objective is equally elementary and fundamental: Have a clear idea of your mission and how you are trying to accomplish it. Simplicity is an important principle, experience having shown that complex plans often fail because of the difficulties of coordination and execution, a generalization likely also to apply to civilian enterprises. The German military scholar Karl von Clausewitz coined the term *friction* for the many different causes for delays and other failures of plans to work as expected. The popularity of the facetious aphorism, Murphy's Law—if something can go wrong, it will—has given wide currency to a major cause of friction. By reducing the number of things that could go wrong, simplicity tended to reduce friction.

Also familiar in industry and commerce is the principle of security. This means keeping from the enemy knowledge of your plans, dispositions, and activities and includes protecting yourself and facilitating your own operations by excellent intelligence of the enemy's capabilities and dispositions. The principle of the offensive asserts the indispensability of the offensive to military operations. This implies its need on the defensive as well. Without the offensive, at least as a potentiality, the adversary would automatically have the initiative.

The last four have such intrinsic interrelationships as to compose parts of a whole. Maneuver does not just affirm that movement is essential to military operations, it directs its use to gain an advantage over the enemy. The principle of mass, or concentration, is the inverse of that of economy of force, which requires employing the minimum force so as to have the maximum available for concentration in space. And, finally, the principle of surprise, like the others, enjoins the least effort because surprise is essential to assailing weakness or being strong on the defensive where the enemy expects weakness.

Implied with the principles of mass, surprise, and economy of force are some related concepts not included among the principles of war. Among these is military behavior that has as its metaphor Newton's third law— every action has an equal and opposite reaction. It is a companion of these because distraction often depends upon it, and distraction frequently provides the means of gaining surprise, economizing on force, and facilitating concentration by drawing the adversary's attention to the wrong place.

The importance of surprise makes clear the supreme value of good intelligence. Illustrative of this is another facetious aphorism, Kelly's Law— the belief in the irony that something will not occur if you are ready for it and surely will if you are not. The usual illustration is that it will not rain unless you have forgotten your umbrella. In warfare the working of Kelly's Law would mean that you dealt with an adversary who, having perfect intelligence, never attacked where you were ready, and was consistently prepared for your attacks, and always assailed you where or when you were unready. Consequently significantly better intelligence would usually forestall being attacked where weak or having your own offensive meet a prepared opponent.

Concentration also implies the concept of a reserve, an uncommitted force available to exploit an offensive opportunity or to concentrate against strength to make an adequate defense. Such a reserve may be subtracted, that is, held back in a convenient location for commitment as the need or opportunity arises. But any force not irrevocably committed to action also constitutes a reserve. Thus a reserve would provide an insurance policy against surprise.

The Allied plans and preparations for the landing in Normandy well illustrated the application of these principles. In spite of its obvious importance, unity of command has often suffered neglect, as, for example, in the United States having two commands in the war in the Pacific. But the Normandy campaign had, under General Eisenhower, complete unity of command of the British, American, Canadian, and many other forces and of the separate armies, navies, and air forces. The objective had received such careful study that the plan projected operations for a year after the landing. Such a plan could hardly be simple, but by prescribing only one landing from the Atlantic and one from the Mediterranean, it adhered well to the principle of simplicity.

Security received meticulous and quite successful attention, and of course the operation was an offensive. Crossing such large forces over water perhaps constituted the most complex maneuver ever attempted. The original plan called for concentration in time of the landing from the Atlantic and the Mediterranean, but concentration in space and economy of force dictated the delay of the Mediterranean landing so that the one in Normandy could use its landing craft. The operation attained surprise, in part due to the elaborate distraction created by an imitation army apparently poised on the English coast ready to land near Calais.

The Allies began with ample reserves, troops for whom there was no room on ships or in the initial landing areas. And throughout they had the ideal reserve, their immense fighter bomber force. These were in action every day; but never irrevocably committed, they were equally available to use their speed and range to act as a reserve by concentrating anywhere in the theater of action.

For the most part, concentration in the principles of war meant concentration in space. But the concentration in time of simultaneous advances could often have achieved a comparable result. The Allies had aimed at concentration in time in France in the summer of 1944 when they projected simultaneous landings from the Atlantic and the Mediterranean. Had they achieved this, a German concentration against either landing would have made them proportionately more vulnerable on the other front.

Nevertheless, in most campaigns concentration in space seems to have eclipsed concentration in time. But, if concentration in time receives a broader construction, it was present in most offensive operations in the form of coordination of all activity to promote the success of the concentration in space. Thus the phony army and the Normandy invasion's other distraction efforts were coordinated and occurred simultaneously with the preparations for the Normandy landing, the operation itself, and the campaign until the St. Lô breakthrough demonstrated to the Germans that there was no other Atlantic landing in prospect. So, typically, good commanders have coordinated all resources to support the main effort, whether offensive or defensive. Hence the principles of war did not prescribe action so much as provide a convenient and important checklist for evaluating campaigns in the past and for checking present military plans. But they did not exhaust the list of ideas that have proved useful for understanding military operations and giving guidance to commanders.

INITIATIVE

The definition of initiative used in this book is rather old-fashioned. It differs from that currently used by the U.S. Army, whose meaning resembles that employed in civil life: the attributes of energy and enterprise in the conduct of business. In spite of its importance, the initiative does not readily fit among the principles of war. The precautions of security or the movements to concentrate in space are under the control of the commander, but he can only rarely act so as to make his antagonist unable to attack him while retaining his ability to assail his foe.

Nonetheless, the concept of being able to act against an enemy who cannot act against you has a close relation to the principle of economy of force in that the initiative may represent a nearly total economy of force. Thus the initiative given to the Allies for the Normandy invasion by the command of the sea, and likewise conferred in all Allied Pacific operations after 1942, permitted virtually an absolute economy of force that made all land forces available for the offensive.

In that the initiative and economy of force have a close connection brings both into relationship with the fortified defense. So when an army fortified itself, it added to its offensive as well as defensive strength. It did this by substituting fortifications for some of the men and weapons needed to defend the area if it were left unfortified. Thus this saving through fortifying released these mobile combat forces for concentration elsewhere. And to the degree that fortification made the area stronger against an enemy attack, it bestowed the initiative on the army that built the fortifications.

A successful distraction could confer the initiative if it made the adversary feel so threatened by an apparently impending attack that he committed his reserves to resisting it. This would eliminate the possibility of an offensive and enable the successful practitioner of the distraction to economize on his forces and to concentrate fully for his attack.

A turning movement could also yield the initiative, once it was successfully in progress. When the turning force was moving convincingly toward the adversary's rear, it usually possessed the initiative because the defender could, reasonably, do nothing other than attempt to extricate himself from his perilous situation. In Normandy, in acting as if they had the initiative by attempting to drive through to Avranches and cut Patton's communications, the Germans only increased their losses to the Allied turning movement.

Often the offensive seemed to grant the initiative, a good example being the German Ardennes offensive of December 1944 and the resulting Battle of the Bulge. Certainly resisting the attack did absorb the Allied reserves and so removed any major threat by these forces to the German front. But the Germans could not take advantage of this because, with their offensive, they were already engaged in exploiting the initiative that the Allies had given them earlier.

ATTRITION

In addition to the initiative, the idea of attrition is absent from the principles of war. Although attrition, the gradual wearing away of the armed forces, has received attention as a type of strategy, all military operations, including troop movements, involve attrition. And because depletion of hostile forces is the aim of military strategy, attrition is hardly a distinct strategy. The concept does not harmonize well with least effort, and typically commanders have used it as a last resort.

It usually has a distinct implication of keeping account of relative losses in military operations and comparing them with the belligerents' ability to continue to suffer them. A strategy of attrition would be one of cheerfully incurring combat or logistic losses when confident that the enemy was losing more. But the combatants must compare both of their losses with their ability to sustain them.

When General Eisenhower rejected the proposal of a logistic strategy to attempt to capture the German Ruhr industrial area in favor of "killing Germans," he doubtless implicitly thought that the Allies' superior manpower and material resources more than offset the heavy losses they would encounter on the offensive under such adverse conditions. This would conform to the strategy of attrition. The comparative idea is essential to the concept. For example, during the Vietnam War, a calculation indicated that it cost the United States $9.60 to inflict $1.00 worth of loss on North Vietnam. But this was a favorable ratio because the United States was more than 9.6 times as rich as North Vietnam, even counting in the aid North Vietnam received from China and the U.S.S.R.

The comparative concept requires a refinement that this example has already implicitly illustrated. The relevant losses could not be based on the physical or economic ability to bear or pay them only, but on the percentage of those resources that each belligerent was willing to commit. To illustrate—if a poor country should use a $1,000,000 cruise missile to demolish a $1,000,000 building of its 50-percent-richer enemy, it would have suffered a defeat in attrition. But, if the poorer country had such an attachment to its war aims that it would, compared to its richer adversary, spend twice the percentage of its resources to win, the use of the missile would represent a victory for attrition.

The case of the Vietnam war parallels this illustration. Because, compared with the United States' elastic demand for victory, the Vietnamese nationalists and Communists had a very inelastic demand, the United States incurred comparatively higher costs than the Vietnamese.

OFFENSE AND DEFENSE

Attack and defense were quite symmetrical, concentration being the motif of both, with concentration in space the more common. Distraction had its value in inducing an opponent to concentrate in the wrong place. The Japanese carrier fleet, which drew Admiral Halsey and the main American fleet away from Leyte Gulf, admirably illustrated such successful distraction.

The reserve offered another tool of concentration. Some commanders thought of a reserve only as a force held back for later commitment when needed and more frequently associated it with the defensive rather than the offensive. Napoleon's operations showed most clearly that any force not irrevocably committed to combat was a reserve. On the defense, he typically dispersed his units and only concentrated them when the enemy had acted, all of his forces thus functioning as a reserve. Before Napoleon's campaigns had demonstrated this approach, most commanders using such dispersions, then called cordons, did not clearly see them as potential reserves nor envision the rapid concentration characteristic of Napoleon.

Reserves showed themselves equally valuable on the offensive by providing the resources for concentrating against enemy weakness.

The turning movement into an adversary's rear usually constituted the ideal objective of an offensive concentration. It had a significant logistic requirement, however, in that, to block an opponent's communications and retreat, the turning force had to have its own source of supplies to enable it to remain on the enemy's communications and fight a defensive battle. The Allied forces that landed in New Guinea at Hollandia and so turned the Japanese at Wewak had secure water communications. These enabled them to wait as long as necessary to repel the Japanese army's effort to recover its supply line.

In the flank position, the defense had a maneuver that had the same attributes as the turning movement. A retreating army might establish a flank position by leaving behind a force on the flank of its adversary's advance. To prevent this detachment from assailing its flank or moving into its rear, the army on the offensive had either to halt or weaken its main force by detailing troops to establish a defense on their flank. Clearly the flank position in operational strategy had the same advantages as cross-fire in tactics.

Whereas the offensive made use of the defensive when it economized on forces to facilitate an offensive concentration, the defensive employed the offensive in the form of the counterattack. More prevalent in tactical than strategic situations, the counterattack in operational strategy had the same advantages as in tactics: catching the enemy disposed for the offensive rather than the defensive and usually otherwise unprepared to defend. A successful counterattack could defeat an offensive, recover lost ground, or inflict serious casualties on an attacker. The successful Chinese offensive in North Korea showed this very clearly.

The World War I opening campaigns in France illustrate most of the elements of operational strategy: the turning movement, the two types of defensive reserves, effective use of the flank position, concentration in space and time, and a successful counteroffensive.

The Germans began their operations with an attempt to turn the French by sending three large armies through neutral Belgium so as to go around the flank of the French armies and into their rear. The French generalissimo, General Joseph Joffre, had prepared for this by posting one army so that it could move rapidly to cover the Belgian frontier and have support from an adjacent army. Thus he had held back troops in reserve to deal with a turning movement if the Germans used it. Meanwhile he assumed the offensive along the German border.

But Joffre had not prepared adequately to deal with the exceptionally powerful turning movement by the three German armies coming through Belgium. These drove back the French army before them as well as the small British army.

Having already used the troops he had held back in reserve, Joffre created new reserves by stripping divisions from the armies on his right along the German frontier, moving them rapidly westward on the excellent French railways, and there creating two new armies to strengthen those opposing the German turning movement. He had made these reserves of units not so engaged with the Germans that they could not disengage and entrain for new assignments. Joffre placed the new 9th Army of General Foch in front of the advancing Germans and the other, the 6th, far to the west where it would be on the German's flank as they continued their movement. To command this army in the flank position, Joffre called from retirement the capable General Michel Maunoury.

When Joffre had finished deploying his reserves, he began a counterattack against the German turning force. When Maunoury made his unexpected attack from his flank position, he threatened to turn the German turning movement. The German army on the flank reacted to this assault by moving to defend itself by facing Maunoury. But, in doing this, it left a huge gap between it and its adjacent German army. Then, as part of Joffre's counterattack by five armies, the British and a French army advanced into this gap. This dangerous situation precipitated the German retreat from this battle, which had involved nearly a million men on a 60-mile front along the course of the Marne River. So reserves assuming a flank position and also counterattacking elsewhere had halted and driven back the German turning movement.

This famous campaign that ended in the Battle of the Marne well exemplified the uses of operational strategy and the role of attack and defense between adversaries pursuing persisting strategies. As in most instances of the opposition of persisting strategies, the strategic defensive dominated. So, although the Germans outnumbered the French 2,000,000 to 1,300,000, Joffre's capably conducted defense prevailed over the well-conceived German turning movement.

This campaign also included a concentration in time as well as space. The German offensive depended on a large concentration in space to conduct its turning movement, but, when the Germans decided also to make a serious offensive along the Franco-German frontier, they added concentration in time when this offensive coincided with the approach of their turning movement to the vicinity of Paris.

Since Joffre had used his interior line of operations to move troops from the frontier to halt the turning force, the German simultaneous attack would face a weakened adversary. But the French armies on the frontier stopped the German frontal attack with the aid of field and permanent fortifications and the uneven terrain, particularly a line of wooded hills. Thus they had a better opportunity to conduct a strong defense than the Germans confronting the Allies' counteroffensive on comparatively level ground.

So the fortified defense and other physical features enabled the French concentration in space to defeat the improvised German concentration in time. Concentration in time had failed the U.S. forces in the Great Sioux War when the natives used concentration in space on interior lines to defeat first Crook and then Custer. On the other hand, it doubtless would have succeeded had the Allies made their Mediterranean landing simultaneously with that in Normandy. Though unplanned, concentration in time did win when the American Central Pacific advance saved the simultaneous landing on Biak, near New Guinea, from the attack of an overwhelming Japanese concentration. The difficulties of coordinating separate forces long made concentration in space preferable to concentration in time.

None of these instances of concentration in space on interior lines exhibits the value of assailing the weaker of two opponents first because of the greater likelihood of gaining a decisive victory over the weaker. The second concentration, against the stronger, could then employ virtually the whole force, and so give the best opportunity of defeating the stronger. Assailing the weaker yielded this advantage not only when engaging forces on the land, sea, or air, but against two countries in a hostile coalition.

The 1914 campaign illustrates the traditional ascendancy of the persisting strategic defensive over the offensive. But an offensive raiding strategy often overmatched the persisting defensive. Yet, formidable as they were, raiders could only function when they had relatively unhampered movement. This lack of restraint enabled them to move in any number of directions, making it fairly easy for them to arrive unexpectedly. Since raiders needed to have no commitment to assailing a specific objective, they had another opportunity for surprise and so to find their adversary weak.

Further, having no need to retrace their route of advance, they could depart in any direction. This made their interception on their withdrawal as difficult as on their advance. But raiders long depended on their ability to move at least as rapidly as their adversaries. Yet, even if pursuit were faster than retreat, raiders might still strike with surprise and accomplish the combat or logistic objective of their raid. But they would have difficulty withdrawing without engaging in unwelcome combat. The strategic bombing of Germany illustrated raiding under disadvantageous conditions: German ground observers and radar warned of the raiders' coming, and fighter planes—faster than the bombers—intercepted and engaged them.

The raids in King Philip's War exemplified skill in their conduct and their effectiveness against a well-organized persisting defense of Massachusetts villages with their garrison houses, well-prepared militia, and mounted as well as foot patrols and reserves. The colonists rarely knew the direction of the raiders' approach, and the patrols never knew their route of ingress or egress. Not only did this uncertainty baffle the defenders, but in the event the English guessed the raiders' way, the natives could change the objective of their raids or the itineraries of their retreats. This gave them unrivaled opportunities to attain surprise and strike the defenders where they were weakest. Although King Philip's warriors failed in the objective of their political-military strategy to make life so difficult for the colonists that they departed for England, they achieved as much as their slender resources made possible.

The success of the Viet Cong before 1961 demonstrated the power of raiding to implement a political military strategy, and the 2,500 Viet Cong assassinations in 1960 show one of the ways a raiding strategy could implement political intimidation. But they did not face an adamant, fortified opposition comparable to that of the New England settlers.

When Alexander the Great faced raiders, he aimed to inhibit their movement by increasing the ratio of force to space. His method, to fortify and garrison all transportation junctions, did not merely impede the raiders' movements but conferred upon the defenders greater strategic mobility because their forces could move through the fortified focal points while their foes would have had to go around them. To have gradually filled a country with strategic hamlets would have implemented the same persisting strategy against raiders.

When raiders could not find a base in the area in which they raided, the defenders endeavored either to cut them off from their base area or to attack the base area itself, or a key part of it. The Allies also did this when they conquered the French and Belgian channel coast to capture the launch bases of the German V-1 flying bombs attacking Britain. At the same time, bombers raided German production facilities for these and the V-2 rockets. Naturally these efforts were not as effective as conquering the enemy's base area, particularly in the case of the virtually bomb-proof submarine docking facilities on the French coast.

Because of the brevity of raids and the transitory presence of raiders on the ground, many raiders could often carry their own supplies and so did not need to operate within a base area or have continuous links with a remote base. Yet their base area offered their only vulnerability and the sole aspect of their situation in which they did not have the initiative. The Virginia colonists immediately perceived this and adopted the logistic raiding strategy of destroying the natives' corn in the fields and smashing their weirs for catching fish.

This successful logistic strategy employed raids and so countered raids with a raiding strategy. But a persisting logistic strategy would have worked well to cut off supplies had the settlers or the army had enough military force to occupy so much territory. In this case the offensive would be the best defensive. This persisting logistic strategy had many applications in the past and was a contributor to the English success in Virginia. As they advanced and cleared land for agriculture, the colonists drove back some natives and converted others into allies and dependents. The settlers secured the fruit of their persisting offensive with the fortified defense of stockaded plantation houses and even by palisading bends in the rivers and an entire peninsula. This steady, persisting advance resembled the pacification practiced in South Vietnam and elsewhere, but the raids against native crops and weirs had more importance than the raids against Viet Cong depots or those by air against North Vietnam.

These historical events demonstrate the comparative superiorities of raiding and persisting strategies. As shown by the operational success of King Philip's raids, they were usually stronger than a defensive persisting strategy, but, as illustrated by the colonists' penetration of the native base area, unlikely to halt a persisting offensive. Raiders usually had, and needed, the initiative and were rarely vulnerable unless they had base areas that, like the native Americans in every case, were exposed to a logistic strategy implemented either by a raiding or a persisting offensive.

Of course the ultimate raider was the long-range ballistic missile. It usually defied interception and could strike any target. But without a nuclear warhead, it could do little more damage than a single bomb. This meant that it rarely had more than political significance. The German V-2 rocket of World War II and its descendant, the Scud missile of the Persian Gulf conflict, illustrate their capabilities as raiders and the limited destructive effect of their nonnuclear warheads.

COMBINATION, COMPLEMENTARITY, AND SUBSTITUTION

In warfare, as in other human endeavors, combination has played an important part. The most obvious example of combination is the weapon system itself. The bow of the Indians who confronted the Englishmen in Virginia was part of a weapon system superior to the settler and his gun in rate and accuracy of shooting. But the colonists could not have used the bow effectively because they lacked the natives' skill, acquired by years of use in hunting. So the native and the bow had a complementary relationship, and the substitution of an Englishman for the Indian would have spoiled the weapon system by turning the bow into a feeble, inaccurate weapon. In World War II the Japanese had this experience in combining good airplanes with inadequately trained pilots.

The complementary relationship, not just in creating weapon systems but also between tactical weapon systems, has provided a foundation for tactics for several millennia. Thus armored vehicles vulnerable to attack by airplanes or helicopters like to have the company of air defense weapons. For example, to accompany armored vehicles and all troop movements, the U.S.S.R.'s army had several self-propelled antiaircraft missiles as well as radar-controlled, self-propelled, quadruple 23-mm guns. The combination of armored vehicles and self-propelled air defense weapons could care for each other, the armored vehicles doing their part by protecting the vulnerable antiaircraft weapons from ground attack.

The complementary relationships characterized strategy as well, the principles of war providing the most obvious application of this idea; only by attention to all of the principles would commanders succeed in implementing their theme of concentration against weakness on the offensive and strength on the defensive.

Tactical combination of arms, long the foundation of warfare on land, had a parallel in the combination of land, sea, and air power. This would hardly need mention had not many prominent students of the strategy of warfare on land overlooked the role of sea power, and some proponents of sea power vastly overstated the influence of the command of the sea. In the twentieth century, enthusiasts for air power urged that they were both wrong, air power being able to win wars unaided. On the other hand, combination of air and land power created the immensely powerful cavalry of the air.

This restored in a far more powerful form cavalry's traditional strategic role in reconnaissance and raiding enemy supplies and communications.

The strategic impact of superiority in cavalry of the air played a major part in Allied victories in World War II and the Persian Gulf conflict and gave a powerful advantage in the Korean and Vietnam wars. With the improvement in the accuracy of the fighter bombers' weapons and the advent of the helicopter, the cavalry of the air now had a more important tactical role.

At sea, the combination of air power with sea power made a tactical revolution in the form of the aircraft carrier and created a new dominant naval weapon system; air power on land, when using appropriate aircraft and tactics, gave the land control of much of the sea. Now the guided missile at sea is beginning to substitute for aircraft based on land or carriers. This illustrates, as does control of the sea by shore- or sea-based aircraft, that substitution is as important as combination.

The use of air power independently rather than in combination to implement a political and logistic raiding strategy did not change warfare as much as its advocates expected. The nuclear warhead, because of its ability to have one bomb substitute for successful raids by thousands of airplanes with ordinary explosives, then made the political and logistic raiding strategy dominant. But the nuclear intercontinental ballistic missile, nearly invulnerable to interception, has substituted for aircraft in this role.

So, overall, the airplane has thus far had more effect in combination with land or sea power than acting independently. But even at sea, missiles have begun to intrude on the aircraft's tactical role as the fleet's and the shore's long-range firepower. But because aircraft carry and launch missiles, substitution and combination go hand in hand.

Land tactics also illustrated combination and substitution well in the case of defense against an attack by tanks. Tanks themselves, if they had good cover behind a rise in the ground, could offer a powerful defense against a tank attack; but so could infantry armed with the wire-guided antitank missile. For a number of reasons a combination of the two was likely to afford a better defense than all of one or the other. The terrain might not have provided cover for enough tanks but would offer an ample number of positions for infantrymen and their missiles. Still, a defender might not wish to dispense with tanks if only because they could help deliver a powerful counterattack.

Normally a commander had some latitude in his choice of combinations of missiles and tanks. He could even array the workable blends on the illustrated curve, called by economists an indifference curve. The combination of missiles and tanks made a curved line because of the operation of the law of diminishing marginal utility. The fewer tanks a commander had, the more value he would place upon each because of their versatility. At the other extreme of the mix, the value of the missiles would increase because there were good fields of fire that only an infantryman with a missile could utilize.

Figure 12.1
Indifference Curve of Combinations of Two Weapon Systems and Its Cost-Ratio Tangent

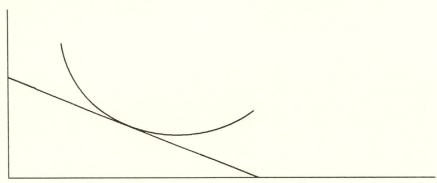

When armies (or customers for any substitutable goods) purchased such weapons initially, price would have had much to do with deciding the relative numbers bought. This is shown in Figure 12.1 by the straight line, the angle of which reflects the relative price of two substitutable weapon systems. Since military judgment had already decided that any of the blends described by the curve were equally effective for antitank defense, relative price dictated the choice among the equally desirable combinations. Here least expense equates with the strategic principle of least effort.

On the field of potential battle the decision lacked such simplicity. The cost of using a tank or missile-armed soldier had no price tag but did have a cost in that the commander could not use it for another competing tactical mission. Thus a commander would have had to compare such considerations as antitank defense on several avenues of approach and the need for tanks as a reserve in another place. Meanwhile, a commander at a higher level might have found what he viewed as a more valuable employment for many of the tanks and antitank missiles.

World War II could have offered a comparable decision in military strategy that would again illustrate that the cost of a weapon system was not just money but also the other uses to which a commander might have applied it. Clearly many of the resources in labor and materials used by the United States to build the huge B-29 bombers and provide and train the men to operate them might have gone, for instance, to support a different logistic raiding strategy against Japan. Instead of inaugurating the aerial raiding strategy of bombing factories, refineries, ports, and shipyards, the United States could have reinforced the success of the submarine logistic raiding strategy.

If such an assessment had taken place in 1943 and the sailors and the airmen could have agreed on judgment of the worth of each kind of raid, they would have made military decisions as to the best combination of raiders to do the most logistic harm to Japan's military power. This might have included any decision ranging from fewer submarines and an even bigger B-29 bomber program to a B-29 program limited to mine-laying, particularly in the Inland Sea, and a few other activities to supplement and complete the effectiveness of the augmented submarine raids. Commanders in the field needed to make the same kinds of military decisions about combination of weapons already in existence rather than, as in the submarine/airplane hypothetical example, those still unmade.

In this case, the hypothetical strategic choice involved two logistic raiding strategies. When General Eisenhower chose to substitute the combat strategy of killing Germans for the logistic strategy of capturing the Ruhr, he made a much more distinct choice but one that also evaluated the comparative efficacy and resource requirements of each.

But the two strategies still involved much overlapping. Thus had he chosen the Ruhr objective, he would still have employed a combat strategy and so have killed Germans as a by-product of the logistic strategy. Almost any military strategy required combat to attain its objective, and General Eisenhower's combat strategy also resulted in conquering German territory. Thus his combat strategy diminished, though modestly, the resource base available to support the German armed forces.

So combat strategy depleted enemy forces as a by-product of implementing a logistic strategy; and usually territorial gains and logistic results came from the carrying out of a combat strategy. This simultaneous operation of more than one strategy also happens by design. Thus the Virginia colonists utilized a logistic persisting strategy in conquering the natives' land and making some of them dependent allies while also employing a raiding logistic strategy against their crops and fish catches. Against Germany in World War II, the Allies used two logistic strategies, persisting with a sea blockade and raiding with strategic bombing. Simultaneously they pursued a combat strategy against the German armies, one that also won major logistic victories, such as the liberation of France and the U.S.S.R. capture from Germany of the Romanian oil fields.

Combinations of weapon systems, even such as cavalry of the air and artillery, rarely produced significant overlapping of function. Artillery performed the tactical role far better, and aircraft properly specialized in what it could do best, strategic raids against troop and supply movements. But there were notable instances of substitution, such as Allied bombing adding much to the effect of the artillery for the St. Lô breakthrough in 1944. With comprehensive strategy, such clear complementary relationships have rarely appeared, duplication and substitution being more common.

THE LAW OF DIMINISHING RETURNS

Just as the economics of consumption offered helpful parallels for understanding the political demand for victory and added a perspective to the strategy of attrition, so the economics of production can contribute a little to our comprehension of the art of war. Long ago, economists noticed an effect in production that they called the law of diminishing returns. This happened when producers used too much of one factor of production.

For example, if ten men with ten shovels were digging a ditch, the addition of an eleventh man might be very productive. Lacking a shovel, the project foreman might use him to give the other men a break, which might increase their productivity by more than the cost of the additional man. A twelfth man without a shovel might be as productive as the eleventh if he worked at increasing the productivity of the eleven by fetching beer or other refreshment. But eventually more men without shovels would add less and less to digging the ditch until they added nothing, and then as the idlers distracted the men digging or got in their way, they would actually retard the progress of the work and reduce output. Clearly the project would suffer diminishing returns to additional increments of labor but could then have benefited considerably by having more shovels also.

Such a situation of inappropriate proportions of production resources often occurred in warfare—an army, for instance, having too much infantry compared to its number of cavalry. In December 1941 both the American and Japanese navies found that they had too many battleships and cruisers compared to the number of aircraft carriers in their fleets. The United States quickly diminished this imbalance by substituting ten small carriers for ten cruisers in the building program. Naturally, similar disproportions occurred throughout the war. For example, the British and Americans found that in 1944 they lacked sufficient landing craft to carry out their plan for using concentration in time in their invasion of France and, comparatively, had a surfeit of aircraft.

The same happened in the strategy for the defeat of Japan when the Allies applied two raiding logistic strategies, by submarines and airplanes, while pushing their persisting strategy aimed at a tight blockade. This resulted in much duplication of effort. In fact, Japan, disarmed at sea and in the air by the three logistic strategies, was to endure a superfluity of defeat by the application of a combat strategy of invasion by ground forces to engage parts of its only remaining military force, the army. If, in fact, the resources applied to the defeat of Japan suffered from diminishing returns compared to those directed against Germany, the Allies might have made a faulty decision in the concentration of their forces against the two adversaries.

Chapter 13

Some Factors Affecting Strategic Choices and Outcomes

Choice typically began with the objective, or Aristotle's final cause, of the war or campaign. The objective should guide the initial decision between a military or military-political strategy, or a combination of the two. The objective also usually influenced the selection of defensive or offensive operations, as well as the choice between a combat or a logistic strategy and whether to implement with a raiding or a persisting strategy.

The four comprehensive strategies were not mutually exclusive and every combination could hypothetically exist. For example, the Virginia settlers utilized an offensive persisting strategy to drive back the natives and occupy and clear the land for agriculture. In doing this, they also relied heavily on the persisting defensive, using the fortified defense in building palisades to defend their farms and fields against Indian raids. At the same time, they took the offensive with a logistic raiding strategy to destroy the natives' weirs and crops.

The importance of attentiveness to political objectives and considerations, to the ideas clustering around the principles of war, and to the alternatives offered by comprehensive strategy summarized much of what people in the Western World had learned from the history of wars and their conduct. The underlying theme of these, and their application to strategy, was winning with the least effort.

Even though the civil environment and tasks often contrasted markedly with those of warfare, in seeking to accomplish its objective with the least effort, the conduct of warfare differed not at all from agriculture, industry, and commerce. In these activities producers or those offering a service also sought the easiest way. And when they had a market economy, price gave them a good guide for accomplishing their tasks with the least effort. Consumers and other buyers also emphasized least effort by making a search for the best relationship between value and price. But, though price could point the way in buying supplies and help in selecting weapon systems and making other military choices, it rarely has had a direct impact on strategy.

So this mastery of the techniques for winning with the least effort depended not on price but, in part, on a knowledge of factors that typically had the effect of independent variables on the conduct of campaigns and wars.

Based on the three strategic considerations of political factors, hostile forces, and physical features, they omitted political factors because they were too diverse and imponderable for easy general treatment. Physical features remained as a major factor, and an analysis of conflict with hostile military forces required dividing this consideration into four distinct factors: tactics, logistics, and numbers and mobility expressed as ratios. Because of the greater variety of the effects of these factors on land war, this exposition gives less attention to sea and air war.

PHYSICAL FEATURES

Physical features include the climate and weather. Weather became less an imponderable with the advent of good forecasting, but foreknowledge had only limited value in mitigating its effects. Storms have so hampered visibility as to make combat difficult, and mud, snow, and ice impeded logistic and strategic as well as tactical movement. The cooperation of rainy weather and soft earth has created mud, which often has precluded military operations. In the American Civil War the temperate climate of the border and southern states facilitated winter military operations. But the region's unsurfaced roads and very heavy winter rainfall created exceptionally muddy conditions. This often crippled strategic movements by road, as exemplified by the halting of one movement by road when cannon actually sank out of sight in the mud.

The Battle of the Bulge offers another example of significant influence of the weather. At that time a long period of overcast protected the Germans from the Allies' most mobile and valuable reserve, the fighter bombers, which would have been particularly effective against an army on the offensive with many vehicles on the roads in daylight. Mountains, deserts, forests, and level grasslands have all affected strategy by their impact on logistics and tactics, as have cities, farmsteads, airports, railroads, good and bad roads, and permanent and field fortifications.

Some features have aided both the offense and the defense. In 1940, for instance, when the Germans wished to invade Britain, the English Channel, guarded by the superior British fleet, constituted an impassable obstacle to the German army. But in 1944 when the Allies wished to invade the continent, it offered not just a variety of avenues of approach but conferred the initiative on the Allies if they could solve the problems of the logistics of landing. Rivers have functioned in the same way as routes for commerce and supply and as tactical obstacles to be defended or overcome. Railroads, airports, and good and bad roads influenced logistics and thus strategy, often aiding the advancing force more than the defending. Other physical features have discriminated in favor of the tactical defensive. Actually, most of the dominance of the tactical defensive in more modern times has resulted from combining high firepower with natural or man-made obstacles.

This kind of deployment, extended to direct-fire artillery and antitank guns and missiles, has diminished importance of elaborate field or permanent fortifications. Such advantageous firing positions, concealed by camouflage and covered by some hasty entrenchments, have provided good substitutes for the more elaborate ditches and earthen breastworks and bastions needed for field fortifications from Roman times through the age of the smoothbore musket. But they do not offer the protection from artillery fire given by field and, particularly, permanent fortifications. All such tactical use of physical features substituted for soldiers.

Permanent fortifications, usually of masonry or concrete, long presented the most formidable obstacle strategists faced. In the nineteenth century the engineers placed much of the forts underground, with their guns in armored cupolas or casemates. After World War I, the guns received better protection, and barbed wire and antitank barriers almost fully supplanted walls. Such essentially underground fortifications permitted a broadening of the concept of crossfire because the defenders' artillery could fire on attackers who would literally be on top of the fort; but the defenders' fire would not harm the fort while killing the assailants and destroying their vehicles.

After the end of the Franco-German war in 1871, the French thoroughly fortified their new border. For the Germans to have attempted to pierce that line of modern fortresses would have meant protracted sieges with the tactical defensive having an overwhelming dominance.

Hence when World War I began, the German plan solved the problem of these obstacles by marching through neutral Belgium. But this solution had the disadvantage of adding Belgium to their enemies and made certain that Britain would join France in the war against Germany. Critics of fortifications say that those of the French failed because the enemy never attacked them. But the builders saw them as fulfilling their mission of protecting the Franco-German border and thus making the Germans take a more difficult route to the French frontier and one with substantial political liabilities. The French had anticipated the German move through Belgium, but, not foreseeing its vast scale, lost much territory before they halted the Germans at the Battle of the Marne.

After World War I, the French recovered their old frontiers, and the French and Germans, neither disillusioned with fortifications, each fortified their new borders. In 1940 the French fortifications failed by the criterion of use because once more the Germans refused to attack them and advanced through Belgium. Again the French anticipated this German move, this time with far larger forces. The Germans' almost inadvertent discovery of the motorized turning movement controlled the outcome of the campaign, which won the war against France for them. On the other hand, the German fortifications succeeded by the criterion of use because an enemy attacked them, but they failed by the criterion of result when they did not halt the Allied invasion in 1944–1945. So the physical feature of permanent fortifications functioned on this frontier, and elsewhere, as an independent variable markedly influencing strategy.

The military operations of the Persian Gulf conflict of 1991 well illustrate the role of physical features in a military operation. The clear winter weather, the essentially level topography of the theater of operations and the terrain's relatively high trafficability made it ideal for the antagonists' motorized armies. Iraq's army sought to create obstacles with field fortifications, but the wind steadily eroded the earthen obstacles and positions and handicapped direct defensive fires. When the Coalition forces overpowered Iraqi artillery, the physical obstacles became vulnerable to clearing by the Coalition forces' sophisticated mine-clearing equipment and methods. The clear weather and negligible rainfall also aided the Coalition, which relied heavily on its superiority in aircraft.

The favorable physical features would make a striking contrast with those found in much of South Vietnam at that time of the year. The persistent overcast would have handicapped air operations, and the mountains and areas of thick jungle would have had the same effect on forces so heavily motorized. These contrasting conditions clearly show physical features as an independent variable of great significance in any campaign or war.

TACTICS

In land warfare the critical relationship was the strength of the tactical offensive and defensive. Between similar forces the defense had an inherent advantage, a modest superiority when resisting an attack in front, particularly when using any but primitive firearms. With infantry this came from their ability to remain motionless while attackers, if not using skirmishing, had somewhat to derange their formation in moving and be more exposed to the defender's fire. Further, movement required effective control and presented opportunities for mistakes that motionless defenders did not face. Moreover, attackers had a disadvantage in shooting because of movement from place to place, including such things as interruptions, poor firing positions, and breathlessness or fatigue from running or crawling. Defenders also had an additional advantage, because the counterattack often dominated the assailants' improvised defense.

The Tactics of Land Warfare

A century ago the magazine rifle and the machine gun were just completing the revolution in tactics in which infantry's enhanced firepower had driven cavalry from the battlefield. Then World War I bore its fruit, overwhelming supremacy of the tactical defensive. This dominance resulted largely from the synergistic relationship between the new firepower and the obstacles of the terrain and field fortifications. This ascendancy of the tactical defensive made warfare between these homogeneous armies quite predictable and diminished the power of the strategic offensive.

But World War I also witnessed the dawn of the mechanized cavalry revolution with the introduction of the tank and airplane. By World War II these had had several distinct effects.

1. Tactics became more complex with the introduction of intrinsically superior weapon systems, the tank over infantry, the antitank gun over the tank, the airplane over the tank and infantry, and the antiaircraft gun over the airplane.

2. These transformed tactics by making armies heterogeneous and combat array dependent on the combination of arms.

3. Further, the tanks and, to a degree, motorized infantry had the same tactically offensive attributes as the old horse cavalry. Infantry had always encountered difficulty attacking the adversary's weakness by assailing its flank. It could move fast enough to catch the defender unready, but then it took so long to go from march to combat order that the defenders had time to reform and baffle the attacker. Yet, since cavalry could move faster than infantry and could do so in combat formation, it long constituted ground warfare's tactically offensive troops. So generals stationed the horsemen on the armies' flanks, poised to use their better mobility and capacity to fight without having to change formation to assault the enemy's vulnerable flank.

Tanks had the same attributes of faster movement and ability to fight as they moved, and motorized infantry in armored carriers could also perform the tasks of tactically offensive troops.

Although aircraft had higher mobility and the capacity to fight as they flew, their speedy passage over the battlefield meant that their tactics resembled skirmishing much more than the line, well exemplified by the defensive as well as offensive capabilities of the tank and infantry. This limitation to skirmishing prevented aircraft from functioning fully as tactically offensive troops.

4. The tactical diversity and the proper combination of weapon systems revolutionized combat, making it extremely complicated as compared with the World War I battles of the essentially homogeneous armies of infantry and their supporting artillery. The changes increased the intricacy of dispositions, the opportunities for error, and the scope for chance and for

making the quality or quantity of a particular weapon system potentially decisive. It also raised the requirements for variations in skill among the now diverse aggregations of soldiers.

5. These tactical changes tended to increase the power of the tactical offensive as compared with the infantry armies. This, in turn, augmented the strength of the strategic offensive as did the huge enhancement of the armies' mobility. The concentration of mobility into armored and motorized divisions of World War II created strategically offensive troops who could use their greater speed to turn an enemy army, winning great victories of depletion for combat strategy. And tactical aviation had much strategic effect by using its tactical skill against logistical targets such as bridges and railway yards and such directly strategic objectives as troop movements.

6. Such heterogeneous armies magnified the effect of physical features on military operations. A prolonged muddy season had long hampered horse-drawn vehicles and artillery, but one virtually fettered the movements of German motorized forces in Russia in the fall of 1941. This delay of the essential motorized elements postponed the entire offensive until cold weather facilitated movement by freezing the ground.

The emergence of the missile since World War II has, like earlier improvements in firepower, augmented the power of the tactical defensive. The wire-guided antitank missile and the heat-seeking antiaircraft missile have seemed to improve infantry's defensive capability as much or more than the emergence of the helicopter has diminished it.

The air-to-ground missile, with excellent guidance, enabled airplanes better to carry out their tactical and strategic missions, bridges no longer being so nearly invulnerable to air attack as they seemed to be in World War II.

The Tactics of Warfare at Sea

The airplane had a very straightforward effect on sea warfare when it made the carrier the capital ship, except in confined waters where it needed the partnership of the battleship. Yet it also introduced more chance into operations because of the fragility of the carrier and the intermittent quality of its offensive capability. But this did not have a major effect on strategy.

The emergence of the missile at sea had a far more profound effect, virtually superseding guns and substituting the active defense of antimissile missiles for the traditional passive defense of armor. The paucity of combat between navies has made it difficult to assess the influence of this or know whether advances in antisubmarine warfare have counteracted the much-enhanced capability of the nuclear submarine.

The Tactics of Warfare in the Air

The cavalry revolution introduced warfare in the air in the first year of World War I. This soon revolved around the attack on bombing and reconnaissance aircraft by the intrinsically superior fighter and the concomitant dramatic contests between the fighter planes, their best pilots becoming celebrated as "aces."

There was still no essential advantage for the tactical defensive in the air, as on the sea, and physical features rarely gave the defense the measure of assistance they did on land. With the increasing predominance of the fighter bomber, the offensive advantage against bombers declined.

Among the many differences between combat on land and that at sea and in the air was the significance of numbers. The absence of the land's physical features on the sea or in the air led to F. W. Lanchester's hypothesis that combat in the air, and usually at sea, would cause the antagonists' strength to vary as the square of their numbers. This was true because in the air or on the sea conditions could approach those in which all combatants could fire at all others. Thus the greater firepower of the larger would destroy more of the smaller's aircraft or ships than it lost, thus rapidly increasing the larger's margin of superiority. This gave an overwhelming advantage to the force with numerical superiority, or its equivalent in quality.

Clearly illustrating this, because of its simplicity, was the exploit of a veteran French pilot in 1940 during the brief military operations of Italy against France. He substituted quality for numbers by flying a modern, 340-mile-per-hour Dewoitine 520 fighter with four machine guns and a 20-mm (.79-in.) cannon. In this plane he faced ill-armed Italian trimotor bombers and 250-mile-per-hour biplane fighters armed with only two machine guns. He vindicated Lanchester and earned the Legion of Honor by shooting down five Italian planes in 30 minutes.

Reasonably informed opinions differed widely in their estimates of the likely course of military operations in the land combat of the Persian Gulf conflict. These ranged from forecasting the quick victory actually attained to a prolonged stalemate engendered by the fortified defense. These illustrated the potential for erroneous estimates of a tactical situation. But good strategic decisions depended on valid estimates of tactical capabilities and the relative strength of the tactical offensive and defensive under different circumstances.

LOGISTICS

Since the aspects of logistics having to do with troop movement more conveniently belong with mobility, this section will treat the movement of supplies, replacement of men and equipment, and the relation to the base area.

In air operations the question of base area has usually been fairly unambiguous. Yet aerial refueling of aircraft has markedly lengthened the airplanes' tether to their bases. U.S. fighter planes illustrated this in 1990 when they flew without stopping from the United States to Saudi Arabia and arrived ready for air-to-air combat.

Naval logistics anticipated this before World War II when oil tankers began to refuel ships at sea. This in turn enabled the United States largely to circumvent Japan's system of fortified bases. Nuclear power, limited to submarines and a few important surface ships, has yet to transform naval logistics.

On land the base situation has had more complexity, with adversaries either or each depending on remote base areas or both campaigning in and using the same base area. Yet sometimes one would use one system and one another, and various combinations and hybrids of the two systems have also had applications. Because of the importance of logistics to strategy, differing relations to base areas have often constituted sources of strategic strength or weakness. Upon the vulnerability of base areas or of communications with remote base areas depended an attack using, and defense against, a logistic strategy.

For most of the history of warfare on land, the opposing armies lived on the country in which they campaigned and thus shared the same base area; but protracted operations might exhaust it and cause one or both armies to leave. When armies long remained in one place, as they would for a siege, they often consumed the supplies in the adjacent area and so had to draw more from a distance. This exposed them to the vulnerability of depending on a remote base area. So, rather than relying on the combat strategy of attacking the besieging army to drive it away by a victory in an offensive battle, a relieving army could raise the siege by the logistic strategy of cutting the besiegers' communications with their base area.

Secure access was also a pivotal strategic element. The immense resources devoted to the attack and defense of Allied Atlantic communications not only clearly illustrates this but shows how effective the German submarine raiders were in diverting far larger Allied resources to the defense.

Access to the base area had important operational significance because it furnished the basis of the turning movement, which implemented a combat persisting strategy. So, for an army, protecting the line of communications from a persisting attack was even more important than securing it from the depredations of raiders: One saved the supplies, the other saved the army. Concern for the line of supply from Normandy to Germany helps explain the German sensitivity to the Caen area, and this made it easier for General Montgomery to distract the Germans by his attacks there.

When the Allied forces broke through at St. Lô, the Germans assailed their communications as they passed Avranches. The significance of this threat calls emphatic attention to the need for the turning force to have its own secure access to a base area; raiders cannot conduct turning movements because they lack the supply lines to base areas to enable them to remain in a foe's rear to block his retreat.

Dependence on remote base areas at sea also permitted turning movements. The Allied command of the sea and, from carriers, the air over it, enabled them to interdict Japanese communications with islands that lacked adequate aircraft to keep the carriers at bay. This made the central Pacific advance effectively a succession of turning movements. Sea power also turned the Japanese in New Guinea, particularly with the Hollandia landing, after which the Allied ground forces fought a defensive campaign that blocked the retreat of a Japanese army along the coast.

When armies campaigned within a base area and were able to supply most of their needs locally, it removed operational strategy's most powerful weapon, the turning movement. Without a line of communications to a base area outside of the theater of operations, an army had no rear; and without a rear it was very difficult to have a turning movement. The U.S. forces experienced this in all of their campaigns against the Seminoles, their summer campaign against the Sioux, and much of their operations against the Viet Cong.

World War II introduced large-scale strategic bombing, the logistic strategy of systematic air raids against the enemy's remote base area. To a limited degree they resembled the raids by Virginia's colonists and those of Colonel Miles against the Sioux in their base area.

Commanders have had difficulty applying a logistic strategy when both opponents campaigned in, and thus used, the same base area. They have usually found that the defensive provided the best opportunities for applying a logistic strategy under these circumstances. To implement this, they would devastate the country along the route of an invading army or in the track of a retreating army. In the American Civil War, for example, the U.S. forces defended themselves against further rebel raids through the Shenandoah Valley in Virginia by destroying the food and fodder resources in its northern part. They implemented this defensive logistic strategy so thoroughly that, as one general expressed it, not only could raiding rebel armies not subsist there but "crows flying over it for the balance of the season will have to carry their own provender."

In Vietnam, the U.S. and South Vietnamese forces faced a strategic problem not so easily solved, even though the United States relied on a remote base area, and South Vietnam to a degree also. Because the Viet Cong had its base area among South Vietnamese people, many of whom were well disposed toward the South Vietnamese government, any logistic raids would strike the government's supporters as well as its enemies.

The experience of the Vietnam War showed the importance of knowing the location of an adversary's base area as well as his logistic requirements. The English invasion of North America illustrated adversaries using the same base area. But the Colonists gained victory through their persisting defensive that gradually conquered the base area. And, while their fortified defense protected their conquests from Indian raiders, they raided the natives' fields and weirs.

The conquest of an enemy's base area with a persisting strategy has usually proven the ultimate and most decisive logistic strategy, and one that often offered positive logistic benefits as well. The German conquest and the Allied liberation of France offer excellent examples of the effectiveness of this strategy. The United States and its South Vietnamese ally could have pursued the same logistic persisting strategy of conquering the Viet Cong's base area and converting its population and output to their use. When they firmly adopted this strategy, called pacification, its slow workings made the Viet Cong and the North Vietnamese troops in the South more and more dependent on the remote base area in North Vietnam. And this, at last, made the insurgent forces in the South vulnerable to the logistic raids against their communications with the North, against the North Vietnamese base area itself, and its communications with its remote base areas, the U.S.S.R. and China.

So all of these different situations derive their significance from the security of one's own supply and the vulnerability of the adversary's. The exposure of a base area to a logistic persisting or raiding strategy could easily have determined the outcome of a campaign or war, and the vulnerability of communications to a remote base area have had the same decisive effect. Moreover, links to a remote base area could have given combat strategy an opportunity to employ the turning movement in land operations and some at sea as well. Thus logistics has always been a crucial strategic consideration, one that usually loomed larger than tactics because supply constituted a daily consideration whereas combat typically occurred only occasionally.

Because the seas had their major importance as arteries of commerce and the transport and supply of military forces, logistics dominated its strategy. Belligerents endeavored to use the sea and deny it to their antagonists. Traditionally the stronger employed the persisting strategy of blockade and the weaker the raid, recently above and below as well as on the surface of the sea.

World War II in the Pacific illustrated turning movements at sea, based—as on land—on using a blockade to interrupt the enemy's supply routes while retaining one's own communications. This is exceptionally difficult for air forces to implement because of the problems of maintaining an air blockade. So its logistics made the airplane a raider only and denied a persisting strategy to any independent effort by aircraft. But it had long been an indispensable and integral part of land and naval action, whether engaged in a raiding or a persisting strategy.

NUMBERS

The factor of numbers of the contending armies also stands for the comparative quality of each force. Thus a few well-trained, seasoned regular troops were usually worth far more than a large number of ill-trained militia, and better-armed forces had an advantage, as the defeat of the Germans at the Battle of the Falkland Islands illustrates.

Yet, independent of quality, having significantly greater numbers conferred many strategic advantages. Beyond adding to tactical strength and facilitating turning movements, numerical superiority gave a measure of the initiative proportionate to the numerical preponderance. It achieved this by requiring a less stringent economy of force to attain a needed level of concentration in space. This force, redundant for the projected offensive, would act as a reserve to give security against an unexpected hostile attack. This situation occurred in Normandy in 1944 when the Germans struck to cut the thin Allied supply line at Avranches; enough Allied troops were there in reserve to halt the attack when, with less numerical superiority, they might have been farther east with the turning movement.

Some have assumed that the offensive had yielded the kind of initiative here produced by superior numbers; but it is likely that such an initiative, when it occurred, actually came from the larger numbers needed for an attack or from the defender refusing to act because he made the assumption that the attacker did indeed possess the larger numbers implied by his taking the offensive. Of course, this is how distraction often worked to give the initiative. But if an adversary had realized the attacker's actual weakness, such an attack to gain the initiative might offer an opportunity for a counterblow. The Allied offensive in late 1944 and the German offensive in the Battle of the Bulge constituted a case of an offensive failing to gain the initiative.

Another very significant numerical relationship was that of numbers to the area of the theater of operations. This ratio of force to space had an important effect on strategy because it had much to do with the character of operations. World War I illustrates the strategic effect of huge numbers in relation to the area of the theater of operations. In 1914 the French, British, Belgian, and German armies fought where Caesar and many others had campaigned before and since. But instead of a few thousand soldiers, the belligerents began with over three million and increased them in subsequent years. This meant that the defenders had enough men to use the fortified defense all the way from neutral Switzerland to the English Channel.

With force multiplied by the fortified defense as well as the huge numbers, automatic weapons, and powerful artillery, no strategy existed that could end the stalemate. So the high ratio of military force to space created a stalemate, making military operations quite indecisive. General Ludendorff, the principal German strategist, summarized the prevailing tyranny of tactics over strategy when he wrote that "tactics had to be considered before purely strategical objectives which it is futile to pursue unless tactical success is possible."

Operations had long been indecisive in part for the opposite reason, a low ratio of force to space. When small armies of 20,000 to 40,000 men, or even 100,000 men, had campaigned in that same area in Europe's wars of the sixteenth through the eighteenth centuries, the primacy of retreat over pursuit meant that the weaker could use the large space to move to and fro, always keeping the stronger at a distance.

The practice of armies living on the country in which they campaigned meant that they operated within their base area and without the constraints of dependence on a remote base area. This had much to do with making such maneuvering possible and the wars so inconclusive. Thus the stronger could only fight if the weaker wished it. So battle occurred rarely, and these conditions also created the same strategic conditions found later in the Seminole War and in much of the Vietnam War.

But in areas where fortified cities blocked communication focal points, they raised the ratio of force to space because they were difficult to capture and sieges incurred high costs in men, supplies, and money. When the stronger captured a city, more equally well-fortified cities usually still remained to besiege. So both a low and a high ratio of force to space created a strategic stalemate.

Such fortifications much increased the ratio of force to space, and this in turn had a marked influence on strategy. A low ratio of force to space enabled the defenders to use retreat to impose a strategic stalemate by avoiding battle; and the opposite, a very high ratio, had created a strategic stalemate in fortified urban areas before it did so on the western front in World War I. But during the era of the French Revolution and Napoleon, operational strategy emerged as the way for the stronger to use concentration and the turning movement to assail the defender when the antagonists had neither too much or too little space and thus had the opportunity to wage a strategically decisive campaign. Figure 13.1 illustrates the operational consequences of differing ratios of numbers to space.

Operational strategy relied on dispersal of force to inhibit the defenders' movements. This also imposed a similar dispersal on the defenders because they needed to protect their flanks from a march around them to carry out a turning movement into their rear. But the defenders' dispersal made them vulnerable to a concentration in the middle of their position. Allied operations in Normandy clearly exhibited operational strategy with concentration in space to overwhelm the German line, spread to protect its flanks by touching the sea on each side. When piercing the line created two German flanks in the middle of the line, General Bradley used much of

Figure 13.1
The Influence of the Ratio of Force to Space

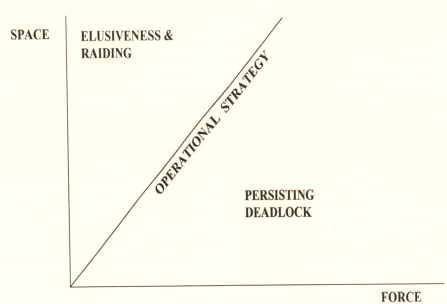

General Patton's Third Army to make a turning movement into the Germans' rear and block their retreat.

MOBILITY

Changes in the cost and speed of movement have revolutionized logistics in the last century and a half. First steam on water and rails and then the internal combustion engine on roads, rail, water, and—succeeded by jets—in the air have enabled large armies to operate at a great distance from their bases. And, though this has tethered armies to their distant base areas, it has also immensely expanded the possibilities for large, far-flung, strategic operations. And these changes in mobility have much affected the operational level, particularly strategic movement.

The strategic mobility of an army had an obviously important relationship with that of its adversary. An advantage in strategic mobility gave the army who possessed it what one might call strategically offensive troops. The 1914 campaign in France illustrated this. When the Germans came through Belgium into France to turn the French armies, they came on foot with horses because the retreating Belgians and French had disabled the railroads. But the French possessed fully functioning railroads and used them not just to concentrate quickly against the slow-moving Germans but even, with General Maunoury's 6th Army, turned the German turning movement. Thus the rail-borne forces were strategically offensive because of their superior mobility. In 1940 a new type of offensive troops emerged when ten German armored and motorized divisions pushed forward rapidly into the French rear, outran French reserves moving westward to block their advance and, by reaching the French coast, turned the British, Belgian, and two French armies. So in 1940 the Germans had the strategically offensive troops and won the opening campaign.

The mobility of aircraft, particularly fighter bombers, showed the strategic value of this high-speed movement throughout the campaign in France when their raids inhibited troop movements and handicapped the transportation of supplies. Only by moving at night, at which the Germans became quite adept, could troop movements take place with any predictable regularity. The same mobility enabled the air forces to concentrate suddenly to meet the needs of offense or defense.

The reduction in the speed of German strategic movement conferred on the Allies the advantage of strategically offensive troops. But the aircraft themselves failed to function as such offensive troops because they could not conduct turning movements. As raiders in strategy and skirmishers in tactics, they could not occupy a position in the enemy rear, assume the tactical defensive, and block his retreat. Efforts to use parachute and glider-borne troops to carry out turning movements failed because these soldiers conveyed by air lacked the artillery, tanks, and antitank guns to hold their positions against fully equipped ground forces.

Mobility usually played essentially the same role in air operations as it did at sea, as the fighter's traditional speed advantage over the bomber illustrated. But in operations on land, strategic mobility clearly substituted for numbers. An army may turn its adversary by so dispersing superior numbers as to open a route around an antagonist's flank and thus into his rear to complete the movement. But the ability to move more rapidly, as by having motor transport for soldiers against an adversary whose troops moved on foot, gave an equal facility for carrying out a turning movement.

Mobility could also substitute for numbers in more ordinary situations. For instance, controlling a country recently acquired by a persisting strategy required holding towns and the other road junctions and otherwise controlling movement over roads. But it also needed patrolling to keep the country under observation and to give evidence of the presence and strength of the occupying power. Fewer but faster-moving patrols on horseback could substitute for more on foot, those with motor transport could replace most horseback patrols, and air would require even less men. But perhaps both ground and air patrols would make a perfect combination, especially if using radio to coordinate their endeavors. So by substituting for numbers, mobility can increase the ratio of force to space.

SOME EFFECTS OF THESE FIVE FACTORS

The principles of war have constituted a valuable checklist for evaluating the conduct of operations in the past and for current use in assessing hypotheses for military operations. So also might these five factors and their potential impact provide a similar checklist and so offer assistance in understanding the reasons for success and failure in the past and for evaluating possible operations in the present.

Like the principles of war, these factors are hardly discrete in their operation. For example, numbers, mobility, and physical features had a number of substitution relationships. So mobility of forces could also take the place of greater numbers and the reverse, and the presence of physical features replaced numbers on the defensive and often mobility as well. And because they facilitated economy of force, physical features aided the offensive as well as the defensive. They also diminished mobility, as when they impeded pursuit more than they did retreat.

Physical features have usually been an independent variable in any strategic situation. The base area, whether remote or in the theater of operations, had this role too. They were independent in that, whereas numbers and mobility might vary and could influence the tactical situation, the physical relationship of the base area and the physical features in the theater of operations were not often subject to alteration.

To illustrate the potential of changes in just two of the five factors on land operations, consider the four possibilities created by two strategically important relationships. In the western world throughout the last two millennia, the comparative strength of the tactical defensive and offensive has had a determining role. And whether or not pursuers could overtake a retreating army also had a major influence on strategy. Using only two hypothetical possibilities for each of these two variables, commanders would face four combinations that could yield the following variety of strategic results:

1. If the tactical offensive were superior to the defensive and pursuit were faster than retreat, the stronger army or fleet would then overtake and destroy the weaker, ending any campaign quickly. This would make the strategic offensive as strong as the tactical. The actual result of the superiority of attack and pursuit would likely resemble the outcome of the ground war in the Persian Gulf conflict.

2. If attack were more powerful than defense but retreat were faster than pursuit, the weaker would use retreat and avoid having to fight. This would produce a strategically indecisive situation.

3. If the tactical defense had a preponderance over the offensive and pursuit were more rapid than retreat, the stronger could overtake the weaker, but the power

of the tactical defense would make the stronger's attack fail. This combination would create another indecisive strategic situation.

4. The fourth combination, dominance for the tactical defensive and retreat, prevailed on land in most of the wars over these two thousand years in the West, and this helps explain why they were so indecisive. It also gives a reason why so much strategy had to do with compelling the weaker to fight and why tacticians sought means of assailing an antagonist's flank or rear. This strategic condition prevailed into modern times, helping to account for the protracted and costly wars of the twentieth century.

Compared to this simple case, the hypothetical variations in each factor create a very large number of strategic environments. It is worth noting these, without listing all of the possibilities, much less describing the resulting strategic environments.

Physical features could have contradictory influences that affect the ratio of the strength of the offensive and defensive, both tactical and strategic, and by their influence on logistics. This yielded four possibilities.

In tactics the ratio between the power of the offense and defense responded to two purely tactical influences, the quite modest inherent strength of the defensive on land and the intrinsic superiorities of weapon systems on land and sea and in the air. This yielded four combinations.

Logistics offered not just the two cases of operating within or from a remote base area. There may have been a significant combination of the two and links to a remote base area may have had various kinds and degrees of capacity and vulnerability, providing at least three cases.

The ratio of numbers, and all they stand for, between the adversaries offered three possible conditions, effective equality and two kinds of inequality, favoring one or the other. Further, the ratio of numbers to the area of operations has had a major impact on strategic conditions and has at least three possibilities, high, medium, and low.

The ratio of mobility between the antagonists had the same three conditions as with numbers and had many of the same strategic influences, including some on the effective ratio of force to space.

Although many of the combinations of the different states of these five factors will not refer to any possible actual condition past or present, enough will correspond to possible or actual reality to give this array of factors some utility for shedding some additional light on strategic situations in the past and, perhaps, some hypotheses about the present.

This list can also apply to tactics and logistics by substitution. To have this kind of glimpse of tactical possibilities, substitute strategy for tactics. Strategy may, for example, prescribe the offensive, defensive, or retreat, each situation affecting tactics. Substituting strategy for logistics would give the same strategic alternatives for logistics, thus giving different effects, for example, for physical features on logistics.

Appendix A

Weapons and Strategy in the Twentieth Century

In part because horse cavalry could no longer fulfill its traditional functions, armies of World War I adopted the tank to fill the role of the armored, heavy cavalry of old. But the soldiers were much quicker to grasp the value of aircraft to carry out the tactical and strategic missions of the light cavalry. Hence the belligerents had developed air forces before World War I and, for their cavalry of the air, manufactured over two hundred thousand airplanes during the war. At first they stressed reconnaissance, gradually making more bombers and learning to use fighters for ground attack. During the interwar period, armies, navies, and air forces operated aircraft over water and developed dive and torpedo bombers and ground-attack aircraft, like the A-20, which used the tactical style employed by the fighter bomber of World War II.

Partially because technological change had not left any large gaps in naval weapons systems, the sailors embraced aircraft far more slowly and first for reconnaissance only. Still, on the eve of World War II, the principal naval powers had equipped themselves with carriers armed with aircraft that could sink battleships.

Many students of air power perceived airplanes as more than a cavalry of the air that could also function exceptionally well over water. Some saw this ubiquity of the cavalry of the air as meaning it could substitute for surface forces, a view General Mitchell espoused with respect to sea power. General Douhet and others went in a different direction, believing that air power had made both land and sea power redundant because aircraft could bomb cities to implement a political-military strategy as well as a logistic one to win a war without significant aid from land or sea forces.

World War II tested Douhet's thesis with the very large Anglo-American investment in strategic bombing. In the bombing of Germany the strategy failed in its political and psychological effects. Even the logistic component of the strategy did not have decisive success prior to the Allied armies winning with a combat persisting strategy. So in World War II the cavalry of the air had a more significant military effect, not only in its part in land war but by extending its influence beyond the land, exercising sea power from carriers as well as from its land bases. It also transformed the relation between land and sea by giving the land more sway over the sea and its commerce than its carrier-based sea power could typically have over the land.

Hence the role of aircraft in exerting such a profound influence over the sea and land proved to be air power's most important achievement in the war. The advent of the jet and of precision-guided munitions continued that steady increase in the airplane weapon system's capabilities that had begun in World War I. So just when nuclear-armed ballistic missiles had assumed much of the responsibility for implementing Douhet's concept of air power, the steadily augmenting capabilities of the air weapon systems brought back the tempting hypothesis that one weapon system, the cavalry of the air, could give victory in war by largely substituting for surface forces.

Yet this hypothesis seemed to overlook the tactical and strategic limitations of the cavalry of the air when operating over land. It also apparently neglected the complementary relation between this kind of cavalry and earthbound forces. Because its nature limited the cavalry of the air to skirmishing tactics and a raiding strategy, it could control the land much more readily by combining its skirmishing and raiding with land power's complementary line tactics and persisting strategy. Thus, as in the past, a combination of weapon systems would have the greatest effect.

The main amphibious operation and naval war since World War II—that between Argentina and the United Kingdom in the Falkland Islands—did not involve any combat of submarines with surface ships beyond the sinking of an Argentine cruiser. The operation reenacted the Allied invasion of Okinawa when the Argentine air force did considerable but not decisive damage in assailing the modern British ships. Argentina's sea-skimming missiles worked well, but ordinary bombs did most of the damage.

The bombing of North Vietnam for the most part failed as a logistic strategy because the bombers lacked many good targets and, for much of the time, were not assailing a remote base area; as a political-military strategy, inhibited by political constraints, its raids failed to raise the cost of the war above what the enemy would pay until the end, when a powerful offensive made a major contribution to expediting the settlement. On the whole, diplomatic and other constraints precluded using the merciless thoroughness characteristic of World War II bombing.

Since World War II, most thinking concerning ground warfare had focused on the potential combat between the ultramodern armies of the U.S.S.R. and its allies and the North Atlantic Treaty Organization. Although no combat occurred between these forces, the wars between well-armed Israel and the Arab powers tested the weapons and doctrines of the armies that confronted each other in Europe. These wars confirmed the value of World War II as a basis for extrapolating the changes in equipment and weapons and their effect on logistics, tactics, and strategy.

The Persian Gulf conflict was one more in this series of Near Eastern wars on a European model. In that conflict the augmented accuracy of fire from the fighter bomber increased the strategic as well as tactical capabilities of the cavalry of the air. Bridges, for example, long almost invulnerable, succumbed quickly to smart bombs.

Yet the vast improvement in weapons and the intensification of the changes wrought by the role of air power in the mechanized cavalry revolution of World War II has had most of its influence on the "conventional" war, which emerged two centuries ago in the wars of the French Revolution and Napoleon. Although European weapons and tactical methods have spread world-wide, they have not usually found as fertile ground as the Near East and have not carried with them the operational strategy of conventional war: a combat persisting military strategy based on concentration in space and time, distraction to facilitate concentration against weakness, and the turning movement as the best means of depleting a hostile force. Even at its inception, this strategy depended on a Western European environment of physical features, political organization, and level of military force, conditions reproduced in the Near East since World War II.

Thus the weapon systems that helped make this strategy so decisive in World War II and in many Near Eastern conflicts have often had less effect in different strategic and physical settings. Most wars since the end of World War II have not had the character of the large-scale operations of World War II. Most have resembled the World War II fighting in the U.S.S.R. behind the German lines and even approached the complex situation found in Yugoslavia where at least six different forces took the field. Among the wars with this aspect were those in the Philippines, Borneo, Malaya, Vietnam, and Bosnia.

Although these conflicts seemed chaotic, their events were not random. They were the typical wars of the past, the present, and—pretty surely—the future. We have called the Napoleonic model of operational strategy "conventional," but it was unconventional when it emerged; this is why it received so much study. And it remains unconventional in the sense that it does not describe the customary conduct of most wars.

Since we have successfully created an archetype of "conventional" war, it is past time to create one for the more frequently occurring "unconventional" war. We badly need it better to understand the past and even to help to give guidance for waging such wars, as well as for choosing wars not to wage.

Appendix B

Maps and Diagrams

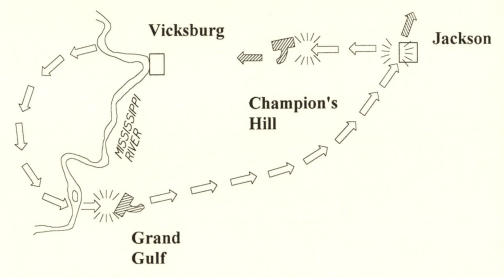

Vicksburg Campaign

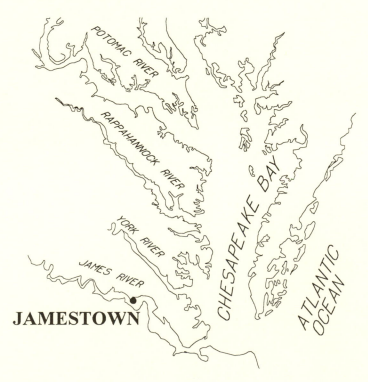

Eastern Virginia

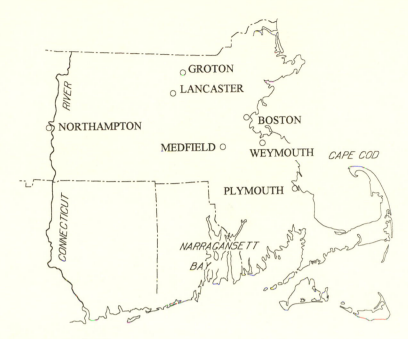

Eastern New England

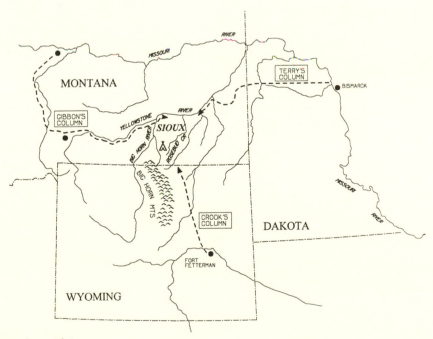

Northern Plains

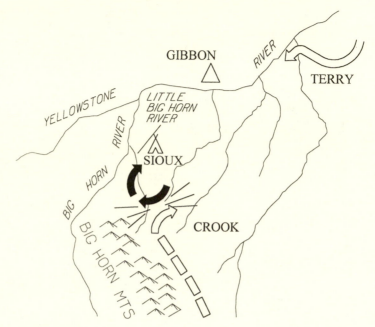

Battle of the Rosebud

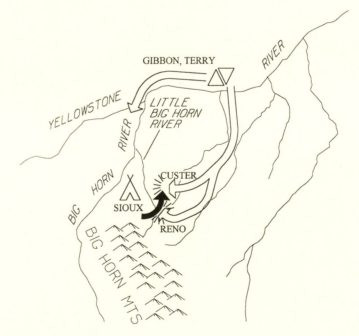

Battle of the Little Big Horn

North Atlantic

Strategic Bombing Area

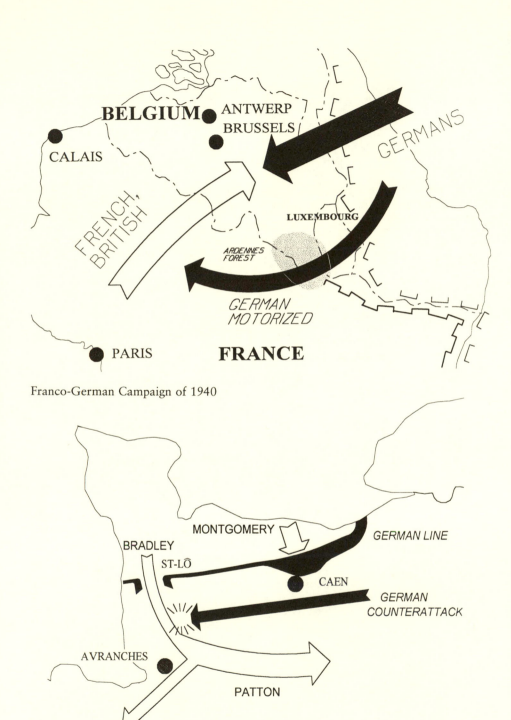

Franco-German Campaign of 1940

Normandy Breakout

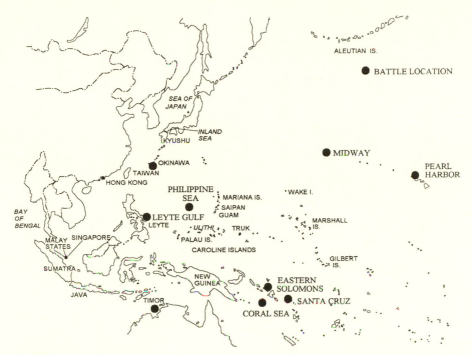

Pacific Theater of War

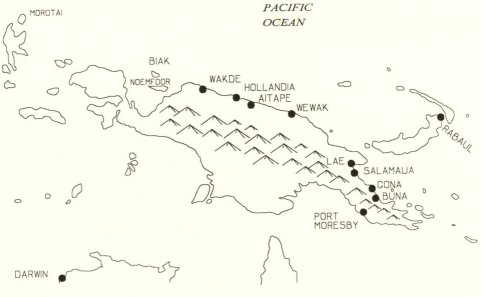

New Guinea

Korea

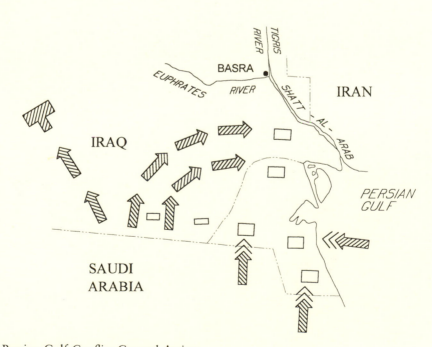

Persian Gulf Conflict Ground Action

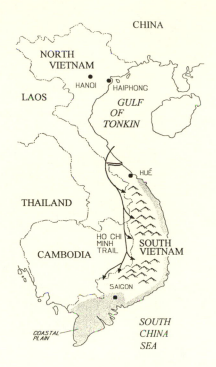

Vietnam

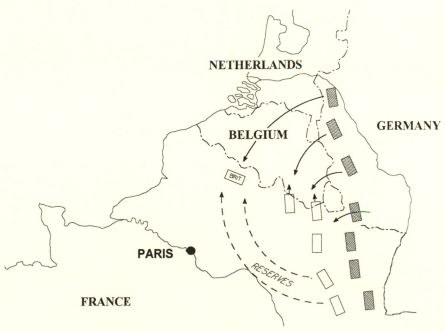

German Turning Movement and Joffre's Response

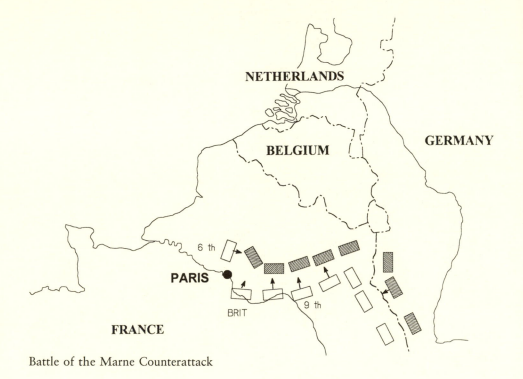

Battle of the Marne Counterattack

Suggested Readings

For the historiography of works on strategy in English, Jay Luvaas, *The Education of an Army: British Military Thought, 1815–1940* (Chicago, 1964) is excellent. John I. Alger, *The Quest for Victory: The History of the Principles of War* (Westport, Conn., 1982) offers a thorough treatment. For the history of military thought, see Azar Gat, *Origins of Military Thought: From the Enlightenment to Clausewitz* (New York, 1989) and *The Development of Military Thought: The Nineteenth Century* (New York, 1992). Of particular relevance is Peter Paret, ed., *The Makers of Modern Strategy from Machiavelli to the Nuclear Age* (Princeton, 1986).

For a concise presentation of the traditional schools of strategy, consult J. C. Wylie, *Military Strategy: A General Theory of Power Control* (New Brunswick, N.J., 1967), particularly pages 37–64. Archer Jones, *The Art of War in the Western World* (Urbana and Chicago, 1987) presents the approach to strategy used in this book. A reader might find Chapter 1 of interest because it shows its origin in and application to ancient warfare. For yet another way of viewing strategy, readers should examine the application by Harry G. Summers, Jr., of the principles of war and the ideas of Karl von Clausewitz to two recent wars: *On Strategy: A Critical Analysis of the Vietnam War* (Novato, Calif., 1982) and *On Strategy II: A Critical Analysis of the Gulf War* (New York, 1992).

For further reading on the history of wars and campaigns, nothing can compare with first putting operational history in its context. One of the best ways to do this is to read Allan R. Millett and Peter Maslowski, *For the Common Defense: A Military History of the United States of America*, revised and expanded edition (New York, 1994). Its selected bibliography will guide readers to books on the wars or campaigns that interest them. Older, but particularly valuable for its biographical emphasis and its notes and bibliography, is Warren W. Hassler, Jr., *With Sword and Shield: American Military Affairs, Colonial Times to the Present* (Ames, Ia., 1982).

Index

Abrams, General Creighton W.: succeeds Westmoreland, 186; mentioned, 188

Aircraft: characteristics of in European warfare, 48; skirmishing tactics limit, 225

Air power: as artillery in St. Lô breakthrough and Persian Gulf, 74, 153; in the Atlantic commerce war, 42–43; bombing less accurate than artillery, 91; British adopt night bombing, 51–52; carriers support Hollandia landing, 122; as cavalry of the air, 215–16; cavalry role in Europe and Pacific compared, 121; combat with North Vietnamese air defenses, 123; command of the sea north of New Guinea, 120; command of the sea permitted turning movements in Pacific, 124; comparison of sea- and land-based, 106–7; emergence of, 237; emergence of the aircraft carrier, 90–91; failure to interdict supply movements, 192; fighter bombers as a reserve, 77; intelligence contribution, 151; and Iraqi troop movements, 152; in Japan's colonial conquests, 99; in last phase of Vietnam War, 192–94; limitations as an offensive weapon system, 234; met logistic needs in New Guinea, 117; New Guinea jungle thwarted, 117; political constraints in Vietnam War, 163–64; relation to operational strategy, 124–25; restored light cavalry to armies, 66; role in defeating North Vietnamese offensive, 191–92; and sea power in Crete, 94–95; successes of sea-based aircraft, 92; has surpassed World War II in logistic raiding strategy, 156, 158; tactical contribution in World War II, 66; tactical limitations, 74; weather favored in Persian Gulf conflict, 157–58; weather handicapped in winter of 1944–1945, 82; wielded sea power, 238; after World War II, 238; World War II aircraft production compared, 110; World War II cavalry of the air, 66; World War II significance for sea and land war, 238; World War II strategic bombing, 51–56, 136, 137

Aitape, landing on, 123

Alexander the Great, how coped with guerrillas, 213

Aleutian Islands, Japanese objective, 103

Antiaircraft defense, explained, 47–48

Antwerp, fall of, 77, 78

Ardennes Forest: German second offensive, 80–81; comparison of 1940 and 1944 offensives, 81

Aristotle, his four causes: applied to military operations, xxii–xxiii, 199; explained, xxi–xxii; final cause as objective of campaign or war, 221

Asdic. *See* Sonar

Attrition: Eisenhower used, 209; inherent in all military operations, 209; not used as a synonym for depletion, 209; not usually in harmony with least effort, 209; requisites as a strategy, 209–10; strategy defined, xiii

Basil II, Emperor, effects of his intimidation of Bulgars, 200

Battles: rarely alter strategic situation, 89; tactical and strategic significance compared, 88

Bazooka, described, 61

Belisarius, Roman general, criticized pursuit, 145

Berlin, British bombing campaign against, 54

Biak, Japanese plan to reinforce, 124

Bigelow, John, Jr., authority on strategy, x

Bismarck, German battleship and its cruise, 92

Bismarck Sea, Battle of, 118–19

Bradley, General Omar: characterized, 73; commands Twelfth Army Group, 75; concept of breakthrough, 76; mentioned, 77

Brussels, fall of, 177

Bulge, Battle of, 80–81

Buna, capture and recapture, 117

Caen, attack on a distraction, xv

Call, General Richard K., operations against the Seminoles, 22

Cannon, changed warfare, xx

Capital ship, battleships and then carriers often combined with battleships; 87, 93

Ceylon, Japanese raid on, 100, 104

Chance, in carrier combat, 102, 103

Civil War, American, vulnerability of railroads to cavalry raids, 58

Clausewitz, Karl von, authority on strategy, x, 206

Climate: and German offensive in the Battle of the Bulge, 80; handicaps aircraft fighting North Vietnamese offensive, 191, 192; inhibits bombing of Japan, 136–37; severe winters in the northern plains, 26

Clinch, Colonel Duncan: at the Battle of Withlacoochee, 21; in Scott's campaign, 21–22

Colin, Jean Alphonse Lambert, authority on strategy, x

Cologne, 1,000-plane raid also concentrated in time, 53

Colonists, Virginia: strategy compared, 189; success of their logistic strategies, 214; used multiple comprehensive strategies, 221

Combat, mounted: New England mounted militia, 15, 17; restored by the tank, 60; tactics and strategy on land and sea distinguished, xxi; tactics on horseback, xx–xxi

Combination: of air and land power, 238; role in tactics, 215; role in weapon systems, 215

Complementarity: of air and land power tactics and strategy, 238; basis of much combination, 215; and principles of land, sea, and air power, 215

Concentration: aircraft rapid, 74, 75, 107; Allies against the Bulge, 81; benefits from distraction, 69; defensive in space by U.N. forces, 145; defensive in space in convoys, 41; defensive of German fighters and firefighting capacity, 53, 54; facilitated pursuit, 77; of Japanese aircraft at Rabaul, 115; offensive by German submarines, 43; on Pacific

lines of operation, 119–20; a principle of war, 206; role in European
sea and air operations, 45; against
successive objectives by Viet Cong,
167; by support groups against wolf
packs, 43, 44; of U.S. forces at Midway, 104; against weakness as the
native's strategy, 8; against weakness
by the Japanese, 101
Concentration in space: by Allies on
interior lines against Germany and
Japan, 57; of British bombers
against Berlin, 54; in British bombing, 52; Japan at Pearl Harbor, 98;
Japanese against the colonies, 98–99;
by Japanese fleet, 99–100; of logistic
resources, 78; by natives in Little Big
Horn campaign, 18, 19; principle for
using interior lines, 212; rejected by
Eisenhower, 79; successfully by U.S.
Navy, 112; Vietnamese failed to use,
195; by Wolf packs, 41–42
Concentration in time: by air raids in
Okinawa campaign, 130; British
bombers use, 52; in carrier combat,
102; chosen by Eisenhower, 79; as
coordination of activity to support
the principal effort, 207–8; failed at
Little Big Horn, 28, 29; by fighters,
49; instances of, 212; Japan against
colonies, 98; in the last raids against
North Vietnam, 194; North Koreans
fail to use against Pusan perimeter,
143; by North Vietnam, 191; in
Opechancanough's offensive, 11:
planned for southern France landing,
78; on Solomons and New Guinea
lines of operation, 116; tactical, 42,
126; in Tet offensive, 184;
Concentration in time and space: both
in German Marne campaign, 212;
compared for winter of 1944–1945,
79–80; Foch used both, 64; lack of
full effect in Pacific, 124; in New
Guinea and Solomons, 119
Considerations, three in strategic decisions, 197, 222
Conventional war: not typical, 239–40;

summarized, 239; unconventional
needs as much study, 239–40
Convoys: Japanese made limited use
of, 133; technique for protecting
merchant ships, 40
Coral Sea, Battle of: account of, 102–
3; tactical and strategic results, 103,
mentioned, 107
Counteroffensive: Battle of the Bulge,
80–81; Joffre employs five armies
along the Marne, 211–12
Crete, German campaign against and
contest between ships and aircraft,
94–95
Crook, General George: his Fall 1876
campaign, 29; in the Little Big Horn
campaign, 27–28; his 1876 campaign in Wyoming, 25, 26
Crossfire: amplified by underground
forts, 233; defended beaches, 68; explained and role in defense, xx; mentioned, 184
Cuba, crisis of missiles illustrated military-political strategy, 201
Custer, General George A., in the Little Big Horn campaign and battle,
28–29

Dade, Major Francis L., defeat of, 21
Darwin, Australia: mentioned, 104;
raided by Japanese, 99
Davidson, General Philip B.: describes
Westmoreland's strategy, 186; mentioned, 191
Depletion, role in military strategy,
xiii–xiv
Destroyers, used skirmishing tactics in
torpedo attack on Scharnhorst, 45
Diem, Ngo Dinh: overthrown, 170;
policies, 164–66; South Vietnamese
ruler, 164
Distraction: bombing of Wewak, 122;
could confer initiative, 231; could
use Newton's third law of motion,
70; effective in Battle of Leyte Gulf,
128, 210; facilitates surprise, 70; by
Montgomery in 1945, 82; by Montgomery's efforts to take Caen, 73;

partner of concentration, 69; preceded Tet offensive, 183, 184; relation to concentration, 210; relation to initiative, 208; relation to surprise, 206; role in Japanese Philippine defense plan, 128; used by Allies in 1944, 69–70; used to cover Coalition turning movement, 155; used to cover U.N. turning movement, 143

Doctrine, combat, characterized, xviii

Doenitz, Admiral Karl, commander of German submarines, 41

Douhet, General Giulio: exponent of air power dominance, 49; his ideas summarized, 49–50; mentioned, 181, 237, 238

Duke of York, H.M.S., British battleship defeats *Scharnhorst*, 45

Eastern Solomons, Battle of, 112–13

Economics, provides analogies for demand for victory, 202–4

Economy of force: less important if numbers are great, 231; relation to the offensive, 211

Eisenhower, General Dwight D.: characterized, 73; mentioned, 218; strategy mentioned, 164; used attrition strategy, 209

Elasticity of demand, for objective of a war, 202–4

Factors affecting strategy, substitution relations among, 235

Falkland Islands, Battle of (1914): account of, 36–37; mentioned, 102, 231

Falkland Islands, warfare between Britain and Argentina, 238

Fighter bombers, description and importance of, 71–72

Fishhook, logistic raid in, 189

Flank position: defensive analog of the turning movement, 210; Joffre places Sixth Army in, 211; strategic analog of crossfire, 211

Foch, Marshal Ferdinand: Allied commander in France, 64; commanded Ninth Army in 1914, 211; mentioned, 81, 202

Force, ratio to space. *See* Space

Fortification: principles of, xx; utility of, xx

Fortified defense: aided French in 1914, 212; in airfield protection, 106–7; at Buna, 117; colonists used to increase ratio of force to space, 14; criteria for evaluating success of fortifications, 223–24; dominant in World War I, 59, 63; effectiveness of Japanese, 114, 121; French and German in twentieth century, 223–24; German in winter of 1944–1945, 68–69, 79; as important physical features, 223; influence of French fortifications on German strategy, 223–24; Iraq relied on, 151–52; at Khe Sanh, 184; in Korean War, 145; Marines used in Vietnam, 180–81; Marines used on Guadalcanal, 114; mentioned, 231; protected U-boats from bombers, 44; relation to economy of force, 208; relation to initiative, 208; role in victory of Virginia colonists, 6, 9, 13, 14, 214; role of permanent fortification in 1944–1945, 79; used by Americans in Philippines, 100; used by communists, 175; used by South against North Vietnam, 192; used by Viet Cong, 195; used for pacified villages, 186, 188; used in strategic hamlets, 169

France, invasion of southern in 1944, 78

Franco-German campaign of 1940: account of, 64–65; U.S. Army's reaction to, 65–66

Fuller, J. F. C., authority on strategy, x

Gibbon, Colonel John, in Little Big Horn campaign, 27

Gilbert Islands: attack on, 116; mentioned, 115

Glorious, H.M.S., carrier sunk by battleships, 92–93

Grant, General Ulysses S.: mentioned,
27; his Vicksburg Campaign illustrates Aristotle's four causes, xxii–
xxiii

Greene, General Wallace M., Jr., strategic views of, 164

Guadalcanal, campaign to capture,
112–14

Guerrilla warfare: factors affecting,
xiv–xv; used raiding strategy, xiv

Haiti, Marine experience in, 176

Halsey, Admiral William F.: commanded in Battle of Leyte Gulf, 128;
mentioned, 210

Hamburg, devastating raids of, 53–54

Hamley, Sir Edward Bruce, authority
on strategy, x

Harris, Air Marshall Sir Arthur, chief
of Bomber Command, 52, 53, 54,
56

Hodges, General Courtney, commands
First Army, 75

Hollandia: Allied objective, 122; illustrates logistic requirement of turning
movement, 210; landing at, 122;
mentioned, 123

Ia Drang, battle at exhibits power of
U.S. tactics, 173

Initiative: conferred by adversary who
eschews the offensive, 206; conferred
by Allied 1944 command of the sea,
69; conferred by command of the
sea, 120, 121; conferred by superior
numbers, 231; conferred by a turning movement, 208–9; conferred on
Virginia colonists by their command
of the waterways, 10; Eisenhower's
concentration in time did not confer,
80; example of pursuer's, 77; exposition of, 208–9; German air force
had in Battle of Britain, 51; given at
Midway by intelligence, 104; given
to Viet Cong by passive defense of
weak hamlets, 169–70; Iraqi weakness gave to coalition, 152; Japan
gained by beginning the war, 97, 98;
Japanese retained it against the colonies, 99; may result from appearance
of superior numbers, 231; military
meaning illustrated in Atlantic commerce war, 44; not necessarily resulting from the offensive, 231;
relation to economy of force, 208;
sacrificed by Westmoreland's strategy, 187; seemed incompatible with
pacification, 87; U.S. forces gained,
77; Westmoreland desired, 176

Intelligence: in Atlantic commerce raiding, 42, 44; can confer initiative, 44;
can take initiative, 44; command of
the air gave Coalition superior, 151;
conferred the initiative at Midway,
104; relation to surprise, 106; value
in preventing surprise, 44

Intimidation, limitations of in treatment of civilians, 200

Jesup, General Thomas S., operations
against the Seminoles, 22–23

Joffre, Joseph, French Generalissimo in
1914, 211

Jomini, Antoine Henri, authority on
strategy, x

Jutland, Battle of: account of, 88–89;
conformed to expectations, 89; hypothetical result of British tactical
defeat, 89; tactical and strategic result, 89

Kelly's Law, illustrates merit of good
intelligence, 206

Kenney, General George C., tactically
astute commander, 117–18

Khe Sanh, siege of, 184–85

Korean War: invasion of the North
and Chinese intervention, 144; last
two years a fortified stalemate, 144–
45; successful U.N. campaign saves
South Korea, 143; U.N. forces establish new defense line, 144

Lae: Allies capture, 120; mentioned, 123; taken by Japanese, 101

Laffey, U.S. destroyer, made a memorable defense, 130

Lanchester, F. W.: hypothesis about sea and air warfare, 227; physical features on land limit the applicability of his hypothesis, 227

Land warfare: long a subject of study, 197; many concepts apply to sea and air, 197

Laos, logistic raid into, 189

Law of diminishing returns, applied to composition of U.S. and Japanese navies and the supply of landing craft, 219

Least effort: conditions when it equals least expense, 217; dictated colonists' choice of logistic raiding strategy, 7; a goal in agriculture, commerce, and industry, 221; guide in application of comprehensive and operational strategy, xv; guided native military choices, 7; guided Seminole strategic decisions, 20; market economy facilitated for civil pursuits, 221–22; motif of best strategy in the past, 221; surprise facilitated, 206; typical criterion in strategic decisions, 197

Lexington, sinking of, 103

Leyte Gulf, Battle of, illustrated distraction, 210

Leyte Island, Allied objective, 127

Libya, aftermath of U.S. raid on, 201

Liddell Hart, B. H., authority on strategy, x

Lines of operation: Allied choice in 1944, 69; Allies had interior against Germany and Japan, 57; Allies in Solomon Islands, 114; comparison of Allied with single, 125; concentration in space and time on New Guinea and central Pacific, 135; concentration in time and space compared, 78; interior in Little Big Horn campaign, 28; Japanese had interior, 125; Japanese navy exploits interior,

99–100; offensive began on central Pacific, 115; principle for exploiting interior, 212; reason for dual Allied in Pacific, 123; summary of Pacific, 119–20; United Nations' interior in Pusan perimeter, 143

Logistics: aerial refueling of aircraft modified dependence on remote base, 227; aircraft moved and supplies forces in New Guinea, 117; base area in Virginia and New England, 18; bombing of Japan changed to night, 136; changed in South Vietnam, 189; China a base area for Japanese forces there, 138; Coalition's air supremacy crippled Iraqi, 151; defined, xvi; description and development since nineteenth century, xv–xvii; dominates Allied strategic decisions, 77–78; a foundation of strategy, xv–xvi; in Great Sioux War, 26; modern importance of the remote base area, 227–29; natives and English, 3; naval base on Pacific atoll, 116; of Okinawa campaign, 131–32; of Pacific war, 87; problem after St. Lô breakthrough, 77; reason for capture of Marianas, 123; remote base area illustrated, 85; significance summarized, 117–30; surface movements more vulnerable at sea, 124; Viet Cong base areas, 167; Viet Cong expand base area, 171; Vietnam in 1967, 182; vulnerability of raider base areas, 214

Lubeck, destructive air raid against, 52;

Ludendorff, General Erich: effect of defeat on, 202; quoted on dependence of strategy on tactical conditions, 231–32

MacArthur, General Douglas: background and performance, 117; commanded forces in southwestern Pacific, 101, 117; commanded U.N.

forces in Korea, 143; commander in the Philippines, 100; mentioned, 101

Mahan, Alfred T.: authority on naval strategy, x; mentioned, 197

Malaya, logistic persisting strategy used with success, 177

Maneuver, alternatives for, 66–68

Mao Tse-tung: authority on strategy, x; his three phases of revolutionary war guided communist strategy, 130

Mariana Islands: landing, 126; objective, 124, 125

Marines, U.S.: in Korean War, 144; mentioned, 186; in Nicaragua and Haiti, 176; in Seminole War, 23; in Vietnam, 166–81. *See also* Vietnam War

Marne, campaign of the Battle of the, 211–12

Marshall Islands: captured, 116; mentioned, 115; raided by U.S. carriers, 102

Maunoury, General Michel, commanded Sixth Army in 1914, 211

McDougal, P. L., authority on strategy, ix

Midway Island, Battle of: account of, 104–5; mentioned, 107; significance for Japanese pilot loss, 104; strategic significance, 105, 108

Midway Island, Japanese objective, 103

Miles, Colonel Nelson A.: campaign compared, 176; campaign mentioned, 229; his winter campaign, 29–32

Military operations, some political effects of, 199–202

Militia: colonial military system, 6; organization for defense and offense, 9

Mitchell, General William: believed aircraft would control the sea, 93; his bombing tests and their significance, 93–94; mentioned, 237

Mobility: of Allied reserves in Battle of the Bulge, 81–82; significance of, 233–34

Montgomery, General Sir Bernard:

characteristics of, 73; decision to make turning movement after St. Lô breakthrough, 76; defensive strategy in Battle of the Bulge, 81–82; his instructive experience in France in 1940, 76

Morocco, example of logistic persisting strategy in, 176–77

Murphy's law, and friction in war, 206

Musashi, Japanese battleship: to reinforce Biak, 124; sunk, with difficulty, 128

Napoleon, his operations illustrate use of reserves, 210

Narragansetts, ally of New England colonists, 15

Newton's third law of motion: in Battle of the Bulge, 82; in British and then German concentration on Berlin, 54; describes behavior in warfare, 69; in enhanced German fighter production, 54; exemplified in Arab and Israeli raids, 200; mentioned, 163, 165, 181, 201; in New Guinea, 122; in politics, 142, 145; relation to distraction, 70, 206; in South Vietnam, 172; in struggle for Guadalcanal, 113

Nicaragua, Marines gained experience in, 176

Nimitz, Admiral Chester W., U.S. Pacific naval commander, 98

Noemfoor, captured, 123

North Vietnam, combat persisting invasion of South Vietnam, 1972: account of, 190–91; faced unfamiliar operational complexities, 191; possible political aspects of invasion strategy, 182; reasons for failure of invasion, 192

North Vietnam, first bombing of, 1965: beginning, 181; constraints on bombing, 181, 182–83; effect of bombing on, 182; poor objective for logistic raiding strategy, 182; re-

sponse to bombing, 182; target selection process, 181–82
North Vietnam, renewed bombing
campaign, 1972: beginning, 192;
changes in, 192–93; final logistic
and political-military bombing campaign, 193; logistic effect of last
bombing campaign, 193
Numbers, significance of, 231–33

Obstacles, examples of effect of various, 223
Offensive troops: Germans used for
strategic turning movement in 1940,
65; U.S. motorized as in strategic
turning movement, 76
Okinawa campaign: account of, 129–
32; Japanese air offensive, 130; logistics, 131–32; role of British
carriers, 130; a siege operation on
land, 129
Opechancanough: death of, 13; native
ruler who warred against Virginia
colonists, 11; peace conference with
colonists, 12
Ozawa, Admiral Jisaburo: commanded
carrier fleet in Battle of Leyte Gulf,
128; commanded in Battle of Philippine Sea, 126; mentioned, 127

Pacification: name for systematic control of South Vietnam's countryside,
169; progress in, 189–91; Vietnam
compared with colonists in Virginia,
214
Parachute troops: fail in offensive toward Ruhr, 79; in Normandy landing, 72
Parrot's Beak, logistic raid of, 189
Patton, General George S.: commands
Third Army, 75; mentioned, 69, 79,
82
Paulau Islands, Japanese base, 123
Pearl Harbor, Japanese raid on: account of, 97–98; failure to sink any
capital ships, 98; lack of strategic
significance, 98; mentioned, 107; po-

litical significance, 105–6; shows
that carriers are the capital ships, 98
Pequots, war against, 15
Persian Gulf conflict: its blockade as
political-military strategy, 201; bombardment of Iraqi combat and logistic targets, 152–55; the contending forces, 150–51; as an illustration, 235; Iraqi defense collapses and
forces retreat, 156; parallels with
Normandy invasion, 157; part of a
series of Near Eastern wars, 139;
significance of differing tactical estimates, 227
Philip, King, chief of the Wampanoag
tribe: his hypothetical demand for
peace, 202; logistical and political
factors in peace with him, 18; his logistics compared with Viet Cong,
196; his raids, 15–17
Philippine Sea, Battle of: account of,
126–27; Japanese plan for, 126
Philippines campaign: air attacks before the landing, 127; battleship action, 128; Japanese plans, 128;
Kuritas fleet attacks and withdraws,
129; landing, 127
Physical features, effect of: enhanced
by cavalry and infantry revolution,
226; favorable climate and terrain of
Persian Gulf, 224; an independent
variable in campaigns and wars,
222; more on land than sea and air
war, 222; summary of significance
of, 222–24; three examples of, 222–
23
Pilots, Japanese failure to train enough,
109
Political aspects: a consideration in
strategic choice, 197, 205; effects of
military operations, 201–4; often the
final cause of a campaign, 199; precluded advance of Coalition forces
into Iraq, 156; treatment of enemy
civilians, 199–200
Port Moresby: Australian base, 107;
Japanese offensive against repelled,
117; mentioned, 102, 112, 118

Preparedness for war, American and
    Japanese compared, 107–10
Princeton, sinking of, 128
Principles of war: deal with combat,
    205; explained, 205–8; valuable
    checklist, 208
Pursuit: aircraft and motorized forces
    strengthened in World War II, 75;
    caused U.N. forces difficulty, 145;
    effectiveness and problems of aircraft
    in, 75; on land, usually inferior to
    retreat, 7; received emphasis in U.S.
    Army training, 76
Pusan, southern Korean port, 143

Q ships, use against submarines, 40

Rabaul: bypassed (turned), 120; Japa-
    nese base nullified by air raids, 115;
    mentioned, 104, 120
Radar, capabilities and use on war-
    ships, 90
Reserve: on defense and offense, 210;
    defined, 71, 206–7; description of
    use after St. Lô breakthrough, 76–
    77; French inadequate for defense in
    1914, 211; helped by superior num-
    bers, 231; Joffre creates new, in-
    cluded two new armies, 211;
    Napoleon's operations illustrate,
    210; role in Battle of the Bulge, 81;
    source of in Battle of the Bulge, 81,
    82
Retreat: dominant over pursuit in Viet-
    nam, 174–75; effectiveness and diffi-
    culties of aircraft in pursuit, 75; on
    land usually superior to pursuit, 7;
    motorized U.N. forces outran pursu-
    ing Chinese, 144; by natives superior
    to pursuit; North Koreans used dis-
    persal to reach mountains of the
    North, 143; reasons for superiority
    over pursuit, 75; strategic effect of
    superiority to pursuit, 232
Rivers, importance of control of in
    Virginia, 14
Rostock, air raid against, 53
Ruhr, German industrial area, 79

Rundstedt, Field Marshal Gerd von:
    German western commander in
    1944–1945, 80; mentioned, 82

St. Lô, account of breakthrough at,
    73–74; mentioned, 218
Salamaua: Allies recapture, 120; Japa-
    nese capture, 101; mentioned, 123
Santa Cruz Islands, Battle of, 113
Savo Island, Battle of, 113–14
Scharnhorst, German battleship, last
    raid of, 44–45
Schwartzkopf, General H. N., com-
    manded Coalition forces, 152
Scott, General Winfield: campaign
    against Seminoles, 21–22; campaign
    compared, 27
Sea power: and air power, 94–95, 121,
    124, 216, 238; and commerce, 40–
    45, 134–35; confers initiative, 69,
    208; effect of weapons changes, 226;
    in Korean War, 141, 143–44; Per-
    sian Gulf conflict, 148, 151; Semi-
    nole War, 23; and strategic mobility,
    10, 14, 50, 57, 58, 66–68, 78, 120,
    124, 222–23; summarized, 230; sup-
    ports land combat, 23, 72, 122,
    178, 191, 238; Vietnam War, 161;
    World War II, 40–45, 95–138
Seminoles and Sioux, lacked remote
    base area, 229
Seminole War, compared with South
    Vietnam, 175, 187–88
Seoul, South Korea's capital falls to in-
    vaders, 142
Sheridan, General P. H., theatre com-
    mander during Little Big Horn cam-
    paign, 27
Sherman, General William T., General
    in Chief during Little Big Horn cam-
    paign, 27
Sioux Indians, their hypothetical de-
    mand for victory illustrated, 203
Solomon Islands, campaign in, 112–15
Sonar, detected submarines, 40
South Vietnam: army of, poor perfor-
    mance, 166–67; change in U.S. mili-
    tary strategy to stress pacification,

186; combat between strategic hamlets and Viet Cong persisting offensive, 170; communists adopt defensive, 185; communists become partly dependent on a remote base area, 189; effects of more dependence on the North for supplies, 189; government has some success with strategic hamlets, 269; government's failed response to Viet Cong persisting strategy, 168; government's inadequate defense of villages, 165–66; government's measures against communists, 165; logistic persisting strategy failed because government went too fast, 177; Marines coordinate with pacification effort, 177; new offensive strategy compared with old defensive, 186; the political-military strategy of the Tet offensive, 183–84; United States responds to Viet Cong persisting strategy with reinforcements, 168; U.S. response to Viet Cong success, 172; Westmoreland's combat raiding strategy lacked logistic consequences for communists, 174

Strategy. *See also* Concentration; Turning movement

Strategy, of attrition: example of, 63; explained, 209–10

Strategy, combat: defined, xiv; difficulties of, 7, 22, 26, 173; Persian Gulf conflict, 150; some other instances of, 79, 83, 144

Strategy, comprehensive: combinations of, xiv, 221, defined, xiv

Strategy, logistic, defined, xiv

Strategy, logistic persisting: colonists use, 11; exemplified in conquests of France, 83–85; at sea, 35, 135; Viet Cong employ, 171

Strategy, logistic raiding: with airplanes, against communications, 71–72, 143, 152, 181–82; effect of airplanes bombing cities, 55–56, 136–37; on foot or horseback against

natives, 10–13, 22, 23, 26, 29, 130–31; with submarines, 40–45, 133–35

Strategy, military, defined, xiii

Strategy, operational: components of, 82; defined, xv; introduction and techniques of, 232; some instances of, 151, 232–33

Strategy, persisting: defined, xiv; employed by Allies in France in 1944, 83; logistical requirements differ from raiding, 67; some other instances of, 9, 14, 121, 136, 168–69

Strategy, political-military: defined, xiv; Douhet advocates, 49; employed by colonists and natives, 10–13; by King Philip, 15–16; some other instances of, 20, 53, 136–37, 148; in Vietnam, 163–64, 181–82, 183–84, 194

Strategy, raiding: advantages of, 8; combat raiding in Vietnam, 173; defined, xiv; Douhet stressed effectiveness of, 49; importance of base area, 214; some other instances of, 18, 165, 175, 214

Strategy, some other aspects of: the Coalition's turning movement in 1991, 150; complementarity of strategies as well as of tactical techniques and weapon systems, 215–18, 238; effectiveness of offensive troops or weapons systems, exemplified in the German success in 1940, 64–65; the law of diminishing returns applied to strategy, 219; some other instances of, 61–62, 225–26, 233–34

Strategy of the Vietnam War summarized, 194–96

Submarine: as commerce raider in World Wars I and II, 40–44; development and capabilities of, 39–40

Substitution: among factors affecting strategy, 235; illustrated by hypothetical substitution of bombers and submarines, 235; of mobility for numbers, 234

Substitution and combination: among

land, sea, and air power, 216; illustrated in tactics, 216–17

Surprise: attained at St. Lô, 74; facilitated concentration against weakness of offense and strength of defense, by Germans in Ardennes, in 1940, 65; in 1944, 80–81; by natives, 16–17, 20; often implied weakness on defense and offense, 70; a principle of war, 206; relation to intelligence, 206; some other instances of, 76, 119, 145, 166; Washington's warning, 20

Tactics, aircraft: and air defense, 53, 193, 197; as cavalry of the air, 58, 62, 66, 74, 117, 118, 102, 124–25, 130, 145, 157; combat between, 55, 102, 117

Tactics, attack and defense compared, 175, 187, 223, 224, 227

Tactics, defined, xvi

Tactics, methods: counterattack, 68; crossfire, xx, 211; enhancement of complexity by heterogeneous armies, 116; of Korean War, 145; line, xix, 5, 6–7, 43, 48, 51, 63; the recent ubiquity of guided missiles, 149, 193, 225, 226; skirmishing, xix, 5, 6–7, 21, 22, 28, 38, 45, 48, 51, 63, 225; Vietnam War, 166, 172–73, 175; World War I, 59–60, 63, 64; of World War II, 58–63, 70–74

Tactics, summary of, 224–27

Tactics, weapons systems: combination and complementarity of, xix, 62, 93, 149, 215; tactical as well as strategic effect of motorized, 224, 226. See also Fortified defense

Taranto, carrier raid on, 92, 97

Tarawa, landing on, 116

Taylor, General Zachary: compared, 188; fights battle, 23

Terry, General Alfred, commanded Dakota column in Little Big Horn campaign, 27

Tet Offensive: events of, 184; significance of, 185, 189, 190, 195; strategy of, 183–84

Thieu, General Nguyen Van: mentioned, 189, 190; objects to peace agreement, 194; South Vietnamese ruler, 183

Thompson, Sir Robert, British commander in Malaya, 177

Thompson, Wiley, Indian agent killed by Seminoles, 20

Tirpitz, German battleship sunk by bombs, 94

Tokyo, effects of 1942 U.S. air raid on, 103–4

Trenchard, Hugh, pioneer British air leader, 49

Truk, Japanese base, attacked and by-passed, 116; mentioned, 120

Turning movement: can confer the initiative, 208–9; effective during pursuit, 77; efficient for combat strategy, 79; explained, xvii; illustrated by Germany in 1940, 65; illustrated in the Korean War, 143; logistic requirement of the turned force, 85, 175, 228, 229; logistic requirement of the turning force, 210; parallels with, 120, 188; some other instances of, 76–77, 80, 85, 101, 117, 122–23, 155–56, 211

Victorious, H.M.S., British carrier that reinforced U.S. Pacific fleet, 114

Viet Cong: base areas of, 167; communist insurgents in South Vietnam, 165–66; development of their army, 167, 168; effective policies of, 164–68; has marked success, 170–71; method of reconciling villages to their rule, 171; military strength in 1964, 171; persisting strategy to expand their base areas, 167;

Vietnam. See also North Vietnam; South Vietnam; Vietnam War

Vietnam, government of South, alienation of rural people, 164–65

Vietnam, physical features, compared with Persian Gulf region, 224

Vietnam War: attrition assessed, 209;
    changes in diplomatic situation, 193;
    strategic problems resembled wars
    against native Americans, 196, 232
Vietnam War, U.S. Marine policies: as-
    sisted in sweeping villages of Viet
    Cong, 178; created combined action
    platoons, 179–80; interfered with
    Viet Cong tax collecting, 178; meth-
    ods of supporting pacification, 177–
    78; sought to conciliate the Viet-
    namese, 178; supported the pacifica-
    tion program, 176–80

Wakde, capture of, 123
Wake Island, raided by U.S. carriers,
    102
Warships, types explained, 36–39
Washington, George, his warning
    about surprise, 20
Wasp, sinking of, 112–23
Weapon systems, attribute of intrinsic
    superiority: defined, xix; examples at
    sea, 36–37, 40, 92, 126; examples in
    the air, 48, 54–55, 226–27; exam-
    ples on land, 60, 62, 149, 225
Weapon systems, interrelationships:
    combination, xix–xx, 215; combina-

tion and substitution, 216–17; com-
    plementarity and substitution, 218;
    complementary relations, 215
Weapon systems, varieties on land:
    cavalry, 7, 225; natives' and colo-
    nists', 4–5; offensive, xxi, 65; World
    Wars I and II and after, 58–63,
    111–12, 129, 130, 133, 139, 141,
    157
Weather. *See* Climate
Westmoreland, General William C.,
    U.S. commander in Vietnam, 173–74
Wewak: bombing of a distraction, 122;
    mentioned, 210
Withlacoochee, Battle of, 21
World War I: effect of war aims, 201;
    effect on warship design, 89–90;
    opening campaigns illustrate most el-
    ements of operational strategy, 211
World War II, its operations and ar-
    mies as models for many later ar-
    mies and wars, 239

Yalu River, divided North Korea and
    China, 144
Yamato, Japanese battleship, to rein-
    force Biak, 124
Yorktown, loss of, 105

About the Author

ARCHER JONES is Professor Emeritus of History and a former dean at North Dakota State University. He is the author of *Confederate Strategy from Shiloh to Vicksburg* (1961), *The Art of War in the Western World* (1987), and *Civil War Command and Strategy* (1992) and joint author of *Politics of Command, Factions and Ideas in Confederate Strategy* (1973), *How the North Won: A Military History of the Civil War* (1983), and *Why the South Lost the Civil War* (1986). He has served as Morrison Professor of History at the U.S. Army Command and General Staff College, member of the Department of the Army Historical Advisory Committee, and trustee of the American Military Institute.

ISBN 0-275-95526-5

EAN

90000>

9 780275 955267

HARDCOVER BAR CODE